Investing For Dummies®, 4th Edition

Published by: **John Wiley & Sons, Ltd.,** The Atrium, Southern Gate, Chichester, www.wiley.com

This edition first published 2015

© 2015 John Wiley & Sons, Ltd, Chichester, West Sussex.

Registered office

John Wiley & Sons Ltd, The Atrium, Southern Gate, Chichester, West Sussex, PO19 8SQ, United Kingdom

For details of our global editorial offices, for customer services and for information about how to apply for permission to reuse the copyright material in this book please see our website at www.wiley.com.

Wiley publishes in a variety of print and electronic formats and by print-on-demand. Some material included with standard print versions of this book may not be included in e-books or in print-on-demand. If this book refers to media such as a CD or DVD that is not included in the version you purchased, you may download this material at www.dummies.com. For more information about Wiley products, visit www.wiley.com.

Designations used by companies to distinguish their products are often claimed as trademarks. All brand names and product names used in this book are trade names, service marks, trademarks or registered trademarks of their respective owners. The publisher is not associated with any product or vendor mentioned in this book.

For general information on our other products and services, please contact our Customer Care Department within the U.S. at 877-762-2974, outside the U.S. at (001) 317-572-3993, or fax 317-572-4002. For technical support, please visit www.wiley.com/techsupport.

A catalogue record for this book is available from the British Library.

ISBN 978-1-119-02576-4 (paperback); ISBN 978-1-119-02577-1 (ebk);
ISBN 978-1-119-02578-8 (ebk)

Printed in Great Britain by TJ International, Padstow, Cornwall

10 9 8 7 6 5 4 3 2 1

Contents at a Glance

Table of Contents

Introduction

So much has happened for investors in almost the twinkling of an eye, it's certainly time for a new edition of *Investing For Dummies*.

Over the past seven or eight years, economic and investment market crises convulsed the world. They include the first ever run on a UK bank in a century and a half; the nationalisation of two of the biggest UK banks; the collapse of some of New York's biggest investment banks; mayhem in the US housing finance market; the bankruptcy of Icelandic banks; the rescue of the Greek and many other smaller European economies in the Eurozone; record low interest rates almost everywhere, guaranteeing that savers get a bad deal; and the rise of emerging market economies such as India and China. And that's only scratching the surface of all the recent changes in the world of investing.

And then, as day follows night, the dark side of financial markets turned sunnier. Share prices in the United States soared to record levels, 'euro' and 'crisis' no longer automatically always appeared one after the other, UK markets perked up – and investors who had placed their faith in the great emerging markets of Brazil, Russia, India and China were disappointed.

Dramatic? Yes. But these big ups and downs have existed ever since financial markets came onto the scene.

On top of all that, UK rules governing what is most people's biggest and most crucial investment – their pension – have changed out of all recognition. So many restrictions have been introduced that I've had to completely rewrite the chapters on what to do about your retirement income for this new edition of the book.

Knowing about investments could almost have been a hobby when I wrote the first edition of *Investing For Dummies* nearly a decade ago. Now, you're out there on your own with pension investment decisions.

But really nothing has changed in the investment world. No matter how chaotic it may seem, or how complex the hedge fund universe appears to all but those with a double degree in investment rocket science, the essentials remain just as they always were.

Investment markets are still a battleground between fear and greed. When fear gets the upper hand, most prices fall – the exception being so-called 'safe haven' investments such as gold. And when optimism returns, everything moves up – except for those 'safety first' assets.

And how investments will fare from here is anyone's guess. No one can be trusted to predict the future. So neither *Investing For Dummies* nor any other source of advice will ever be right all the time. The essential aim is to get more than half of your decisions right and beat the averages. If you can do that then you're doing as well as you're likely to. This applies to the so-called experts and professionals as well.

This book gives you the facts up front and honestly. So you'll find no magic formula for wealth here. Besides, even if there were a get-rich-quick recipe, I wouldn't be telling anyone about it; I'd be using it.

No one can predict which shares will do well (although that doesn't seem to stop people from asking me for sure-fire tips at parties). But what I can provide is guidance to help you make sensible decisions that suit your circumstances.

Investing involves more than understanding an economics textbook or balance sheet. It involves understanding a whole lot about human reactions to the ups and downs of money, plus (really important) understanding how you react. And it's fascinating because it's where you find all the drama of human life: investment values represent nothing other than the combination of the minds of all the people involved in investment markets.

Over all the decades that I've been writing about money, I've continued to find investing a fascinating subject and endeavour, and I've become moderately more well off than I would've otherwise been. I hope that this book helps you become fascinated with investing too. And I also hope that by reading it you'll be better off than you would've otherwise been.

About This Book

This book is designed to be read in several ways. It's a reference book, so you don't have to read the chapters in chronological order, from front to back, although of course you can read it cover to cover, like a novel, to gain appreciation for the huge variety of investment opportunities that are available. (If you approach the book this way, I suggest doing so with pen and paper at the ready so that you can note areas for further research on the Internet or from publications such as the *Financial Times*.) Or you can just pick a topic that interests you or go straight to a section that answers a particular question you have.

But my preferred way for you to read this book is to go through Part I and *then* pick up on the investments that concern or interest you. For example, after reading Part I you may want to go straight to Part III to find out what

collective investments are because, say, an advert about collective investments has caught your eye or a financial adviser has suggested one or two
of them. Reading this section helps with your pension choices. But you may
want to skip the chapter on buy-to-let properties because, say, being a do-
it-yourself landlord is the last thought on your mind. Or the one on betting
opportunities because they're simply too scary.

Conventions Used in This Book

I've tried to avoid jargon as much as I can, but know that the investment
world is full of it. Like all professions and occupations, finance and investment have their own insider language that's intended to mystify outsiders.
When I do use the industry's language in the text, I *italicise* the term and
define it for you in an easy-to-understand way.

Foolish Assumptions

While writing this book, I made some assumptions about you:

- ✔ You're either completely new to investing or have limited information
  about it, and you want someone to help you understand what investing
  is really about and what types of investments are available.

- ✔ You don't want to become an expert investor at this point in your life.
  You just want the basics – in informal, easy-to-understand language.

- ✔ You want to make up your *own* mind while using a guide through the
  investment jungle. You want enough pointers for you to risk only what
  you can afford to lose and for you to make a worthwhile return on your
  hard-earned cash.

Beyond This Book

Find out more about investing by checking out the bonus content available
to you at www.dummies.com. You can locate the book's e-cheat sheet at
www.dummies.com/cheatsheet/investinguk, where you'll find handy
hints and tips.

Be sure to visit the book's extras page at www.dummies.com/extras/
investinguk for further information and articles.

Icons Used in This Book

 I've highlighted some information in this book with icons:

This icon points out useful titbits or helpful advice on the topic at hand.

 I use this icon to highlight important information that you'll want to keep in mind, so don't forget this stuff!

 This icon points out just that – a warning – so take heed. The investment world is full of sharks and other nasties. I don't want you to lose your money to crummy schemes and criminals.

You'll find this icon next to, well, technical stuff that you may want to skip. I've been sparing with this stuff because investment can be pretty technical anyway. (Note that even though you may want to skip this material on your first reading, and please feel free to, this info may be worthwhile coming back to later with your greater knowledge of the fundamentals.)

Where to Go from Here

This book is set up so you can dive in wherever you want. Feel free to go straight to Chapter 1 and start reading from the beginning to the end. Or look through the Table of Contents, find your area of interest and flip right to that page. Or better yet, read Part I and *then* flip right to that page of interest. Your call.

Wherever you go from here, if you find a piece of advice or a warning that you think applies especially to you, copy it down and then fix it to the fridge with a magnet, or pin it on a board.

And as you read through this book, either in part or in whole, why not practise some dry-run investing? Buying a dummy portfolio using pretend money is always a good way of getting familiar with investment without the worry of losing money. You'll find plenty of resources online to help you establish and plan your pretend portfolio.

Part I

Getting Started with Investing

For Dummies can help you get started with lots of subjects. Visit www.dummies.com to learn more and do more with *For Dummies*.

In this part . . .

- Find out all the things you always wanted to know about investing.

- Discover what the term investment really means.

- Look at the five basic investment choices – the foundation of most portfolios.

- Discover how to increase the benefits and shrink the drawbacks of investment choices.

- Learn that the small print is vital in understanding what you invest in – ignore it at your peril!

Chapter 1

First Steps on the Money Trail

*T*his chapter explains the first steps you must take in your investing ventures. But take heed: in this chapter (and throughout the book, for that matter) you need to think deeply about some personal matters, to understand yourself better and know where you're going in your life and what makes you tick. In other words, you need to wear two hats – that of investor *and* that of self-examining philosopher. So be prepared for some tests that ask just what sort of person you are, what you want for yourself (and those around you) and what you're prepared to do for it.

And if you don't run into a test, such as a risk profile from a financial adviser, that's no bar to testing yourself. Many 'risk profiler tools' online can help, but no matter how you go forward, the final decisions you make are down to you and no one else.

Understanding the facts and mechanics of investment decisions is just a start. Knowing how to apply them to your own circumstances, and to those of your family and other dependents, is what will make your strategy succeed.

What's Your Reason for Investing?

This section is very basic, comprising just one simple *Investing For Dummies* test question: why did you buy this book? Chances are you probably did so for one of these four reasons:

✔ **You have no money but want to make some.** Most people fall into this category. You want to invest some money and accumulate funds but don't know where to start. How you go about it depends on how well you can discipline yourself. Take heart, though: even the most confirmed shopaholic can build up a nest-egg for later use.

✔ **You have some money, want it to make more and currently make your own investment decisions.** You're the traditional investor who wants to make your personal wealth grow. You already make your own investment decisions and want to get better at it. How you go about it depends on who you are, how you made your money and where you hope to be in 5, 10 or 20 years.

✔ **You have some money, want it to make more and currently have others handle the investment process for you.** Maybe you have fund managers or investment advisers handle your investments so you can gain tax advantages or because your savings are lumped together with those of others in a pension or similar fund. Or maybe your life is just too busy or complicated for you to do the investing yourself. Regardless, you now want to understand how investing works so you can either take over your own investment decisions or monitor what others are doing with your hard-earned cash. I'm not sure many people will pick up this book just to check up on the professionals, but I could be wrong.

✔ **You're now in charge of your pension decisions.** Unless you work in the public sector, the chances are that you now have to take stock of your own pension arrangements. What you get when you retire is now largely up to you rather than your former employer or employers. And the new pension freedoms extend this choice into your retirement years. Because building up and then winding down a pension are likely to be the biggest investment decisions you make, Chapters 14 and 15 are devoted to helping you construct your retirement funds and then make the most of your pension's nest-egg.

What's Your Personality Type with Money?

Some people spend all they have each month (and then some on top – ouch!). Others put away a bit in the bank or building society on a regular basis. And still others buy and sell stocks and shares, with some going in for some very complex investments.

Test time: you need to decide whether you're a spender, a saver or an investor. Doing so isn't as easy as it looks, though. Spenders can be savers or investors. Savers can be spenders and investors. And investors are generally also savers and must, at some stage, be spenders. But most people are predominantly one of the three types – spender, saver or investor. Which category you think you fit into determines what you do from now on, how you react and how you progress.

Spenders have fun

Spenders are generally people who live for the here and now. They may want more than they can have and end up borrowing money, probably on plastic cards. For many spenders, accumulating cash for the future has no priority.

Here are ten attributes of spenders. If the majority of them apply to you then, yep, you're a spender:

- You don't look forward to the end of the month.
- You love new things: you'll queue all night for the latest smartphone and your friends gasp when you tell them how much your new handbag cost.
- You have more than one credit card – maybe you use one to pay for the other.
- You can't resist two-for-one offers, even if you throw half of what you buy away.
- You buy unnecessary clothes.
- You're always first – and last – to buy a round of drinks.
- You believe in living a lot now.
- You see the future as a foreign land.
- You worry about money at times but then go out to the shops to stop fretting.
- You buy glossy magazines as much for the advertisements as the articles.

If you're in this category, your first priority is to recognise that investors can't always be spenders. Getting familiar with investing is a good way to accomplish this priority because it offers an alternative use for your cash.

Know that while on your way to becoming a saver or an investor, you can start with very small sums. You can become a saver with £1. And some regular stock-market-based investment plans start at £50 a month less than the cost of a coffee-chain cappuccino a day.

Savers have cash

Savers are people who want to keep their financial cake and eat small slices at a later date. Here are ten saver attributes. Tick those that apply to you, and if the majority do then you're probably a saver:

- ✔ You have a surplus at the end of each month.
- ✔ You go to the supermarket with a shopping list.
- ✔ You don't have a credit card, or you pay it off in full each month.
- ✔ You're prepared to put off purchases.
- ✔ You'd rather buy second-hand than run up a debt.
- ✔ Your property is more important than your furniture.
- ✔ You look at the display windows at banks and building societies.
- ✔ You know what the current interest rates are.
- ✔ You believe in the saying 'waste not, want not'.
- ✔ You've read *Sorting out Your Finances For Dummies* (published by Wiley) – or, if you haven't, you'll get a copy the next time you buy a book.

Saving is a stage you must reach before investing. You can be a saver as well as an investor, but you can't be an investor without first saving up some money to invest.

'Hi, it's me, Spender. Can't I just use my credit card to finance an investment?'

You can't use a credit card to buy investment products over the phone, via the Internet or in other circumstances where you can't send a cheque. Some of the reasons lie in the complexity of consumer credit legislation. Another factor is that financial companies only want you to invest what you can afford, although unauthorised, illegal and probably fraudulent offshore investment firms may try to sucker you into schemes by telling you to use your credit card.

But the most important reason you shouldn't borrow to invest or save is that doing so only makes financial sense if the return is going to be higher than the interest rate charged. Paying 29.9 per cent annual interest – and that's by no means the top credit card rate – is pointless unless you can be very sure that your investment will grow even faster and that your original capital will be safe. Both now and in all of history, no such investments exist.

And note that even if you could borrow at 0 per cent annual interest, you'd still have to be sure of getting your money back with one of those rare investments that can't fall, in order to be better off.

Investors build up future funds

Investors are people who are prepared to go the extra mile to try to ensure that their wealth goes the extra thousands, tens of thousands or even more. Investors want control over their money but are ready to take a risk provided that they're in charge and know the odds. They want their money to work hard for them – as hard as they worked to get the money.

You don't need an MBA, a posh old-school tie or stacks of money. However, know that although you can sleepwalk into just saving your cash, you must be wide awake to be an investor.

As a pure saver, you really don't have to know what you're doing. You can just stash your cash under the bed, for example. As an investor, you *must* know what you're doing and have the self-discipline to follow your strategy, even if the strategy is doing nothing, buying and forgetting, or benign neglect.

So are you an investor? Check out these attributes to find out:

✔ You have spare cash.

✔ You have an emergency fund for the day the roof falls down or the car collapses.

✔ You want more than the bank or building society offers.

✔ You think about your money-making strategy and tactics.

✔ You can face up to bad days (and there'll always be some) on investment markets without worry.

✔ You're ready to swap certitude for a bigger potential reward.

✔ You can afford to lock away your spare cash for five years at the very least.

✔ You understand what you're doing with your money.

✔ You're prepared to lose money occasionally – knowing it's an occupational hazard.

✔ You're ready to invest your time into growing your fortune.

All these attributes belong to an investor.

Working out where you fit

So, what's your bottom-line personality type when it comes to money?

✔ **You decided you're an investor.** Congratulations! You're ready to embark on the road to growing your money. It won't be easy. You may face stiff climbs, vertiginous falls, rocky surfaces, long deviations and dead ends. But give it enough work and time, and I promise that investing will work out.

✔ **You didn't qualify as an investor.** You got as far as a saver and no further. Or you're really stuck as a spender. You're wishing you'd spent the price of this book on something else or stuck it in your savings account, where at the current virtually invisible savings rates it'll double in about 100 years. Well, don't regret your purchase or vow to send this book off for recycling, or try to recoup some of the price by selling it in a car boot sale. Stick with it. The very fact that you bought this book shows you're ready to move on to investing when you're financially and psychologically ready.

And even if you decide you never want to buy a share, sell a bond, invest in a unit trust or check on foreign exchange rates, this book is still for you. Why? Because you're almost certainly an investor already. (The following section tells you how, if I've piqued your curiosity.)

Surprise! You've Probably Been Investing Already

Your financial fate already depends on the ups and downs of the stocks and shares markets. Few people can escape this fact, and every day the number of people who can ignore the investment world diminishes. You may be an unconscious investor or even an unwilling one, but there's no running away from it; you're already an investor.

Investing through your pension fund

The biggest amount of investment money you're likely to have is the value of your pension fund. And whether you pay into it yourself, rely on your employer or build it up via a partnership with your employer, it all rides on investment markets.

Just to give you an idea of how much you may have, suppose that you earn £25,000 a year and put 10 per cent of your earnings each month into a pension fund that grows at a 7 per cent average per year. Here's what your fund is worth over the course of 45 years (I've ignored tax relief on pension contributions, future wage rises, inflation, and fund and pension management charges to keep this example simple):

Number of years	Value of fund
5	£14,915
10	£36,059
15	£66,032
20	£108,525
25	£168,762
30	£254,157
35	£375,214
40	£546,827
45	£790,111

That's serious money! And it all started with a first monthly payment of just £208! Of course, the assumptions I make are foolish. No one continues on a flat salary for 45 years – some see earnings soar and others stop work. And although the annual growth rate I've used is an average based on the past, whatever happens in the future, it won't be smooth!

Most people haven't a clue that they have the potential for anything like the preceding example over a working lifetime. But even if you're aware of what you could achieve, I bet you didn't know that you have a good chance of taking some investment control over that sum. Even if you don't want to, at the very least you should be able to check up on what the pension fund managers are doing with your money. Understanding what other people are doing with your money can help you increase your own pension fund in good markets and prevent it from going down when the investment world turns sour.

Note that your pension plan isn't the only area where you may be an unwitting stocks and shares investor. Endowment mortgages and other investment-linked insurance schemes also revolve around stocks and shares.

Investing in your employer

Millions of people are potential and actual investors in the company they work for. Most big stock-market-quoted companies, like British Airways or Wal-Mart's UK offshoot Asda, offer employees option plans that give workers the chance to acquire a stake in the firm. To acquire that stake, workers buy *shares*, also known as *equities*, which I explain in the section 'Get your share of shares', later in this chapter.

The original idea was that giving someone the chance to buy shares in the future at a price fixed in the past would help motivate staff members and make them put in more effort, but in reality the idea only works if all colleagues work *equally* hard.

The original idea aside, the option plan is just a pay perk, but one that can be valuable. A variety of schemes are available, but the most common one is linked to a savings account known as Save As You Earn (SAYE). SAYE schemes have a monthly limit to encourage you to tread carefully, because putting all your investment eggs in one basket would be really daft. You don't want your savings to collapse if your employer goes bust or makes you redundant.

In an SAYE scheme, you save from £5 to £500 a month in a special account that earns interest. When you start, you're given a price, called the *exercise price*, at which you can buy the firm's shares in the future. The account continues for three or five years (with an option to go to seven years). At the end, you can use the savings plus interest to buy shares in the firm at the pre-set price. If the price has risen, you make a profit, although you don't have to sell until you want to. But if the price has dropped, you can walk away from the whole deal with the cash you've saved in the account. But you won't get any interest at the present time – rates are just too low.

Some employee share option schemes aren't a perk. They're a danger – especially in small companies whose prospects sound brilliant (on paper, at least). You can easily be lured from a well-paid, secure job into risky employment with the promise of share options sometime in the future but a substantially reduced salary now. Most option plans lock in employees for a number of years, and by the time they take their options the shares could be virtually worthless, assuming that the company is still in business. Putting all your eggs in one basket is always an error, so never tie your fortunes so closely to one company. No matter how attractive the deal sounds, a wage packet bird in the hand is worth several options in the bush.

Being part of the economy

We're all part of the investment scene, whether we know it or not. Every time you decide to buy an item or save your money or work harder or work less or go on holiday in the UK or abroad or do nothing, you're part of the big picture that makes up the economy. You can't avoid it, so find out how that economy can work for *you* rather than just working for others.

Between a rock and a hard place

Investment hasn't had a good image recently. It started with the Northern Rock disaster back in 2007, where small investors in what should've been a rock-solid business saw their shares go down to the very hard place of zero. Northern Rock was only the beginning, followed in the subsequent year by the collapse or near-collapse of some of the UK's and the world's biggest banks, and their subsequent rescue with billions of pounds of taxpayers' money. The media can characterise anything to do with finance – the City of London and New York's Wall Street especially – as greedy, self-serving and even a threat to the planet. And yes, a lot of that's true. Investment bankers have paid themselves bonuses to equal the earnings of football internationals and Hollywood stars. Since the banks started collapsing, scandal after scandal has ensued, with bankers accused of rigging just about anything they can get their hands on, including interest and currency exchange rates. Many global banks have been fined sums hitting billions. Somehow, unlike footballers or actors, they manage to pick up huge wage packets for failure, or unbelievable 'severance packages' should they actually be forced to quit. After all, hardly anyone else, and certainly not their bosses or their shareholders, has a clue what all their esoteric investments are about.

And when serious professional investors fell for Bernie Madoff's $50 billion investment scam, you seriously had to wonder what it was all about. Madoff ran what seemed to be a very successful fund, although it turned out to be a *Ponzi* scheme. Named after 1920s swindler Charles Ponzi, these plans offer very high returns that they can only give to investors by using new money coming in to pay out anyone who wants to withdraw. When the new money stops or is slowing, the whole house of cards collapses. The scheme invests in nothing – other than the promoter's secret bank accounts.

We've yet to come up with anything to replace the financial system we have at the moment, but the great crash should teach us some lessons. Firstly, never, ever take even the supposedly biggest and brightest investment brains on trust. Secondly, although no one will again fall for the mess of offering complex financial instruments and dodgy mortgages to people who had no hope of ever repaying, other financial bubbles will occur in the future. There'll even be those who claim to have learned from the mistakes and who come up with an even better way of packaging these home loans.

So when it comes to your hard-earned money, never sleepwalk your way to ruin. As the old saying goes, 'if it looks too good to be true then it almost certainly is'. No safe route exists to a quick buck; highly paid City types eventually run out of luck; guarantees given by the seemingly most august banks can turn out to be worthless; and you can't even rely on governments to always back their promises.

Look out for the warning signs. Shareholders in Northern Rock, Bradford & Bingley, Halifax Bank of Scotland and Royal Bank of Scotland had plenty of chances to get out with something before the shares went down to zero (in the case of the first two banks) or down to pennies (with the second two), before government-sponsored rescues. Warnings were spread over a number of months.

So why did so many private investors ignore the signs? For some, their holding was so small that selling would have cost more than it was worth. But most had an irrational hope that things would get better and go back to 'normality' where prices keep rising. If the global financial crisis that started in 2008 has taught people anything, it's that 'normality' includes disastrous crises as well as good opportunities.

Five Basic Investment Choices

All your money decisions, outside of putting your family fortune on some nag running in the 3:30, simply involve making up your mind as to where to put your money. Literally tens of thousands of choices are available online. And at least a thousand choices appear in many daily newspapers.

But you can cut that number down to just five possibilities by considering basic investment choices only. Get these right, or even just right more often than wrong, and you're well on the way to financial success:

- Cash
- Property
- Bonds
- Shares
- Alternatives

Here's a big investment secret: most professional fund managers – yes, those City of London types who pull in huge salaries and even bigger bonuses for playing around with your pension, savings or other investment money – don't wake up each morning asking themselves which investments they should be buying or selling that day. Instead, they reduce the investment world to five big buckets that they call *asset allocation*, which simply means that they divide up investment money into the five areas in the preceding list – cash including foreign currencies, property, bonds, shares and alternatives. They take your money and allocate a portion to shares, another portion to property and so on. The fund managers, and especially the people who run large pension funds, know that if they get their asset allocation decisions right and do nothing else, they'll beat the averages over the long term.

Can this theory fail? Yes, especially over the short term, by which I mean up to two or so years. In the great global financial crisis, almost everything went down. You couldn't just move from one thing to another because whatever you switched to was equally under pressure. No single investment theory works all the time. The best I can do is to point you to those that have a good chance of working most of the time.

You can't go wrong with cash

Having cash under the mattress can be very comforting when everything is going wrong in your life. But keeping cash under the mattress, or anywhere else at home, isn't a good idea from a security point of view. Nor does it make sense for investors. Putting your cash in a bank protects it from thieves, fire risks, and perhaps the temptation to grab it and spend it in a shop.

You never earn much money just leaving your cash in the bank. Most bank account money is in current or cheque book accounts, which often pay just 0.1 per cent, an interest rate that, transformed into pounds and pence, gives you the princely sum of £1 for each £1,000 you have in the bank for a full year. And if you're a taxpayer, that £1 may be worth as little as 55p after HM Revenue & Customs take their slice. Ouch!

Better ways of investing the cash that you don't want today are available, including building society deposit accounts, online cash accounts, telephone banks and postal accounts. With all these options, you can get a higher interest rate but you have to give up flexible access to your cash in return. And you won't make much. Since interest rates hit their lowest ever in March 2009, savers have struggled to get anything much, losing out to rising prices. But the situation won't always be like that.

The longer you're prepared to tie up your money, the better the rate of interest you receive. You can lock into fixed rates so you know exactly where you stand, but you must be prepared to hand over your money for a set period, usually one to three years, and throw away the money box key. Granted, some fixed-rate deals let you have your money back early, but only if you pay a big penalty.

Whatever you earn is cut back by income tax on the interest unless you're a low earner or use an Individual Savings Account (or ISA). But does this matter? No. The best you can really hope for from a cash account is that the interest equals the *rate of inflation* – that's the amount the price of things the average person buys goes up each year – after the tax charge on the *annual interest uplift*. If inflation is 4 per cent, then a 20 per cent taxpayer needs a 5 per cent headline rate to keep up with price rises – work it out and see! Suppose, for example, your savings account of £1,000 earns £50 interest, or 5 per cent, in a year. Take off the basic rate of tax (20p in every pound) and you end up with the £40, or 4 per cent, you need just to keep up with the rate of inflation. If you're well off enough to pay tax at the top 45 per cent then you probably work for a bank and pull in big bonuses!

The whole point of cash investing is to use it when you're uncertain or everything in your life looks awful. It's a security blanket you can retire to during periods when all else is confusion or contraction.

Don't disrespect this fact. Keeping a firm hold on what you have isn't just for fast-falling markets. It's a vital concept in the months ahead of retirement or any other time when you know you'll want cash and not risks. You lock in the gains made in the past and can go ahead and plan that big trip, your child's wedding or the boat you want to buy. Cash is what you can spend, and expenditure is the endgame of investment.

Property is usually a solid foundation

The property you live in is probably your biggest financial project – assuming that you don't rent it from someone. Typical three-bedroom semis now change hands at £500,000 or more in many parts of the UK. And at the higher end of the market, no one blinks an eye any more at £2 million homes (not that most of us can afford one).

But is property an investment? Yes, because you have to plan the money to pay for its purchase, buying can help you spend less than renting and because you can make or lose a lot of money in property.

Property beyond your home can also be a worthwhile investment. Stock market managers run big funds like property because it rarely loses value over longer periods, often gains more than inflation and provides a rental income as well. Commercial property, such as office blocks, shopping centres, business parks, hotels and factories, is usually rented out on terms ensuring not only that the rent comes in each month (unless the tenant actually goes bust) but also that the rent goes up (and never down) after each five years, when the amount is renegotiated.

Bricks and mortar are as solid an investment as you can find outside of cash, as long as the bricks and mortar are real. A fair number of property schemes take money from you for buildings that only exist on the architect's plan. This is known as *off-plan purchasing*. In many cases, these buildings eventually go up, although you may sometimes struggle to find a mortgage lender or a tenant – or both. Some don't, however, and these cases leave you nursing a loss as the developers and their agents gallop off into the sunset with your cash. This bad buy-to-let industry reputation puts off many mortgage lenders even where the building is finished to specification. Additionally, problems with loans can make tenants wary – they know they can be evicted if landlords don't have satisfactory financial arrangements.

Besides building up value in your own home, you have three main routes to investing in property:

✔ **Buy to let.** You become a landlord by purchasing a property that you rent to others.

✔ **Buy into a property fund run by a professional fund manager.** You can do so through personal pension plans, some insurance-backed savings plans and a handful of specialist unit trusts. These nearly always invest in commercial property although some now specialise in student accommodation.

✔ **Buy shares in property companies.** This is the riskiest method but the only one that can provide above-average gains.

WARNING!

Every week I get emails offering me 'guaranteed returns' from property or forests or farmland in some distant country. In many cases, the returns are promised over ten years and are truly enormous. I always delete these as trash. A 'guarantee' is only worth as much as the organisation backing it. And I don't reckon too much on the chances of an offshore company being around in a few years' time, let alone paying me what it promised.

Bonds are others' borrowings

A stock-market-quoted *bond* is basically an IOU issued by governments or companies. Loads of other sorts of bonds exist, including Premium Bonds, which give you the chance to win £1 million each month at no risk, other than losing out on interest. But here we're talking bonds from governments and big companies, which go up and down on stock exchanges.

Bond issuers promise to pay a fixed income on stated dates and to repay the amount on the bond certificate in full on a fixed day in the future. In other words, you pay the government, say, £100, and the Treasury promises to give you £5 a year for the next five years *and* your £100 back in five years' time.

Sounds simple, right? Well, it's not at all. Bonds are complex creatures with many traps for the unwary. (I devote a big slice of this book to the ups and downs of bond investment.) But if you reckon price rises will be kept to a minimum and interest rates will stay where they are or go down, then bonds are a good bet if you need regular income.

Diversifying is no monkey business!

Diversify across asset classes such as property, bonds and equities – that's the standard advice given to long-term investors. The theory is that when one asset is down, another goes up. So in the early 2000s, shares disappointed while property prices, both residential and commercial, soared skywards. Bonds and commodities, such as wheat and copper, also did well. But every once in a long while, investment theories break down. In the great 2008 financial crisis, virtually everything went down.

Will that happen again? I don't know. Nor does anyone else. But a London-based firm of financial experts called – and I'm not joking – No Monkey Business says that we should dump the diversification model. Its basic line is that all you need is a mix of shares to provide higher risk and higher reward, and index-linked government stocks to give total stability. I go into this further in Chapter 18. (The firm has now changed its name to something more mainstream – Fowler Drew – but not its way of working.)

Bonds are becoming more common as well. The reason is partly because many investors have been taken with the relative safety and steadiness of bonds compared with shares and the relatively higher income they offer compared with cash. (Everything in investing is relative to something else, by the way.) But the reason is also because the people running big pension funds need the security and regular payments so they can afford to write cheques each month to the retired people who depend on them.

The easiest way to buy into bonds is through one of the hundred or so specialist unit trusts. But don't take the headline income rate they quote as set in stone. It can go up or down, and no guarantees or promises exist. Some even cheat by hiding costs away. Always remember that the capital you originally invest in the bond fund isn't safe either. It can go down or up along with investment trends and the skills of the manager.

Get your share of shares

Shares make up the biggest part of most investment portfolios. They can grow faster than rival investment types and produce more. They're probably your best chance of turning a little into a lot – even if the first ten years of this century was a shares disaster, it's got better into the second decade.

Shares are what they say they are – a small part of a bigger picture. Buying shares (also known as *equities*) gives you partial ownership of a company. You can own as little as one share, and if that's the case and the company has issued 1 million shares, you have a 1-millionth stake in that enterprise.

You can't chip off that 1-millionth portion and walk away with it. What you get is 1-millionth of the profits and a 1-millionth say in the future of the company. But you won't have a 1-millionth share of clearing up the mess if the firm goes bust. You can never lose more than you put in.

Ownership rights are becoming more important and more valued. Put a lot of small stakes together and companies start to notice you, especially if you have a media-attractive project, such as protesting against excessive pay for fat-cat executives who fail to deliver to shareholders and collect big bucks if they're sacked.

Most people buy shares because they hope they'll produce more over the long term than will cash, property or bonds. They've generally done just this, although no guarantees exist. Shares are your best chance for capital gains and the top choice if you want a portfolio to produce a rising income. But take heed: they can also be an easy way to lose your money.

Want to know the most dangerous sentence in investment? 'It'll be different this time.' Sometimes, that becomes 'the new paradigm'. What people mean is that they've found a magic formula to find an investment that goes up but not down. People trot out that sentence whenever prices rise rapidly, and brighter investors start to question how long it can continue. The thing is, the situation never is different. Anything that people promise is a one-way bet is bound to run out of steam sometime, whether you're looking at property prices, the price of wheat or shares in African economies. Share prices, and the values of every other single investment in this book, go up with greed and down with fear. As long as these human emotions exist, 'It'll be different this time' will be the same nonsense as the last occasion someone said it. Expect to hear this phrase many times during your investment life!

Alternatives are a hodgepodge to consider

This investment area covers a rag-bag of bits and pieces. For some people, alternative investments concentrate on items you can physically hold, such as gold bullion, works of art, fine wines, vintage cars, antiques and stamp collections. But for an increasing number of people, the term means hedge funds, which are about as esoteric as investment gets. Put simply, you hand over your money to managers who, by hook or by crook, hope to increase it.

In most cases, don't even ask how those types of managers hope to gain cash for you. They won't tell you. Or they won't be informative, instead just coming up with some meaningless jargon phrase. And don't even ask what'll happen if they fail. They don't like to talk about this possibility, even though you could easily lose all the money you have with them.

So is there a plus side? Yes. Hedge funds can make money out of shares when prices are falling all over the place. Once they were the only way to do this, but now 'absolute return' funds claim the same.

In the section 'Surprise! You've Probably Been Investing Already', I explain in detail that, well, you've probably been investing already – without knowing about it. On that same line of thinking, you may also unknowingly have some of your wealth riding on hedge funds. Hedge funds make their main pitch to really big investment and pension funds, as well as to private investors with lots of spare money. Chances are that a hedge fund or hedge fund type of tactic is in your pension plan.

You can't invest directly in a hedge fund unless you're seriously, seriously rich. Some funds work on an invitation-only basis, so you wait until you're asked! But you can sometimes put your money into a fund of hedge funds. This is a special vehicle that buys, holds and sells hedge funds. They're sometimes offered to the general public – or at least those with the minimum £10,000 they usually require.

Commodities consist of a totally different category. On the one hand they are the essentials of life – anything from coal to cocoa or copper – so they are hardly alternatives. But investors see them as an alternative to stocks and shares, property and cash because you can bet on the price of any quoted raw material, from potatoes to potassium, and from olives to oil. This facility attracts many professional investors, and therefore attracts money.

You can make a fortune quickly in these commodities markets, but just as easily lose your shirt. No one can foretell who the winners and losers will be, or when or how or where. That's the fascination of investment. It's always changing but it always relies on the same basics of greed versus fear and supply versus demand.

Chapter 2

Checking Your Personal Life Before You Invest

Investment truth #1: Losing money is easier than making it.

Investment truth #2: More domestic break-ups and rows are caused by money, or rather the lack of it (or the spending habits of one partner), than anything else. Money is more important than love, any day.

Investment truth #3: You'll be a better investor if you've secured your home base – getting a roof over your head whose costs are sustainable is the vital first move. Buying, if you can, is usually better than renting, so a mortgage is the number one investment. Provided, that is, that you can find the deposit.

Investment truth #4: Paper profits have no more value than the piece of paper they're written on. What your investments are worth on a statement is just a row of figures. Until you turn that investment into cash by selling, it won't put a roof over your head, put food on your table or provide an income if something happens to the breadwinner.

Investment truth #5: Borrowing money to buy investments can be a very fast route to the bankruptcy court, as can gambling on stock markets.

Feeling down after reading that? Wondering why Chapter 2 doesn't launch straight into how to analyse stock futures and double your money in minutes? Or how to clean up with a simple, can't-fail formula?

You've every right to be depressed and puzzled. But it's a good thing you are. Investment knowledge has as much to do with *when not to do something, when to hold on to what you have, and when to hold back and let the next person pick up the problem* as it has to do with plunging headfirst into financial markets.

And that's what this chapter is about. Before you invest, you need to consider all the above truths. You need to take a close look at yourself, and those around you. You should be aware that no easy routes exist in finance. But more importantly, everything revolves around you and your family – not the commission needs of assorted advisers and hucksters who claim to have the solution to all your problems.

There's nothing new under the sun

I've probably been involved in investment writing for far too long. I've seen it all and then all over again. I can remember the great 1970s bust and boom, the 1980s boom and bust, and the 1990s boom that, inconveniently for my neat decades, only bust just after the decade ended in 2000. Then, back in 2008, we saw the great banks' boom and bust. Add to that more than a few property bubbles, and some crazy ups and downs in gold, oil, wheat, sugar and just about everything else under the sun. Every time share or other financial market prices advance to new highs, I ask myself just how long it can last.

Unfortunately, those running our finances never see it that way. They learnt nothing from the great 2008 banking crisis (or any other). This isn't surprising: they can't own to up the fact that finance runs in cycles of up and down because that's more than their very highly paid job is worth. Asking them, 'Just how do you do it? Where does the money come from and go to?' is like asking the emperor about his new clothes. 'Don't worry. Nothing will go wrong,' they reply. After all, these people control some of the world's biggest firms, so how could they not know? How could they be anything other than full of wisdom? How could anyone taking home millions a year in bonuses be anything other than supremely able? But reliance on these people was wrong, wrong, wrong.

Despite what politicians and bankers often say, the world will never usher in a new financial era in which boom and bust have been abolished. I wish this age could exist, but wishes don't turn into investment success. The rules of investment that I lay down in this book must catch up sooner or later.

Everyone who tried to convince me that we were into a new world with new rules probably earned 10 or 100 times as much as I did. But they could take this devil-may-care attitude because they were playing with other people's money (known as *OPM* or *opium*). They didn't care what happened because they made sure that they were number one. By the time it went horribly wrong, they'd made their cash and locked it away somewhere impenetrable.

The morals of all this? Don't chase fads. Never assume a quick or easy route to riches exists. And never give up the day job, no matter what someone offers!

Assessing Your Personal Wealth

Before you start investing, take a long, cool look at your personal wealth. Draw up a balance sheet (Figure 2-1 shows an example) so you can check how much comes in each month from work, interest payments, dividends and/or pensions. Then look at where the money goes.

Income	£
Your earnings (after all deductions)	
Your partner's earnings (after all deductions)	
Interest on savings	
Dividends from investments	
Child benefit	
Social security payments	
Pensions	
Other sources of income	
Total	
Outgoings	
Mortgage/rent	
Supermarket bills	
Children's school expenses	
Public transport	
Car – petrol, insurance, tax	
Gas and electricity	
Eating out	
Phones, broadband	
Pension contributions	
Insurance premiums	
Newspapers, magazines	
Cinema, theatre, downloads	
Sports, gym and leisure interests	
Interest on credit cards/loans	
Rainy day fund	
Total	

Figure 2-1: Use a balance sheet like this one to keep track of how much money comes in each month and where it all goes.

Repeat this exercise over three to six months so that you balance out low-spending months in one category with months in which you had to lay out a lot. Also take into consideration months in which a big bonus or overtime payment boosts earnings. Averaging means you even out these peaks and troughs.

An essential first step before investing is knowing what your incomings and outgoings are (how much money is coming in and going out). This knowledge helps you focus on your goal of increasing your wealth. And what if your outgoings leave nothing left over? Well, you know you should consider holding back from active investment at this time. But you can still use this time to look at, find out about and get a real feel for financial markets.

Taking Care of Family before Fortune

Investing involves taking chances. Serious investing, as opposed to taking a wild punt on a short-term stock market move, ties up your money for a length of time. Assuming that you have some spare money (see the preceding section to find out whether you do), think about how investing it rather than spending it will affect your household.

Weigh up the happiness quotients for all concerned. For example, compare spending the money now on piano lessons with investing it for later use on university tuition fees. I don't pretend this is easy.

What you do with your money should have a goal. Investment is intended for future consumption. It's not a game where you concentrate on ego-boosting by building up a big cash score. Plenty of phone apps and computer games exist for that.

Talk over investment strategies with adult members of your household. You'll feel much better if you get them on your side. But if they aren't happy with your strategies and you can't convince them then hold back.

If you have some spare cash but don't want to take chances with it, or maybe you're tempted to spend it, go for National Savings, now renamed National Savings & Investments. National Savings offers a number of products where you can put your money away for a set time, ranging from one to five years, and more flexible accounts are available as well. The rates are rarely chart-topping, but you have the security of the UK Treasury and Exchequer backing your decision. And for anyone who went through the misery of bust banks in 2008, that's a great comfort blanket.

Studying How to Save without Sacrificing

Almost everyone can save some money without sacrificing too much lifestyle. Even small amounts each day can soon mount up. Here are some initial ideas – and how much you can save each week:

- ✔ Give up smoking. A person who smokes 20 cigarettes a day will save £60 a week.

- ✔ Buy milk at the supermarket instead of using home delivery. You'll save £6 a week.

- ✔ Take a sandwich from home instead of buying one at work. You'll save up to £15 a week.

- ✔ Go shopping with a list and stick rigidly to it. You'll save at least £10 a week – and probably avoid some fattening snacks as well.

- ✔ Ditch pricey cable or satellite TV stations you hardly ever watch. You'll save £3 to £10 a week. Freeview has more channels than you can watch.

- ✔ Put every £2 coin you receive into a box. When you have £50, put the money into a special bank or building society account. I did this when I was saving for my bike. I put away over £800 without noticing it.

- ✔ Buy a copy of *Sorting Out Your Finances For Dummies* (published by Wiley). You'll save yet another fortune each week!

Think about your lifestyle and then make your own additions to the list, from saving on transportation (walk? cycle?) to checking the market for gas, electricity, mobile phones, landlines and broadband, and always using a comparison website for insurance policies. You can create big savings with some discipline – it's the same style of discipline you need to be a winning investor.

Savings quickly mount up thanks to compound interest

Pennies really can turn into pounds and pounds into thousands. And they can grow even faster thanks to *compound interest*, which is interest on interest.

Suppose, for example, that you manage to save £10 a week and put it in the bank. That's more than £40 a month and £520 a year. These sums can start you on an investment habit.

Here's how much various weekly savings would be worth after five years with a modest 2.5 per cent interest paid each year.

- ✔ £10 a week: £2,733

- ✔ £15 a week: £4,099

- ✔ £20 a week: £5,466

- ✔ £30 a week: £8,199

- ✔ £40 a week: £10,932

- ✔ £50 a week: £13,665

Looking After Your Life and Health

None of us knows how much time we have left on this planet. The good news is that your chances of living longer have never been better. Most people nowadays are likely to live to around 77 to 82 years of age. The bad news? You can never forecast when you're going to be hit by a bus or succumb to a mystery virus.

So you should always make sure you have sufficient life insurance and cover to replace at least some of your income if you succumb to a serious illness or worse. Life insurance won't replace you, but it will replace your money-earning capacity.

Always shop around for all insurance. Look at any comparison site. You can easily pay twice as much for life cover of exactly the same amount with one company as with another. What's the difference? Nothing. You have to die to get a payout with both, so the conditions are identical. No one wants to buy insurance – it's not fun – but if you have to then don't waste your cash.

Before buying life-insurance cover, decide how much you need. One rule of thumb is four to five times your yearly take-home pay. But also look at any death or illness benefits that come with your job. No point exists in doubling up cover unnecessarily. And know that if you have no family commitments or that your wider family will rally round if trouble occurs then life cover is just a waste of time.

As well as life cover, you can purchase *critical illness policies* that pay out a lump sum if you have a serious illness, such as a heart attack or cancer, and survive for a month. A huge range of prices exist for policies with standard terms, so never, ever go for the first quote you get and be careful of exclusions. Knowing what's covered can be a minefield so taking expert advice first is worthwhile.

Some policies, known as *income protection plans*, promise to pay a monthly sum until your normal retirement age or for a shorter set period if you can't work due to illness or injury. These policies can be expensive. Also be aware that although some policies pay out if you're unable to do *your own* job due to illness, less generous ones only pay out if you can't do *any* job at all.

Always look at all your family and personal circumstances before signing up for a policy. If you don't really need it then don't buy it. You could use the monthly premiums to help build up an investment nest-egg.

Paying into a Pension Plan

Your pension plan is an investment for your future but with tax relief in the here and now. This means that, if you're a basic-rate taxpayer, you pay £80 for each £100 that you get in investment going into the plan – a pretty good deal.

If you're a 40 per cent taxpayer then the setup is even better because you only have to pay in £60 to get £100 into your account, thanks to government tax rebates.

The pension picture is changing. Under a scheme known as *auto-enrolment* employers have to offer all those in employment a pension plan and pay in a percentage – admittedly small – of salaries up to around £45,000 a year, provided the employee contributes some earnings to the plan as well. If you don't want to pay in from your salary, you have to make the conscious effort to opt out. And then you don't get the employer contribution. None of this helps the self-employed.

Those with larger sums and a do-it-yourself attitude to investment can opt for a *self-invested personal pension* (SIPP) where the holder gets to choose what goes in. You can start a SIPP with anything from £5,000, although £50,000 is a more normal minimum. However, on the downside, the costs can be high and if your strategy goes wrong, you have only yourself to blame.

Chapter 14 contains loads of hints and tips on how to deal with your pension, whatever the level of involvement you want.

Taking Care of Property before Profits

The roof over your head is probably your biggest monthly outlay, whether you rent or buy. And it's also likely to be your biggest investment if you own your own home. So don't begrudge what you spend on it. In the long run, your home should build up to be a worthwhile asset. (At the very worst, it'll shelter you from the elements!)

The best way to save money when it comes to home-owning is paying it off early. Imagine I say to you, 'Want an investment that pays up to 80 times as much as cash in some bank accounts but is absolutely safe and totally secure? And what about a 100 per cent guaranteed return that can be higher than financial watchdogs allow any investment company to use for forecasting future profits?' Sounds like a snake-oil salesman scam, doesn't it? But if your first reaction is, 'You've got to be kidding', then you're wrong. Paying off mortgage loans with spare cash offers an unbeatable combination of high returns and super safety.

To see what I mean, take a look at the following mathematics. In this particular example, I've used interest-only figures for simplicity, although anyone with a repayment (capital and interest) loan will also make big gains. And, again for simplicity, I've assumed that the interest sums are calculated just once a year. Six per cent is at the higher end of mortgage interest now. But it's very possible that over the life of a mortgage six per cent will be at the low end. That said, here's the scenario:

> # Your home is your castle
>
> If you rent, always look at what it would cost each month to buy the same property – assuming you can find enough for a deposit. Purchasing incurs substantial costs, such as stamp duty and legal fees, so you have to factor those in if you can afford to buy, but don't intend to hang around for long in any one place. Whichever – buying or renting – works best for you, putting aside any cash you save through your choice for the future is always a good idea.
>
> Homes have generally been a good medium- to long-term investment. They've beaten inflation over most periods and more than kept up with rising incomes in most parts of the country.
>
> Some areas have seen spectacular gains. But even in the worst parts of the country, you'd have been very unlucky to lose over the long run, even counting the big price falls of the early 1990s and, more recently, the collapse in values following the 2008 financial crisis.
>
> Whether the next decade will see the spectacular gains of the first years of the century is impossible to say. But homes should continue to be a good investment and at the very least keep up with rising prices over time.
>
> However, although your home is the essential roof over your head, never see it as a conventional investment, no matter how appealing any price rise may be. Buying and selling costs a fortune – legal fees, estate agent charges, removal vans, stamp duty – as well as taking up time and requiring saintly patience. You don't need to own shares or bonds or hedge funds. But you do need somewhere to come home to.

Someone with a standard mortgage and with £100,000 outstanding at 6 per cent pays £60 a year, or £5 a month, in interest for each £1,000 borrowed. On the £100,000, that works out to £6,000 a year or £500 a month.

Now suppose that the homebuyer pays back £1,000. The new interest amount is £5,940 a year or £495 a month.

Compare the £60 a year saved with what the £1,000 would have earned in a bank or building society. The £1,000 could have earned as little as £1 at 0.10 per cent. And even at a much more generous 3 per cent, it would only make £30 – half the savings from mortgage repayment.

'But you've forgotten income tax on the savings interest,' you rightly say.

Ah, but the money you save by diverting cash to your mortgage account is tax-free. It must be grossed up (have the tax added back in) to give a fair contrast. Basic-rate taxpayers must earn the equivalent of 7.5 per cent from a normal investment to do as well. And 40 per cent taxpayers need a super-safe 10 per cent investment return from their cash to do as well.

Now where else can you find a 7.5 per cent a year guaranteed return, let alone a guaranteed 10 per cent a year? Nowhere.

Reducing your loan makes sense if your mortgage rate has fallen to a tiny percentage and you now have more spare cash each month than you previously allowed for. After you make a payment to cut the outstanding loan, you reduce this year's interest as well as that for every single year in the future until you redeem the mortgage. If interest rates go up, you'll save even more. But if they stay low, you'll keep on having extra and be able to afford to pay down your mortgage even more.

Some flexible or bank-account-linked mortgages let you borrow back overpayments so you can have your cake of lower payments with the knowledge that you can still eat it later if you need to. Alternatively, you can remortgage to a new home loan to raise money from your property if you need it. This sounds very attractive in bank account publicity, but dipping into the value of your home should only be a route when other solutions to your financial difficulties have failed.

Setting Up a Rainy-Day Fund

Before investing for the longer term, you need to set up your own personal emergency (or rainy-day) fund for contingencies that you can – and, more importantly, can't – imagine but couldn't pay for out of your purse or wallet. The fund should contain enough money to pay for events such as a sudden trip abroad if you have close family in distant lands, any domestic problem that insurance wouldn't cover, a major repair to a car over and above an insurance settlement or a substantial vet's bill not covered by insurance.

Here are some additional snippets from experience for you to keep in mind:

- ✔ Don't put your emergency-fund money in an account that offers a higher rate of interest in return for restricted access, such as not being able to get hold of your money for five years. The problems and penalties associated with getting your cash on short notice outweigh any extra-earning advantages.

- ✔ An emergency cash reserve serves as reassurance so you can more easily ride out investment bad times such as a fall in the value of shares.

- ✔ Monitor your potential emergency cash needs on a regular basis. They can shrink but are more likely to expand.

- ✔ Know that you may not be able to access some investments in an emergency. Don't be put in a position where you're forced to sell.

- ✔ Know that your credit card can be a temporary lifeline, giving you breathing space to reorganise longer-term investments when necessary. The key word here is 'temporary' – maybe up to three or four months. Using plastic for long-term borrowing is a certain road to financial ruin.

Chapter 3

Recognising What Makes an Investor Tick

*N*eedlework and carpentry are among the skills where you need a firm hand and a good eye as well as technical ability. You need technical ability in investing too. But as well as a firm hand and a good eye, you need an understanding of investor psychology – how you tick and how the other investors who make up the market tick as well. This chapter looks at psychology – but don't worry, you don't have to read huge tomes or understand long words.

Good investors know all about the mechanics of buying and selling stocks and shares. They know how to tell a positive company balance sheet from a looming disaster. And they understand that a relationship exists between interest rates, inflation and what they end up earning on their investment cash.

Great investors do all that *and* something more, something far more vital. It doesn't involve learning how to interpret share earnings forecasts, how to understand credit risks or how to evaluate the future of small companies. What it involves is far more basic – and far more essential.

This extra something is investor psychology, and it's what this chapter is all about. In this chapter, I tell you what investor psychology actually is and explain some specific emotions that make an investor tick. In addition, I explain that although gambling and investing share certain similar characteristics, they're actually very different ventures. And for those of you whose emotions range from cautious to scared stiff, I provide some starting-point investing advice.

Understanding Investor Psychology

Investor psychology comes in two parts – the psychology of the marketplace and the psychology of the individual. This section helps you understand each part – and their interaction, because you can't define where one stops and the other starts.

The psychology of the marketplace

Investors' research is usually directed toward where companies are going, what their likely future earnings would be and what shape their business would be in three to five years in the future. This remains essential. But a new dimension is appearing in stock-market analysis, especially that coming from the United States. This new way of thinking recognises that even the brightest and best investors make mistakes and lose money when they should have made profits. Why? Perhaps their judgement was clouded by the comfort of being with the crowd or by hating the idea of standing alone or by refusing to accept early enough that they made an error. In other words, they went for the comfort blanket of conformity.

You need to stand back from the crowd and its noise, including investment cheerleaders in the media and online. Instead of following the herd, understand how it works so you know where investment values are going and why. Winners think 'outside the box'. Losers act like sheep.

The psychology of the individual

Knowing how you'll react to what goes on in investment markets is vital. As you read this book, you'll experience some very basic emotions, such as 'I'm comfortable with this' or 'I wouldn't touch this investment with the proverbial bargepole' and a whole range in between.

Couple these emotions with setting your own investment goals. Depending on the sort of person you are, your goals could range from the reasoned ('I want to make my spare cash grow a little over the next five years') to the 1 in 10,000 chance ('I want to quit work in three years' time and live on a paradise island').

Working out where you are on the line that goes from a need for complete comfort and security to wild gambling enables you to make more rational decisions, including probably the most important one – the decision that at times walking away is best. The psychological aspect of investing is what separates figuring out investing from figuring out plumbing or gardening.

Looking at the Emotions That Drive Investors

Two specific emotions drive investors to make the decisions they do. These over-riding emotions are greed and fear, basic emotions that lead to a financial market tug-of-war. Everyone has both to some extent or another. Knowing the effects these feelings can have on investors is a powerful tool.

Greed is the accelerator

Greed is what you want beyond pure need. Granted, negative connotations are sometimes associated with greed, but consider these facts: without the greed for more and better food, we'd still have the monotonous diet of cave-dweller times. Without the greed for spices and other treasures, Columbus would never have set out for the east and landed in what became America. And without the greed to go faster, we'd all still be on foot. Greed drives us forward. But no two investors act identically.

Fear is the brake

People often ask me why share prices move so wildly during a very brief times-cale when little, if anything, has changed in the underlying company. They also want to know why downward movements tend to be more violent than upward gains. I reply that the stock market is like the first day of post-Christmas sales in posh department stores. If someone shouts, 'Designer frocks are reduced by another 75 per cent!', hordes rush to the women's clothing floors. That's the greed factor in action. But note that not everyone joins the rush. Men, for example, may just stand and stare.

But there's another factor to consider. If someone at that same posh department store shouts, 'Fire!' (or the alarms ring), then *everyone* rushes for the exits. That's the fear factor in action. And it takes only one or two people to panic for even more people to panic, thus reducing the hope of an orderly evacuation. Fear is always a stronger driver of emotions than greed.

Coming full circle here, the scenario is much the same with investment markets. And the point I want to stress is that fear is a stronger emotion than greed. When fear, justified or not, gains the upper hand, pandemonium can break out as investors rush for the exit or for safety-first investments.

The anatomy of some mad markets

'Every age has its peculiar folly; some scheme, project, or fantasy into which it plunges, spurred on by the love of gain, the necessity of excitement, or the mere force of imitation,' wrote Charles Mackay in 1841. What was true then is just as true now – or even truer given the speed at which information and financial decisions cross the globe. So take a look at some of the irrational madness and greed that has convinced some very bright people into a bubble investment. And we all know about blowing bubbles from childhood – they're really attractive and they grow in front of your eyes, but they have no substance and burst at the first pinprick.

✔ **The Dutch tulip mania of the 1630s:** Dutch merchants noted that rare tulip bulbs were expensive. So they started to buy and sell them. And the more they bought, the higher the price went. Mostly, the buyers just held on and watched their paper fortunes soar to the extent that one bulb could be worth more than a solid middle-class house in Amsterdam. But when one or two tried to sell, the price collapsed. That brought in more sellers, so the prices fell even faster. The economic ruin of the tulip mania in the Netherlands was so far-reaching that it pushed the Dutch out of 'New World' exploration, leaving it all to the English, French, Spanish and Portuguese.

✔ **The South Sea bubble in 1711:** People made and lost huge fortunes betting on the shares of the South Sea Company, which had never traded and was never going to. Much of the trading took place in Exchange Alley, City of London, which still exists today. People set up other bubble companies at that time to erect windmills and purchase lead mines. Fine, assuming they actually existed. Worse, far worse, was to come, though,

such as the company set up to 'make a wheel of perpetual motion'. At the height of the bubble, companies were set up 'for matters so secret that no one should talk about them'. Many of these companies took in over £1 million – a vast sum at the time and equal to around £500 million nowadays.

✔ **The UK railway mania in the 1840s:** Like so many technological ideas, railways were destined to change the way people lived in a very short time. They transformed travel and even changed the way wars were conducted. But changing lives isn't the same as making profits to justify share prices. People set up companies that had no hope of ever laying a rail, let alone running a train. And other companies simply overstated their earnings potential.

✔ **The US radio bubble in the 1920s:** Radio was the big change in the United States during the 1920s, and the share prices of any firms connected with radio went higher and higher. The more share prices soared, the more investors jumped on board. As a result, the shares went up a lot more and, inevitably, even more investors were suckered in. But eventually, no investors were left with dollars to buy from people wanting out of their investment. In October 1929 the market in radio shares collapsed and took everything else with it. The US stock market didn't recover fully until after the Second World War.

By the way, radio shares – and some really appalling investment trusts – boomed after the great Florida land bubble in the mid-1920s burst. Somehow, speculators were led to believe by clever promoters that land was running out fast in the Sunshine State. Nearly a century on, there's still plenty of it.

(continued)

(continued)

✔ **The Japanese stock-market boom of the 1980s:** Japan's stock market multiplied four-fold between 1984 and 1989. A combination of falling interest rates, soaring property values, a rising currency and money rushing in from investors elsewhere looking for the fastest-moving market all helped. At the height of the boom, Japanese phone company NTT was worth more than every company on the German stock market taken together; the Tokyo market was worth one and a half times the value of the rest of the world's shares excluding those in the United States; and the value of the land that the Canadian embassy occupied in Tokyo was worth more than all of Montreal's property. The bubble burst, although fairly slowly. Now the Japanese market has fallen around 75 per cent from its peak and trades at the levels seen before the mania started.

✔ **The dotcom boom of the late 1990s:** This is probably the best documented example of investor psychology going to extremes. Share promoters from the world's top investment banks convinced enough investors that they'd found a new paradigm using the undoubted potential of the Internet. These million-dollars-a-month bankers told investors that basics such as assets, earnings and profits were old economy, as were companies such as builders, food manufacturers and engineering firms. Internet-related stocks didn't need profits as long as they had a concept. Investors bought into this – because if they didn't, they feared being left behind by others. So share prices were propelled upward. But reality intervened, as it always does. Dotcom became dotcon or dotbomb. Many shares joined the 90 per cent club, meaning their prices fell by that amount. Others made the 99 per cent club. A lot went bust. But a few survived, prospered and became among the world's biggest companies.

✔ **The property boom of 2003–2007:** Yet again, those masters of the financial universe trumpeted another new paradigm – this time one where real-estate values could only rise and never, ever fall. The banks built onto this assumption amazing investment structures: houses of cards. The boom couldn't last because these complex investments were built on shifting sands. Many of these so-called top-rated investments, such as the infamous NINJA ('no income and no jobs') loans, were based on lending money to Americans who hadn't the slightest hope of keeping up payments. The bankers had believed their own sales pitch! By 2008 many of the world's banks were in crisis if not bust. And economies shuddered.

So, as an investor, how do you deal with the market pandemonium caused by fear – and with the prices that are falling all around you? Well, first, know this fact: when a real stocks and shares panic is going on, don't even think about beating the professionals to the selling exit. Their training makes them faster and heavier than you. And they have a direct line to the stock-broking professionals who'll deal with their £10 million selling order before they even pick up the phone or look at the screen for your £1,000 worth of business.

So if you can't beat the herd as it thunders to the exit, you need to develop other strategies for the inevitable bear markets. (Falling share prices are known, for reasons now lost in history, as *bear markets*. Investors who think prices will fall are *bearish*. The opposite, rising share prices, are called *bull markets*. Optimists are, of course, *bullish*.)

Here are some strategies to consider (check out Part II of this book for specific directions on buying and selling shares):

- ✔ Sit tight. If you don't need to sell, don't. You don't make a loss until you sell. Paper losses are just that – a minus number on a piece of paper.

- ✔ Look at your investments and assess whether they're directly affected by whatever is behind the panic or whether they're just being pushed along by the market as a whole.

- ✔ Be counter-intuitive. Use the panic to buy selected investments at knockdown prices.

- ✔ Consider potential tax bills if you decide to sell. The UK's capital gains tax can take up to 28 per cent of your profit.

- ✔ Use a bear market period (when shares are falling) to hone your research. Filing away all the negatives that come out during this time is valuable for future reference in a bull market, when all you hear is positive talk.

- ✔ Don't sit up all night worrying. It won't help!

And here are some tips to keep in mind during this tough time:

- ✔ Time is the healer. Share prices have always eventually recovered in major markets such as the US and UK, although you'll have to be patient.

- ✔ You're probably still earning dividends from your shares. These regular payouts often hold up better than the share price.

- ✔ If you fancied an investment at £1, it could be better value at 75p, assuming nothing else has changed. If you're really sure, buy some more to reduce the average purchase price.

- ✔ This year's big losers are often next year's major gainers.

Debunking the 'Stock Market as a Casino' Psychology

Stock-market columns in newspapers often refer to investors as *punters* and talk about *having a fun flutter*. So it's not surprising that many people see the stock market as a giant casino, admittedly without the overblown decorations of the Monte Carlo model. And you can take bookie-style bets on stock-market moves (I look at spread betting, as it's known, in Chapter 20). This section looks at how things really work in both gambling and investing, because they're very different ventures.

How things work in gambling

In gambling, you're totally dependent on random acts or a series of events that have an unknown effect taken together. For example, in a roulette game, you have no control over the wheel and no way of knowing which number will turn up after the wheel stops spinning. All you can do is ration out your bets in such a way that you minimise your losses.

You may gain in the short term on a few lucky choices. But if you play long enough, you'll lose, thanks to the zero on the wheel, because when it turns up, the house wins everything bet on black or red, on odd or even and on individual numbers. Because zero turns up once in 37 times, it's equal to chipping away approximately 3 per cent of all the money bet. And wheels that contain a double zero, well, they double that tax.

Now consider for a minute another gambling game – the fruit machine. In theory, the fruit machine is a zero-sum game. It can only pay out what people have put in. But even the most optimistic gambler knows that those machines are built to repay only about 80 per cent of what's put in, so the casino company is bound to win. It's said the older machines are, the meaner they become.

Once, people bet on horses, greyhounds and football matches. Now you can bet on anything including the name of the next prime minister and the winner of literary prizes. But so many unknowns exist in such betting – the voters, the judges – that the result is all down to chance.

How things work in investing

Here you aren't totally dependent on random events like the drawing of a card or the spinning of a wheel. You know beforehand many (although not all) facts about where you're placing your money. Your skill comes from evaluating these facts and then allowing a percentage for the unknown.

Equally important, time is on your side. You aren't forced into an instant appraisal. No one is (or at least shouldn't be) hassling you to make a decision on what to do with your money. And the game isn't over when the fruit machine shudders to a halt or the roulette wheel stops spinning or the horses go past the winning post. Stocks and shares have very long lives – most have no set expiry date. As an investor, you always live to fight another day unless your investment goes bust.

But most important of all, investment isn't a zero-sum game. New money comes into the market all the time. New investors put in fresh cash, and in addition, either knowingly or from pension-fund deductions, the companies into which you buy also put fresh money into the equation through dividend payments on shares and interest on bonds.

Most investors just look at the share price but forget the *dividends* – the half-yearly (sometimes four times a year) payments where companies divide out part of their profits for the benefit of shareholders. That's a big mistake. Money is money, wherever it comes from. All those small amounts add up to big cash over time. Always remember that a dividend bird in the hand is money in the bank, unlike the share's value, which is only cash when you sell.

Two dangers investors share with gamblers

Even though gambling and investing are two quite different ventures, two dangers exist that investors sometimes share with casino-frequenters.

The gambler's fallacy

The *gambler's fallacy* is that the past can affect the present and the future. Say, for example, that you have a £2 coin fresh from the mint. You toss it once. It lands heads up. What will the next throw bring? You really have no idea. So you toss the coin again, and it lands heads up again. How will it land next time? You're not too sure, but you think it may land tails up. After all, it's landed heads up twice and the coin is perfect. But it doesn't. And with each successive head, you get more desperate and your belief grows that it should go to tails.

Suppose, also, that you're betting on these coin tosses. With each loss, you double up your original stake in an increasingly desperate attempt to make your fortune. After ten losses in a row, your original £10 bet has now become £20,480. The coin has no memory and so each subsequent toss has no relationship with the previous. True, tails will come up some time, but can you afford to wait? That's the gambler's fallacy in action – and the negative result it can bring.

You can see the gambler's fallacy in investments. So-called experts quoted in newspapers say the market is going up (or down). On what do they base their assertion? Often it's no more than that the direction last month has to repeat itself this month; or that it's time the market changed direction. Distrust this – it's no different from the coin-tosser hoping for tails after a run of heads or the coin-tosser who believes that a run of heads will result in another head.

The gambler's fallacy is also present when so-called stock-market historians attempt to call the market by reference to the number of months since an event took place. They will say, for instance, that because the market has fallen in four consecutive months, it must almost certainly rise in the next four weeks because the market has fallen five months in a row only twice in the past 100 years. The trouble with this approach is that these once or twice in a century events have a habit of happening more often – think of floods in the UK – and exactly at the moment when everyone believes the opposite. The past is no guide to the future.

Trading too much can backfire!

One of the wonders of investing is that the fundamentals driving those involved – a mix of greed and fear – never, ever change. So although the following case comes from a 1998 study by researchers Brad Barber and Terrance Odean and is based on American experience, the story is as relevant today and in the UK as it ever was.

The researchers showed how many investors earn poor returns because they overtrade with too many buy-and-sell decisions. Additionally, they make matters worse because they tend to go for smaller companies that are both more volatile – that's bigger ups and downs – and cost more to buy and sell.

Barber and Odean looked at the trading records of 60,000 small investors in the US. They found that these individuals managed to beat the averages of all share prices and indexes such as the UK's FTSE 100 (the *Footsie*) or the US Standard & Poor's 500 by 0.6 per cent per year. Not a lot, no, but it builds up to big sums over a lifetime of investing.

So far, so good.

Now for the bad news. Because these investors tended to buy and sell often, and because the gap between the price at which you buy a share and that at which the share is sold to you is wider in small-company stocks than big-company stocks, the average investor paid more than 2.4 per cent of his money into trading costs. So the original 0.6 per cent gain turned into a 1.8 per cent loss per year. What's worse, the most enthusiastic traders lost 5.6 per cent in costs, so they underperformed the averages by 5 per cent per year.

For some investors, overtrading occurred because buying and selling shares had become a hobby, and those investors had become addicted. Psychologists say that over-activity is a way some people control their environment. But sadly, this psychological requirement some people have (and it's close to compulsive gambling) runs counter to the need for good money discipline.

The moral? Don't overdo share buying, or trading in and out of collective investments such as unit trusts or investment trusts. Each time you switch, there's a cost. In the UK, the cost is stamp duty and maybe capital gains tax as well. So always think before you swap investments. Doing it occasionally is fine because you've come up with good reasons for your decision. But buying and selling often erodes profits.

History tells you about the past. And it suggests that all empires eventually crumble. But could anyone have used the longevity of the Roman Empire, which lasted over 1,000 years, to predict the two to three hundred years the British Empire would last?

Overconfidence

Overconfidence leads you not so much to magnify possible gains but to minimise the effect of losses. 'It can't happen to me' is the way people express this kind of overconfidence. But, oh yes, it can. Overconfidence can also cause you to keep increasing your investment stakes to recoup previous losses. Doing so is really easy if you trade electronically via the Internet. Just a few clicks and you've committed yourself to a deal.

Combine the gambler's fallacy with overconfidence, and you could move into short-term investment tactics such as spread bets and options and end up with a demand for more than you were prepared to invest.

Sound Tips for the Cautious Investor

Having doubts as you consider investments is only natural. Having doubts is actually a good thing. Otherwise, you'd run into the overconfidence trap (see the 'Overconfidence' section, earlier in this chapter).

So if you're not quite sure about whether to invest, why not invest *part* of the cash you have and keep the rest for later when you gain more experience? Or maybe look for a lower-risk alternative. For example, instead of making investment choices yourself, look for a low-cost collective fund such as an investment or unit trust. Dealing with one diversified fund is easier than attempting to build your own portfolio.

If you think the time is right for venturing outside of cash, you may want to try one or some of the following. (I examine all these options in later chapters of this book, spelling out the advantages and drawbacks of each one. This list provides a starting point for your research.)

- ✓ **A bond fund:** Your money goes into fixed-interest securities tied either to governments or companies.

- ✓ **A cautious managed fund:** This type of fund focuses on a mix of lower-risk shares, bonds, cash and property. Don't confuse this with *absolute return funds*. These may have some of the same assets but can be higher-risk ventures.

- ✓ **A no-loss fund:** You put your money in a special fund, usually for five years. At the end of the specified time, you either get your money back without any deduction or, if the index has risen, your original money enhanced by the percentage rise. These can have masses of small print so be careful you know what you're getting.

- ✓ **A tracker fund:** This type of fund follows a stock-market index such as the FTSE 100 up and down. This option is a good idea if you want to be in shares but have no idea which ones to buy or which fund manager to back. But you still have the risks of shares.

For those of you who are seriously scared, your motto should be safety first. Here are a few suggestions:

✔ If the thought of losing any of your money gives you the heebie-jeebies then don't invest in anything that could cause you grief or sleepless nights. It's as simple as that. Worrying yourself sick is pointless.

✔ Don't just go for the savings deal your bank or building society offers. Instead, shop around for the best deal using Internet comparison sites.

You can invest up to £15,000 a year per person into a tax-free cash fund through the New Individual Savings Account (NISA). Besides paying no tax on the interest, you don't have to put it down on a self-assessment tax return form. You can also use the account for stock market investment.

Chapter 4

Squaring Risks with Returns

· ·

· ·

*W*hen we walk down the street or drive a car, we're aware of the risks. We know, for example, that we may risk life and limb crossing a road when the pedestrian signals are red. And we know that our safety (not to mention driver's licence) is threatened if we drive 60 miles per hour in a 20 zone.

Granted, if we run helter-skelter down the street or drive recklessly down the road, ignoring everyone and every rule, we may arrive more quickly at our destination. But the faster we go and the more corners we cut, the greater the chance of losing everything. So generally we take simple precautions to avoid risks. That way, we make some progress through life.

But what if we never took risks at all and, instead, wrapped ourselves in cotton wool? If we only walked on perfectly kept, deserted fields and drove on empty roads at exactly 10 miles per hour? We'd simply not get anywhere, and our lives would be boringly empty. We'd be taking the risk of missing out on something interesting and perhaps profitable.

You can say the same about investing. Investment risk is no different from the risks of daily life. There are steady-as-you-go investments that give a moderate rate of return with perhaps the occasional loss (after all, even the most careful driver can have a bad experience). There are hell-for-leather investments that can offer massive returns or huge losses. And there's the investment equivalent of surrounding yourself with layers of cotton wool – where nothing will happen at all.

In this chapter, I examine investment risks – specifically, the benefits and drawbacks of various investment possibilities and ways to increase your odds of successful returns.

Examining Two Investing Principles You Should Never Forget

Here are a couple of clichés that sound banal but should be carved in mirror writing on every investor's forehead, so they can read them first thing each morning when facing the wash basin:

- ✔ *There's no gain without pain.* To achieve something means you have to forego something else. If you want to build up your finances, you'll probably have to stop partying so often.

- ✔ *You have to speculate to accumulate.* If you don't take some chances with your money, you'll never get anywhere.

Financial markets – indeed, all of capitalism – work on these two principles.

Here's an example to help you see the importance of these two thoughts. Suppose that you're running a company and need £10 million to finance a new product. You could borrow the money from the bank, knowing that you'll pay 10 per cent interest a year whether the new venture works or not. If this new venture fails, you still have to pay the bank its £10 million plus interest, even if it means selling the rest of the business. But if your business idea turns out to be a winner, the bank still only gets its £10 million plus interest while your fortune soars.

Alternatively, you could raise the cash through an issue of new shares, where the advantages for you are no fixed-interest costs and, if the project is a flop, your investors suffer rather than you. They could lose all their money. And so could you! That's the risk everybody runs. But if the venture is a success, the shareholders receive dividends from you and see the value of their stake rise due to everyone demanding a share of the action. You shared the risk with others, so now they get a big slice of the reward. In each case, there are different winners and losers.

Now suppose that no one had taken any risks. You decided not to expand into the new product so you have no need of bank loans or share investment. There'd be no pain – no one would lose – but there'd also be no gain for you, the bank, the investors or the wider economy. Either the new idea would never see the light of day or maybe someone else would do it instead.

By doing nothing, all these potential participants could have argued that they'd taken a risk-free stance with their cash. But had they? No. They'd taken the very severe risk of missing out on something positive. They didn't speculate. They didn't accumulate. Risk isn't just about losing – it's also about missing out on gains.

Taking the tests to show your profile

Financial advice used to start with questions such as, 'Do you want to invest in the UK or Japan?' Now it commences with tests to show your *risk profile*. The goal is for you to understand yourself, to know how you feel about taking the risk that you may gain, the risk that you may lose out and how far you want to go in each direction.

Risk profiling, which leads to measuring your tolerance to risk, is subjective. But capacity for risk, which should come first, is objective. *Capacity for risk* is the amount of risk that you must take to achieve your objectives. Suppose you want to fund your grandchild's education expenses of £500 a month and that this is your most important goal for your investments. The test here is whether you can achieve this with a very-low-risk investment such as interest on bank accounts, or whether you need to be the right side of a very volatile investment or dip into your savings (and the effect that would have on your other finances). Capacity-for-risk questioning ensures you get the basics of your personal finance right.

Then you move on to the risk-profile exercise. Usually you answer twenty questions on a scale of one to five (strongly agree via neither disagree nor agree to strongly disagree). So you rank your response to phrases such as 'I consider myself average', 'In the past, I've been extremely cautious in my financial dealings', 'I think taking risks with my money is totally stupid' and 'I'd rather get a guaranteed rate of return, even if it's low, than take the chance of losing my money'. Sometimes, questions may sound similar, such as 'I'd be happy investing a large proportion of my income/capital in a high-risk investment' and 'I'd feel comfortable investing in shares', but they're subtly different and designed to sort out your thinking.

No right or wrong responses exist – the objective is that after all the questions, investors and advisers have a better understanding of the investor's financial risk appetite. Advisers then match this knowledge to investments that they've previously assessed for risk/reward levels.

Risk profiling, coupled with capacity for risk, is seen as the first building block of any portfolio, with many advisers now realising that their abilities to see into the future are, at best, very limited. Investment is no longer like a computer game where the object is to score as many points as possible. Now it's all about ensuring that your resources and your goals match up.

Determining the Return You Want from Your Money

The starting point of any risk–reward assessment is to determine the return you want from your money. The harder you want your money to work, the more risks you need to take.

You may want your money just to maintain its buying power – to keep up with inflation. Or you want to see it grow in real terms by a relatively small amount – just enough to keep ahead. Or you may want some aggressive growth to fund a pet project.

Suppose, for example, that you have a 10-year-old child who's been given a £30,000 lump sum by an adoring relation who has one proviso: the money must be spent on university education when the child reaches 18. The most basic education costs £30,000, but most will need more – especially if they want to study for a post-graduate qualification. So what rate of return over the eight years would you need to produce the result you want? (I've ignored inflation, which erodes your target figure in real spending terms, investment fees and taxation here to simplify the figures.)

£30,000: 0%

£36,000: 2.31%

£42,000: 4.3%

£48,000: 6.05%

£54,000: 7.62%

£60,000: 9.05%

£75,000: 12.14%

£90,000: 14.72%

£105,000: 16.95%

£12,040,000: 18.92%

The higher figures – those over the rate of return you need to produce £54,000 – are more than what you're likely to earn on your money unless either of the following apply:

✔ You're prepared to take big risks, including losing your original capital.

✔ Inflation returns with a vengeance, so you appear to obtain substantial gains even if they don't translate into real spending power at the shops. But then, the recipient of your generosity will need even more.

To show you how your money might grow, I want to give you recalculated figures using the official growth rates for salespeople from the Financial Conduct Authority (FCA), the watchdog and successor to the Financial Services Authority. These rates are intended as examples of what could happen and not what will happen (which no one can predict). These growth rates are stated as percentages and they are recalculated from time to time. They are intended to prevent unscrupulous sales folk from coming up with the first big number they can think of and then multiplying that by their phone number (and yours as well if they really fancy earning extra commission that day) to show what a great investment you could buy. Here's a rundown of the rules:

✔ Providers must use growth rates in projections that are appropriate to the investment potential of the product, so they can't claim that a no-risk fund could ever grow at the highest rates allowed.

✔ Growth rates are different for taxed investments and for tax-exempt products (largely pensions and individual savings accounts). If you pay no tax on the returns which are subject to tax, you are bound to make more than the same investment where you have to pay tax.

✔ If an investment is taxed, the annual growth rates that providers can show are 1.5, 4.5 and 7.5 per cent (they used to be 4, 6 and 8 per cent). But don't try checking those numbers against paperwork from a few years or more ago – the figures have been cut down to reflect a lower return environment. And if the investment isn't taxed then the rates, primarily for pensions, are 2, 5 and 8 per cent (dropping from a previous 5, 7 and 9 per cent). As very long-term investments, pension projections must also show the effect of inflation at a series of rates. It's all very complex and you would need a super spreadsheet to work it out.

What's the point of these figures? None of these projected rate calculations comes with any guarantee. Your money could go backwards or zoom ahead at top speed. They could change if the cost structure of your investment was varied. And if even the rates used for these illustrations in key feature documentation can alter with time, you're best treating them as little more than an amusement rather than relying on their coming true. Quoting these figures is a requirement with certain products but many professional advisers suggest you ignore them. Those that do look at them say you should concentrate on the middle point of the growth rate you are quoted.

The real – and perhaps only – point is to prevent financial advisers promising the earth from an investment that ends up with a very average performance.

You won't find these supercharged investments, of course, if you buy shares or most packaged stock market investments such as unit trusts or investment trusts where gains or losses tend to be down to earth.

So take a look at FCA growth figures to see how long it would take your £10,000 to grow into a number of target figures assuming a 4.5 per cent annual return. I could keep going but I reckon 25 years is long enough.

£10,000: No time

£12,000: 4 years and 1 month

£14,000: 7 years and 8 months

£16,000: 10 years and 10 months

£18,000: 13 years and 4 months

£20,000: 15 years and 10 months

£25,000: 20 years and 11 months

£30,000: 25 years and 0 months

Investments are for the medium to long term – from five years upwards. So, over this timeframe, what can you expect? The following sections tell you.

The likely return from shares

Anyone reading newspaper headlines or watching television news can be forgiven for believing that shares only go in one direction. And that direction goes through 180 degrees from time to time. It veers from 'everyone pile into a one-way bet' to 'run as fast as you can from shares'. Oddly enough, the euphoria tends to come after a big price rise while the misery memoirs all too often come after a huge fall in values.

This tells you two things about shares. Firstly, the media fails to present a balanced view. Secondly, and more importantly, the media fails to understand that shares work for the long term.

Shares are volatile, but over the very long term, say the whole of the 20th century, a basket of typical equities has produced average annual gains of around 12 per cent before tax.

Using different start and finish dates can produce almost any other figure you care to think of. But however you cut it, the trend in share prices is upward provided that you're patient. No one would bother to take the inherent risks with shares if they didn't expect to make greater gains than with bonds, property or cash over the longer term. But past performance is never a guide to the future. So this is just an illustration of what's been the very-long-term performance.

The return from shares comes in two forms, although neither is guaranteed, let alone even promised:

- ✔ Dividends
- ✔ Capital gains

Dividends are the way companies return part of the profits they make, or the reserves they've built up over good years, to the part-owners of the firm. That's you, the shareholder.

These are small amounts compared with your initial investment. But if reinvested into more shares, they can boost your holding. A 3 per cent annual dividend, after any tax, reinvested would add around 40 per cent to your shareholding after ten years.

When the shares pay more than the savings

Don't stick your money in a bank; invest in bank shares instead.

As UK interest rates – and hence the return from savings – sank to virtual invisibility in the months following the 2008 financial crisis, savers started to look for other ways to maintain their battered finances. Leaving the cash in a deposit account was a guaranteed loss. If you received 1 per cent (and that's before tax) from a savings vehicle while inflation was running at 2.5 per cent then each year the value of your money would fall. Many accounts paid less than 1 per cent – some as little as 0.10 per cent. One alternative was to buy the shares of the bank you may put your money into via a savings account. You couldn't do this with every high street bank – Nationwide had no shares and Lloyds and the Royal Bank of Scotland group were in finance's equivalent of 'special measures'. Those you could buy included Barclays, HSBC and Santander. All these shares offered shareholder dividend returns well in excess of saver interest.

There is, however, a two-way risk with this strategy. If the value of bank shares fell then you wouldn't get your original money back if you needed to exit. This is a serious no-no for many. But if the shares rose, you'd gain twice over. Besides extra income, your investment would have grown. An added advantage of the share route is that banks, like other businesses, hate cutting or abandoning their dividends because it sends such a bad signal to investment markets. Instead, they expect to increase them gradually over the years – you can't say the same for savings rates.

The beauty of dividends is that you should get them whether share prices as a whole are going up or down. Dividends are regular, and a company cutting out or missing a payment is a very bad sign indeed. So, with a lesson from history, holding up the dividends can stave off the day of reckoning, even if that means running the rest of the business on worse than empty. Missing dividend payments was the only thing Northern Rock didn't do as it fell from grace in 2007. Even when Northern Rock was in severe trouble, the bank maintained its ambition to pay shareholders their twice-yearly cheque. The bank cancelled the payment only when this dividend would have been paid from rescue money supplied by the Bank of England.

The second return from shares is that the capital goes up. Is this a sure thing? No. But should it happen? Yes, although only over the long term. The first decade of the present century was a shares disaster and the only one since the Second World War where shares fell after inflation.

What you get from a share depends on the exact price you paid and when you purchased. If you buy at the top of the market and the share subsequently halves in value, it could take the best part of a decade before you're back on the growth track.

The likely return from bonds

Are you an avid reader of Victorian novels? If so, you know that the heroines always know the value of the hero's (or villain's) fortune by turning his lump sum wealth into so much per year. And the figure selected is always 5 per cent because this was the long-term return the Victorians expected.

And how do heroines of Victorian novels always know this? Because in Victorian days, most money went into bonds. Those from the government were the safest. Those from railway companies and iron works were riskier. So although the Victorian novel heroine may not be able to recognise all that much of the world around her, she is at home with the finances on bonds. The more world-aware villain also knows the value of a lady's fortune and the likely income if he can lay his evil hands on it.

With lower rates over the past years, 5 per cent is probably on the high side, but it could be near enough right looking 10 years or more ahead. Whatever the rate that villain looks for, he knows he'll get a little less in the super-safety of UK government bonds, or *gilts* as they're known in the money trade. And he'd get a percentage point or two more aiming for *corporate bonds*, bonds issued by commercial companies raising loans.

But how do you get the 6, 7 or 8 per cent on offer from some bonds and bond funds? Easy! You just aim at bonds – known as *junk bonds* – from firms that have a dodgy track record. In addition, the bonds of some countries have junk status because the country's underlying finances are a mess. Nations from Latin America or south-east Asia have often been guilty parties.

If you're willing to take the risk that they'll miss a payment or, worse, fail to give back your capital on time or at all, then you may be rewarded for your bravery plunging into these junk offerings by the potential doubling of your return over safe bonds. But although you could end up with more, you could equally get your financial head blown off in a crisis. And plenty of those have occurred.

Investors who like to sleep at night should look at bonds paying out a maximum of 4 to 5 per cent. Bond fund purchasers should go no higher than 3.5 to 4.5 per cent. Why the gap? Because the fund carries an annual fee, typically 1 per cent, which must be paid out from somewhere! These costs come directly from the bond's income, hence the reduction.

The likely return from property

According to the Nationwide Building Society, the average price of a modern property throughout the UK was around £186,500 in summer 2014. In 1992, the price of that same typical home stood at £51,630. Track back to 1983, and it was just under £26,000. And three decades or so ago in 1973, it was £9,800.

Of course, these are averages. In summer 2014, London-area properties were £400,000 and substantially up on 2007, and those in north-west England were £144,000 – virtually unchanged over the years, although some areas were still cheaper than seven years previously.

But for the purposes of this discussion, leave aside what you may make from your own home, because you have to live somewhere, don't always have much choice on where you live and would be paying rent if you weren't buying. Instead, think in terms of commercial property.

Professionals invest in commercial property, such as factories, office blocks and shopping centres. You can't go out and buy a business park unless you have tens of millions and the ability to manage your investment. But you can tap into commercial property through a number of funds.

What you get from a property investment comes from two sources. One source is the rent tenants pay. You won't get this straight into your pocket, though. You'll have to fund management costs, perhaps repairs, interest on borrowings and tax. The second source is the hoped-for gain in the underlying value of the buildings. Add the two together, and you get the full return.

Since 1971 the overall annual returns from property have only declined in years of financial crisis and severe economic downturn, according to figures from experts Investment Property Databank. These were the financial crisis in 1974, three years during the economic downturn at the start of the 1990s, and in the years 2007 and 2008 when almost everything went down.

In present-day conditions, you can expect to earn around 4.5 to 6.5 per cent a year averaged over long periods. So you can expect more from property than from bonds but less than from shares. However, you don't need to repair a bond, have security guards for bonds or worry about a bond going out of fashion.

Commercial property is different from domestic property. Figures for the two seldom go in tandem.

The likely return from a cash account

Don't expect too much from a cash account. Many pay a pittance – and that's before tax. You should only invest in cash for safety, never for the long term unless it's of paramount importance that you know exactly what you'll have in the future to meet a known financial need, such as a child's education.

Since 1971, cash has only been the best performing asset type during two years – 1974 and 1990. And both years, the financial system was in trouble. Cash was the worst place to put your money during at least 12 separate years. And over almost any long period, cash has been easily out-gunned by bonds and property, and it's been beaten out of sight by shares.

The building society, bank or National Savings is the starting point for any calculation of whether a risk could be worthwhile. Investing in a speculative enterprise is pointless if the best you can foresee is a fraction of a percentage point above the bank branch.

Leaving medium- to long-term money in a current bank account is a guaranteed loser. Rates can be as low as 0.1 per cent, and yes, that's before tax on this virtually invisible return at 20 per cent for most people and 40 per cent for the better off. Inflation means your money is worth less each year.

The government inflation target is 2.0 per cent, so your money needs to earn that much after tax to stay level. For a basic-rate taxpayer, that means a headline rate of at least 2.5 per cent, and a top-rate taxpayer needs around 3.2 per cent just to go nowhere. At the time of writing, it's hard to find any account producing more than around 2.5 per cent – and that's with shopping around and restrictions on withdrawals.

The likely return from other assets

Investors have seen spectacular returns at certain times from gold, diamonds, works of art and even special shares offering guaranteed tickets at the centre court at Wimbledon for the All-England championships. Others have made big money out of racehorses, vintage wine and stamp collections.

But all these ventures demand a whole lot of specialist knowledge combined with a whole load of luck. Fans of this sort of thing tend to flag up the good times and ignore the bad years.

Figures are fairly unreliable because you're always comparing apples with bananas. A painting by Pablo Picasso may double in value over a year, but that doesn't say anything about a Salvador Dali or even other works by Picasso.

 People have offered many illegal investment schemes in areas such as stamp collecting and fine wines. These schemes offer big gains for supposed small risk. The authorities have shut down some of these ventures but usually not before hapless investors have lost their savings.

Increasing Your Chances of Successful Returns

You can't separate risk and reward, risk and regret. You must take risks and put your head above the cash investment parapet if you want to win.

Now turn risk on its head and call it opportunity. It's really the same thing, but now you have a positive phrase. You can increase your chances of success by diversifying (not putting all your investment eggs into one basket) and being patient.

Plenty of factors affect your chances of success

Suppose that you acquire shares in ABC Bank and XYZ Insurance, perhaps as a result of free share handouts. Obviously, you have to work out whether the opportunities in each company are worthwhile. And that's something I look at in detail in Part II.

But for now, you need to consider the bigger picture altogether. No company is an island, and none lives in a vacuum. Plenty more factors can enhance your opportunities or increase your chances of making a mistake:

- **Currencies:** Foreign exchange markets can have an impact on your investment. They have a habit of moving in slow trend lines, although they jump about at the umpteenth decimal place all the time. Each day, even each minute, exchange rates can go either way by very small amounts. No investment straight lines exist!

- **Interest rates:** You may invest in a brilliant company, but if interest rates go up, the company will be less attractive because the cash it needs from the bank for expansion will cost it more. Rising interest rates are bad news for almost everyone other than holders of cash.

- **Stock markets:** When share prices are generally booming, even badly run companies do reasonably well. But when share prices are falling, even the best organised firms with the greatest prospects tend to lose out, although not by so much (ignore what happens in days of total panic when, besides the bad and the ugly, good shares slump fast because alarmed investors sell quality because they can't find buyers for rubbish).

- **Inflation:** Nope, not car tyre pressure but rising prices. Inflation can be good for some sectors, such as retailers, because it takes the pressure off, meaning they don't have to run perpetual sales and price cuts. When people have more pounds or euros or dollars in their pocket, they will spend them before prices go up even higher. If prices are falling – that's deflation – then people put off purchasing and that's bad for stores.

- **The economy:** You can't really beat it. If it looks good, everything shines; when it turns down, only a handful of assets manage to hold their heads up.

Diversification is your best friend

Diversification is putting your eggs in many baskets. So if you trip up and choose a poor investment, you still have some capital left to help your finances recover. Or at least, that was what people thought before the credit/ banking crisis in 2008.

Now everything remains up for questioning – including some of the assumptions I've made in this book. Fact is, no one knows when or whether what previously passed for normality will return. Or what will be the new normal. Or whether there'll be a normal at all.

So, in the meantime, diversifying may still be better than sticking everything in one asset type.

Understanding the multi-layered approach that professionals use

Professional investors consider what the fund they manage is supposed to achieve. If the fund's main role is to provide a regular pension income for those whose retirement needs it has to meet, the fund goes, in the main, for safer assets, such as bonds, property and cash. But if the fund advertises itself as a route into, say, higher-risk Far Eastern share markets, it must restrict itself to these investments, with a little cash to give it flexibility.

Those running a fund with a wide remit, such as a cautiously managed fund (the basis of many retirement plans as well as the cornerstone of investment bonds sold to older people), work out their asset allocation as percentages of the whole fund between the main asset classes, including shares, bonds, cash and property.

When diversification turned out to be worthless

Big investment institutions traditionally put money in a variety of assets that were 'uncorrelated' with volatile equities such as bonds, property or currencies. *Uncorrelated* means that they kept going steadily even if shares were all over the place. But they still believed shares would win out over the long term.

The 2008 credit crisis threw those assumptions up into the air. So-called uncorrelated assets turned out to be correlated because they fell as far and as fast as shares. And equities lost their shine to bonds – partly because of the growing number of pension-fund recipients who needed the predictable income stream that bonds, not equities, could provide.

These mega-investors matter. Private investors – sorry to say this – have very little influence at all because most of their money is channelled into professionally run funds.

Will life settle back to business as usual? Or are we into uncharted territory? Only time will tell, but it will take a very bold investor to tear up the diversification book just yet.

Within each of those asset areas, they buy a wide range of investment assets. The idea is not to be caught out if one area catches a cold. Within property, for example, a fund manager may buy some office blocks, shopping centres and industrial premises. Within shares, a well-diversified fund manager may have holdings in the UK, the US, mainland Europe and the Far East.

Wide-remit managers then further subdivide. Say, for example, that a fund manager has holdings in the UK, the US, mainland Europe and the Far East. Regarding the fund focusing on UK shares, the fund manager may decide to have a percentage in different stock-market-company sectors, such as bank stocks and engineering companies.

Only after looking at all those various things do fund managers look at individual shares, deciding to hold pharmaceutical company A rather than B. This is called the *top-down approach*.

Concentrating too much on one or two investments is a mistake. Another mistake is not looking at all your wealth. If your pension fund is riding on UK shares then you should consider other areas in your own investment strategy for money under your direct control.

Spreading your money in practice

Suppose two of your ancestors each invested £100 in 1899. Both said the money was to stay in the family whatever happened. But one allowed you to spend any income while the second decreed that you had to reinvest all income. For simplicity, we'll assume no taxation at all. To simplify matters, these distant ancestors both said you could choose between just three investment types: cash at the building society, UK government bonds and the UK stock market.

The results of each strategy have been widely different. The timeframe is well over the span of four generations, so plenty of ups and downs have occurred (and booms, crashes, wars and peace treaties). They're all well documented by Barclays Bank in its excellent annual number-crunching exercise, the Equity-Gilt study, whose figures I use here.

Let's have a look first at what happened to that first bequest from way back – the one that said you could spend all the dividends and interest the day they popped into your back account. If you had put the money into shares, the £100 would have been worth £14,915 at the end of 2013 if invested in UK equities with the dividend income spent. But those Victorians who trusted their government bonds came out far less well. Their £100 would now be worth just £52. The £100 in the bank would still be £100.

But if you had re-invested all the income year on year without fail – the object of the second bequest from all that time back – then everything would look brighter. The shares would now be worth £2,214,856; the government bonds £30,591; and the building society/bank account would be valued at £20,363. All this is before the tax authorities take their substantial slice.

Of course, prices have increased a great deal since the last days of Queen Victoria. Adjusted for inflation, the equities, including re-invested income, would be worth £28,386, so their real value was multiplied 284 times, but the gilts would only buy goods worth £392 in 1899. The cash is even worse at £261. Even over the past 40 years, average prices rose more than tenfold.

This is really long-term stuff, but the theory 'whatever you do, you have to have assets in shares' works on shorter periods as well. So even if your ancestors were cautious, dividing their £100 in shares, bonds and bank accounts, today's balance would still be a lot higher than if the money was either all in bonds or, worst of all, just left in the bank. Most investment gains come from shares, despite their bad performance in the first decade of this century.

Even over just 40 years, shares have proven best. But what if you'd been a real speculator, believing that you knew the best home for your money each 1 January for the following 12 months? If you had perfect foresight, you'd be more than 2,000 times richer (ignoring tax and costs). You may have managed to pick the worst option, however, in which case your money would have halved in paper terms – or gone down 95 per cent or so in buying power.

Note that the great outperformance in shares wasn't gradual. It came in fits and starts. During 11 of the past 40 years, the index made 20 per cent or more in gains in a 12-month period. But bad years were really bad – down as much as 50 per cent in the very worst 12-month period. And if you scratch those figures more closely, you find that the big gains in equities were concentrated on just a relatively low number of days in that period. If you missed them because you were moving in and out of the market, you may have fared little better than keeping your money in the safe and solid building society.

One thing all the figures show is the power of re-investment. If you'd spent your money as you earned it rather than putting it back, your fortune would be a tiny fraction of these figures – whatever investment you chose.

Patience is your pal

To be a good investor, you need to have a good strategy and good diversification, but to be a savvy investor you also need patience and time. Your investments may need years to mature. There may be more days when your investments go nowhere or down than when they rise. But when they do increase, they can do so by substantial amounts over a short time.

Your own time horizons determine the risks you can afford to take. Investment isn't a short-term punt on financial markets. It requires at least five years, preferably longer. Short-termism can also increase your costs and your tax bill.

Chapter 5

Being Aware of Small Print – and of Print that Isn't There

. . . .

In This Chapter

▶ Knowing that shares can go down as well as up

▶ Knowing that bonds can go bust

▶ Understanding that super-strategies can turn into sand

▶ Being aware that property investments can crumble

▶ Avoiding the tax-freedom trap

▶ Putting a stop to scamsters

. . . .

So you've taken a long, hard look at how ready you are to take the risks inherent in investing. You know that you have to take chances and step, a little or a lot, into the financial unknown. And you know that if you aren't prepared to take a risk, you stand no chance of beating the bank or the building society. And now you've made up your mind to invest rather than merely save. (If you *haven't* taken a long, hard look at these things then you really, really need to. Look through Chapter 1 to make sure that you're even ready to invest and check out Chapter 4, which is all about investment risk.)

Congratulations on making an informed decision. Now you have just one hurdle to cross before you're ready to look at the nitty-gritty of investing. That one hurdle is getting into the habit of reading the small print in investment situations before looking at the headlines. You're in the right place because this chapter tells you all about those nasties.

'Um, Where Do I Actually Find the Small Print?'

Small print exists in virtually all investment situations. You'll find the small print in places like the bottoms of adverts and way down through official documentation. Small print is virtually invisible for a purpose. It has to comply with the law (which has never defined how small is small) but doesn't draw attention to itself.

At times, you won't always understand what you read. When that happens, ask the person you're buying from. If the reply is still incomprehensible then shred the deal. Plenty of other opportunities are out there with words that make sense.

Know that if small print exists, you'll be deemed to have read and understood it, even if it's located on page 199 of a document and written in language only the lawyer who wrote it could possibly follow. The Financial Ombudsman Service (the last port of call before the court for complaints about financial products) won't look kindly on you if you complain that you lost your money through not reading the small print, although you may have some cause for complaint if the full version of the legal stuff wasn't available or if it really is gobbledygook.

And know that even if you're buying and selling shares for yourself without professional advice, you'll probably have to sign a piece of paper accepting all responsibility for your own actions. Buying without a broker or adviser giving specific advice is called *execution-only* dealing. Expect to see phrases such as, 'You are responsible for selecting the stocks and shares, and you take full responsibility for the outcome of your investments and your actions.' Signing this disclaimer doesn't stop the broker charging you!

Shares Can Go Down As Well As Up

Seems simple enough: shares can go up and down. Yet that information takes many people by surprise because they were lulled into a false sense of security by the silver-tongued investment sellers who convince customers (and possibly even themselves) that share prices will go on rising forever. 'Treat any price reverse as a reason to buy more,' they say. Remember that it's the investment seller's job to sell investments just as it's the farmer's job to produce food.

You need to be prepared for the value of your shares to go down, and the small print in investment documents addresses this very issue. The wording is often something like this: *The value of your investment and the income you receive from it can go up or down, and there is no guarantee you will get your full investment back.*

The small-print people could add that there's no guarantee you'll get anything back at all (and sometimes that happens – ask all the folk who had shares in Bradford & Bingley or Northern Rock at the time of the banking crisis for confirmation). But otherwise, this information is clear and means what it says. So take it to heart.

Of course, shares can go up too! Individual shares can go to zero, but shares as a whole have never become worthless in any one country outside of cataclysmic events such as the Russian Revolution back in 1917.

Even the best companies' share values go backwards when shares are falling all around. Sometimes the top companies suffer unduly. When share purchasers want out quickly, they sell the good stuff first because the rubbish is harder to shift. (Think of which properties in your area would be easiest and quickest to sell if the owners needed to raise cash.)

Besides being prepared for the value of your shares to go down, be aware of the following truisms about past performance:

✔ **Past performance isn't necessarily a guide to future performance.** The Financial Conduct Authority (FCA) says that no relationship exists between the future and the past. All too many funds like to sell their wares on the basis of past performance, and they show this in the most flattering light (surprise, surprise!). Investment companies, not surprisingly, disagree with the FCA because they spend a fortune advertising their past successes, hoping customers accept that the future will be the same. Academic research supports the FCA line, with some experts reckoning that the past of a fund has no more relevance to the future than using past winning lottery numbers as a guide to winning the next draw. At the very least, a good fund manager may have moved elsewhere to be replaced by a dud.

Three degrees of falsehood exist: lies, damned lies and investment statistics from companies trying to sell you something.

✔ **Past performance may not necessarily be repeated.** Even if an investment remains successful, it's not likely to be successful in the same way as before. The investment may do better or worse. In any case, it all depends on which time period you use for the comparison.

You also need to know that if you buy individual shares, you normally only receive specific warnings if you buy during the initial public offering (or flotation) period or other times such as when a rights issue is launched when an official prospectus covers new shares. Keep in mind that any forecast of future business is based on assumptions that the directors of the company consider reasonable from their point of view, which will be optimistic.

The specific warnings from the company that you find in prospectuses or other cash-raising documents may be worded something like this:

✔ *The price you get for your shares should you wish to sell may be influenced by a large number of factors, some specific to the company and some extraneous.* This type of small print covers almost everything.

✔ *Competitors may arise and make large investments to enter the market this company is focusing upon.* Patents and present success protect little.

✔ *The directors and their connected interests will be interested in 55 per cent of the share capital and be in a position to control the outcome of certain matters requiring a shareholder vote.* Forget shareholder democracy and voting at annual general meetings where it's one share, one vote on any issues raised. Your views will always be outvoted if the board and their mates (who are usually the big investment banks and fund management companies) have more than half the shares – unless you can persuade any of them to change their minds.

✔ *The company may require further funding to achieve profitability.* In the future you and other shareholders may be asked to put your hand into your pockets again or risk the company flopping from a lack of cash.

In recent times companies have started to tell investors more than they used to reveal. They update more often and are under a duty to comment on unusual share price moves (even if it's to claim they have no idea what's going on) and to 'correct' market assumptions such as forecasts of future earnings made by stockbrokers' analysts. These usually take the form of a *profits warning*, serving to dampen down expectations. Companies would rather ease investors down gently over a few months than let them fall with a big bump. Equally, although this happens less often, firms that are doing better than the market predicts tell investors to upgrade their forecasts.

The Best Bonds Can Go Bust

Fixed-interest securities, or *bonds*, can fail to pay their regular promised income or the final repayment of the original capital, a scenario called *default*. You need to be aware that the higher the payout, the greater the chance of a default. Here are some bond warnings that you'll find in bond-fund litera-ture, and sometimes in the legal material that accompanies a bond issue. You won't find anything about these risks if you simply buy a bond through a stockbroker.

✔ *This fund invests in higher yielding bonds (non-investment grade).* The risk of default is higher with non-investment grade bonds (also known as junk because they could go bust or fail to pay out on time) than with investment grade bonds (they're the ones from really respectable gov-ernments and top companies). But what you can't know is how much higher this risk will be. Seasoned investors can remember Argentina defaulting on its bonds, and many Russian bonds went bad as well.

✔ *Higher yielding bonds may have increased capital erosion than lower yield-ing bonds.* This small print means that your chances of losing serious money are greater with higher yielding bonds.

✔ *The level of income on offer could indicate a likely loss of some of your capital.* Some bonds offer a high income now but with the chance (or perhaps almost certainty) of capital loss later on. This may not matter to

> some pension funds, but it could be bad news for your tax bill because you have to pay income tax on the income you get, but can't claim anything back if you make a loss when you sell the bond or it comes to the end of its life.

Great Ideas Don't Last Forever

The investment world is full of bright ideas that once worked but no longer do. You won't receive any specific warning about this fact, so you need to be aware of it all on your own. Not to worry. That's what I'm here for. A couple of examples will help you understand what this concept is all about.

One now-defunct investment firm came up with a bright idea. It had a list of 30 big company shares, and it looked at which shares offered the highest dividend payments for a £1,000 stake. The firm decided to hold for one year whichever three shares fitted this recipe on 1 January each year. Then, 12 months later, the firm would repeat the whole exercise. At that time, the firm would sell shares that had moved out of the target area and buy whatever new high-dividend payers suited its formula.

When this idea was launched, the firm could show that it worked using historical data, a process known as *back-testing*. The firm then stretched its initial idea so investors would get five shares that most fitted the profile and then shrank the concept to just one share a year.

Moving the goalposts like this usually suggests desperation on the part of the concept's promoters. They move the goalposts so you hopefully don't notice that their scheme isn't making money. Surprise, surprise. High ones, threes, fives (as these schemes were called), and probably any other number they might've come up with all failed to produce the desired effect.

What worked in the past has no more chance of working in the future than any other idea.

Another brainwave was the January effect. Someone noticed that shares went up in January, so an idea was born: buy the day or so after Christmas Day. Problem was, when the idea got around, it ceased to work. Clever share buyers decided to anticipate the January effect by purchasing equities *before* Christmas. Then another group decided to pre-empt those clever share buyers by putting in orders at the end of November. Give this practice a few more years and it would have got back all the way through the year to January!

When more than a tiny handful of people know about an idea, it ceases to work.

Property Investments Can Crumble

Whether you read it or ignore it, a lot of small print exists around bonds and shares. But when it comes to property, hey, you're out there on your own. Scant documentation is available for you to consider, even for those with the sharpest eyesight.

So here are the warnings property purveyors would put in, if they were obliged to do so:

- ✔ *No one may want to live or work at this location.* The danger here is when a new project doesn't attract any tenants or doesn't attract tenants of the quality and deep pockets expected.

- ✔ *No one may want this property in the future.* Properties can fall out of fashion. I can't be the only person to live near a 1930s shopping area that once hosted top retail names but now is a mix of low-rent takeaways, even lower-rent charity shops and zero-rent boarded-up premises. And more than one 1970s shopping mall is only suitable for the bulldozers.

A good property fund or property company whose shares you've bought work all this out and come up with a value for the building or rent for the tenant that better reflects reality. Low rent is better than no rent; £5,000 per year rent on a property without bank debts that cost £50,000 to build decades ago is a lot better than turning a recent unwanted building still in hock to the banks that cost £10 million to build into a skateboard park or demolition zone.

Know that property funds often have a small-print clause that allows them to freeze investors into the fund when the going gets really tough, meaning that anyone 'wanting out' has to wait until the managers allow them to escape. This could be next year or next decade.

Plenty of property opportunities aren't well managed or require you to put all your bricks onto one site without diversifying your risk.

Property sales people get their money from selling real estate. After they have their commission, they're unconcerned about what happens next.

Tax-Free Can Be a Dead Loss

I hate paying taxes. You hate paying taxes. Any people who can legally cut their tax bill generally try to do so.

The government has a number of legitimate tax-saving schemes, primarily pensions but also Individual Savings Accounts (ISAs), which are intended to encourage people on modest incomes to put money away for the future.

Also available are a number of more obscure schemes involving everything from high-tech start-up companies to conifer plantations. The rationale for some of these schemes has been lost in the mists of antiquity.

'Tax-free investment' or 'pay no tax with this plan' are such powerful draws that they're featured as huge headlines in a large number of investment ads. The obvious idea is to grab your attention. But you need to know about the hidden subtext.

Some investment-product firms use tax benefits as a 'feel the width, never mind the quality' approach. These sellers hope that you'll be so impressed by the chance to get one over on HM Revenue & Customs (HMRC; the tax authority) that you won't look too closely at what they're really pushing. So be very aware of the following:

- Product providers and sellers use phrases such as 'government-approved tax savings' to imply that the scheme has state approval or that it's as solid as the Bank of England. But in reality, the tax benefits are a few pennies a week and the risk still exists. If your investment falls, you won't get any government handout. Some investments into pensions are touted as 'approved' by HMRC. That's true – except that virtually anything other than residential property can go into a retirement plan. So the approved bit means nothing.

- The advertised tax benefits may only apply to a minority. Sometimes, they may be positively harmful to others. For example, non-taxpayers can actually lose out on some deals because they can't claim anything back. HMRC reckons that if you pay no tax, you can't get a refund.

- Many tax deals come with a deadline. Product providers know that no one wants to miss out on a bargain. They hope you'll buy in a last-minute rush and not look too critically at what's on offer.

If you're tempted by saving tax (and who isn't), consider the following facts: basic-rate taxpayers now gain nothing from tax freedom on the dividends on equity ISAs. Higher-rate taxpayers may save a few pence a week for each £1,000 on equity dividend payments. Bond ISAs are a better deal tax-wise, with basic-rate taxpayers typically saving £12 a year (25p a week) for each £1,000 invested.

Stock-market ISAs also give you freedom from capital gains tax (CGT), which may be worth something if your holdings and potential profits are large enough to warrant it. *Capital gains tax*, which is designed to get the government a slice of your investment success, can grab up to 28 per cent of any gain you make. However, everyone has an annual CGT exemption of around £11,000 to set against profits (it can change each year, so look at the HMRC website, www.hmrc.gov.uk, to see the latest figure). CGT only applies when you sell. So if you're a long-term holder, don't get too fixated on it. The way this tax works has changed a lot over the past decade or so. And it could continue to alter over the next years.

The worth of any ISAs held on your death counts toward the value of your estate and any inheritance-tax bill. So if HMRC doesn't grab your money while you're living, it could collect from your estate when you die. Great thought, that.

As an investor, you must calculate whether the tax saving on offer is sufficient to attract you into a deal that you'd otherwise let pass you by. It'd take a big tax-freedom cushion to protect you against falls in your money. The tax relief isn't the cake or even the icing on top of it. It's just the decorative finishing touch.

Foreign Scam Operations Are Bigger (and Trickier) Than Ever

All previous sections of this chapter paint a grey picture, meaning they warn you that promises of top investments can actually prove to be average or just plain mediocre investments. But this section paints a flat-out black picture, meaning it warns you of scamster investments that guarantee you'll lose every single penny. You may even lose more if you're persuaded to run up a big credit-card bill in an attempt to get your money back. You won't. You'll just be even poorer. But despite the fact that many scams are run by organised crime, the mob just loves the veneer of respectability, so some of these scams come complete with their own warnings. So just like with the more legitimate investment plans, scamsters can say you should've read the small print.

Beware the boiler rooms

A *boiler room* is a collection of guys (hardly ever gals) in a cheap building somewhere, usually abroad, who spend all day working through phone numbers – the so-called *sucker list* because they expect to sucker people on it into paying big money for phoney investments. They expect most people to slam down the phone, but for those who show interest, they read prepared scripts on the wonders of the asset they're pushing. It's called a boiler room because some are down in the basement but also because they send out a lot of high-pressure steam to scald victims.

Boiler rooms may state that they're based somewhere like Beijing, Barcelona, Belgrade, Mexico City or Mali. It doesn't matter. Wherever they claim to be and wherever they really are (rarely the same place as they claim), they're outside UK jurisdiction.

With a particular type of scamster, you're dealing with organised crime that makes the bad guys in *The Godfather* films look like amateurs. This crime was perfected in Toronto in the 1970s. Now, it's bigger and nastier than ever and operates from all over – although don't ever believe them or their websites if they give an address.

The scam can start with a simple letter. It may say that you're an investor in a company, which it names, and that you may like to receive a special research report on that firm, compiled by investment experts. Or the letter may be more general, simply offering a regular investment newsletter compiled by experts. The report or newsletter is, of course, free.

Those who reply are required to give details, including phone numbers. The company's return address is often in the UK, although that means nothing because it's just a mailbox. A UK phone number is equally meaningless because diverting calls to somewhere way beyond UK legal protection is easy. In addition, the company isn't regulated under UK investor-protection laws, so you can't go complaining to anyone.

Watch out for a dodge in which a foreign scam firm gets a regulated UK firm to supposedly authorise it. A loophole in UK law allows legitimate firms to 'approve an advertisement for marketing purposes'. So all the UK firm is really doing is saying it agrees that the advert details are correct. These usually only run as far as having a name, phone number and possibly address with the briefest description of what the firm purports to do. Such authorisation means nothing. It gives no compensation rights. It guarantees nothing. It's a sham.

A variation is the European Union financial firm passport. Under EU law, a firm regulated in one member country can operate in another. Scam merchants set up a regulated firm in a country that has lax rules – often claiming they're in something called 'insurance mediation' (whatever that is). You still don't get any compensation if you're caught by one of these outfits.

Instead of an expensive letter, many use spam emails. They offer a free report on a currency or stock market, always supposedly compiled by expert analysts. A third approach scamsters use is to send millions of junk emails (usually from Asia or Eastern Europe) lauding the prospects of a company you've never heard of. The scamsters try to cover themselves by revealing that the email senders were paid a sum such as $30,000 for their work. In very small print.

However they do it, the scamsters now have your interest. Often, they leave you alone for some weeks to receive your newsletter. You may notice that 75 per cent of the four-page letter is devoted to mainstream shares and economics. But the back page gives lavish praise to the money-making opportunities in a share you've never heard off, usually with a high-tech or scientific bent. The scamsters use all this stuff for the next stage of suckering cash from their victims.

Now, here's the really dangerous bit unless you're prepared: the phone call. The caller may make some pretence of discussing your investment needs, but he's really trying to probe how much he can take you for. The representative tells you that your investment could double your money in 30 to 60 days, or make ten times as much by this time next year. It's a straight appeal to greed, and it works because these firms continue to proliferate. Of course, the shares or whatever else is on sale are worthless and you never see your money again.

Scamster representatives use hard-sell tactics to persuade you to buy the shares, commodities, currencies, wine, precious stones or works of art they're touting. The Financial Conduct Authority is aware of *experienced* investors who've been pressured into buying things from these representatives, which shows just how persuasive these salespeople can be. If the representative sells you a commodity or currency deal, he may ring you back shortly afterwards with news of your winnings. The purpose is purely to persuade you that the firm is safe and that you can make really easy money. Don't bother asking for your winnings back in cash, however. You'll never get them. He'll suggest you re-invest. If you insist on your money, the representative will ignore you, and because you won't be able to find him, he'll pocket your money. But if his appeal to your greed works and you want more, the scamster will just 'trade' your cash until he has it all.

Alternatively, the representative sells shares in a tiny company, usually one with a miracle cure or technological wonder. Invariably, the boiler room buys the shares at their true worth – usually one-tenth of a US cent – and sells them to you at $1 each (boiler rooms always use US dollars). They're *restricted shares* too, meaning that you can't sell them without the company's permission (never forthcoming) until a year has passed, by which time the company will have disappeared, assuming, of course, that a real company existed in the first place.

After buying the shares, you generally experience delays and difficulties obtaining your share certificates. The shares turn out not to be the great deal you were promised. When you try to sell the shares, the representative usually tells you to wait a few weeks because really important news that will transform the price is about to emerge. This is just another tactic to keep you holding on.

But even if you do appear to have sold the shares, you nearly always have difficulty obtaining the proceeds or are put under a lot of pressure to buy other shares from the same boiler room with the money, so you never get to see the cash. Or you may be contacted by an organisation with another name that offers to get the money back provided that you pay an upfront fee.

These follow-up firms are known as *recovery rooms*. They're usually linked with the boiler room that ripped you off – otherwise how would they have all your details? But linked closely or not, their aim is a second bite at your bank account. The usual story with the recovery room is that it has an investor prepared to pay $20 a share to acquire the whole company. Now, because you only paid $5 a share, you're convinced that this is the miracle exit you've been waiting for. You calculate that you'll have made $50,000 profit. You have to complete just one piece of paperwork, the recovery room tells you, and pay a share transfer fee of $10,000. Pay that and then the 'buyer' and the recovery room both evaporate with more of your money.

Knowing the phoney deals that scamster companies sell

To catch you out – and the typical victim loses £20,000 – scamster companies need to both convince you that they have an asset that will soar in value and that they're real investment brokers. Many sell assets that are outside of financial services regulation, such as wine, carbon credits, land, rare earth minerals and, most recently, 'litigation' or your share of the results of a series of legal actions. They have a script that's designed to break down any scepticism – and to appeal to greed. Here's how the scamsters operate:

✔ **Wine:** The scamster company says that great vintages are limited in amount (true), that the Chinese are buying (maybe true) and that the Chinese are so rich they'll dilute their top chateau claret with cola (total nonsense). The story goes that because of all this, wine can only ever go up in value. The company quotes 'experts', but that's rubbish. If a big demand exists for one wine then either wine producers will make more or drinkers will switch to another vintage. In any case, the wine these scamsters sell is overpriced, may be phoney and, in some cases, may not even exist.

✔ **Land:** Scamster companies buy land from a farmer and convince victims it's about to get planning permission for housing. They sell it at ten times what they paid for it, but tell investors they'll get their money back twenty-fold. Needless to say, the land never gets planning permission.

✔ **Carbon credits and rare earth minerals:** The scamsters blind you with science – and the old story that big shortages are imminent. They sell credits at 10 to 20 times their real price and the minerals, assuming they even exist, are also grossly over-priced.

These companies tell you they have a City of London address (you can hire these by the day) and that they have 40 years of experience – difficult when the typical director is aged under 30. Every year, scores of these companies emerge and scores shut down. Don't expect any compensation, even when they're wound up in the public interest by government departments. These folk have spent your money long before.

Dealing with boiler-room operatives

Boiler-room operatives don't worry about their phone bill. International calls are dirt cheap anyway but spending $50 on calls is immaterial if they can convince you to part with $10,000. The longer they talk to you, the more persuasive they get. So just tell them that they're crooks and hang up. Don't worry about their feelings. They haven't got any.

Absolutely no reason exists for any overseas organisation to call you in this way other than to scam you out of your money. I've been writing about and tracking boiler rooms for more than 20 years, and I've yet to find an honest organisation with this approach. I won't. Ever. Why? There isn't one.

You have no protection whatsoever when dealing with boiler rooms. After you part with your money, you've lost it just as if a mugger stole your wallet or purse on the street, except the amounts involved are far greater than anyone carries around with them. And no theft-insurance comeback exists. Sadly, complaining to the UK authorities is pretty pointless. They can do nothing for you whatsoever. All you may get is the doubtful good glow from knowing that your experience may warn others.

Steering clear of onshore boiler rooms

Boiler and recovery rooms are nearly always based offshore. But some UK-registered and -regulated firms use the same tactics to sell dodgy shares of dubious value. Some are quoted on the AIM market, which has very easy listing rules. These firms may also try to sell you high-risk, high-cost *contracts for difference* – a specialised casino-style bet on a share that I explore further in Chapter 20 – where the only certainty is that they'll make more than you.

Onshore boiler rooms have different ways of getting your attention that you should know about:

- ✔ **By cold call:** They phone you. They shouldn't do this, either under Financial Conduct Authority (FCA) rules or if you've registered with the Telephone Preference Service to avoid junk calls. They get around this by saying you completed a 'research survey' some months ago. When pushed, they say they aren't sure which survey that was. That's because the survey never existed.

- ✔ **By post:** The other way of getting around the rules to get your attention, used less often than the cold call, is to get a list of shareholders in a very big company – perhaps one that was privatised – and then offer you 'research' or 'analysis' on the company. By returning the form, you agree they can contact you. And as for the 'analysis', it's generally something a school leaver could have cobbled together from the Internet. In other words, it's not worth the paper it was printed on.

The FCA shut down a number of these firms, but only after they brought misery to investors. It fined some, but because they were bust they never paid the penalty.

No one contacts you out of the blue for your own good. Stick to what you know.

Part II
Shares, Bonds and Other Investibles

Shares that don't behave as they should

When markets move up or down, it's usual for most shares to follow the trend. Those who watch stock-market screens talk of a 'sea of red' when prices are falling or an 'ocean of blue' when they're on the way up. But a few always defy the trend.

- Interest rates go up? This means inflation and higher prices. And, believe it or not, supermarkets actually welcome that (although they won't admit it). If prices start to rise, they can adjust the stickers on the shelves even faster and further in the knowledge that not too many people will notice. That way, they increase profits and benefit shareholders.

- Higher VAT? Again, no problem for supermarkets because so much of what they sell – more than half – is VAT free.

- A really bad winter that hits everything that moves (or rather, doesn't move!)? Bad for all sorts of shares including transport, high- street stores and insurance companies, but great for drug companies, which will sell a lot more cold cures.

- Market hit by a fall in the value of sterling? Don't worry. Companies that do loads of business abroad using other currencies will shine out from the gloom.

- Share prices pushed up by really good news? Well, don't expect that to extend to water and power companies, where prices are subject to regulation. In any case, although you may celebrate good economic data with a bottle of champagne, you never toast happy statistics by leaving more lights on!

For some online extras about Investing, head online and visit www.dummies.com/extras/investinguk.

In this part . . .

- ✔ Learn what you need to know about how stock markets work.

- ✔ Discover more about stocks and bonds and how they differ from each other.

- ✔ Look at some of the numbers investors have to deal with.

- ✔ Identify the professionals you'll need to employ to carry out your investment strategies.

Chapter 6

Comprehending How Stock Markets Work

. . . .

In This Chapter

▶ Unravelling the mysteries of shares and your ownership rights

▶ Explaining bonds and the rights you don't get

▶ Looking at the basics behind price rises and falls

▶ Discovering whether you can predict price moves

▶ Going behind the scenes to see how the stock market operates

. . . .

Ⓐll financial strategies, including those to keep all your money in cash or property, are based on what happens on stock markets – they're the big drivers of the world's finances. Many stock markets exist across the world, although the most important are in New York, Tokyo and London. What unites them all is that they're where shares and bonds are traded and, hence, the prices are determined. That sounds simple but stock markets can appear to be places of great mystery – even more so nowadays because most don't really have a physical presence at all. This chapter unravels the mysteries of the stock market. I explain what shares and bonds are. I spell out the reasons for the ups and downs of the market and offer tips for predicting market moves. And I describe the basic mechanics of the stock market so you can better understand those newspaper columns or online blogs you read every day.

Looking at the Evolution of the Stock Market

For centuries markets existed where people bought and sold items. Many of them, such as cattle and other livestock markets, were open to public scrutiny. They didn't require membership or passing exams. All people had to do was walk in with some money, and they'd walk out with an animal – or vice versa. If they knew what they were doing, the deal worked. If not, they ended up with the famous pig in a poke – not a good idea.

Markets in companies started off much in the same way, often in City of London coffee houses. But they became specialised as people set up more sophisticated companies that needed to raise money from investors. Share dealing had to be centralised (helped by inventions such as the railway and telegraph).

After centralisation happened, share-dealing became the plaything of the professionals who did what all professionals do – setting systems to ensure that they kept the work for themselves at the terms they considered suitable. Stockbrokers formed partnerships and controlled the work through the stock exchange, which they collectively owned.

Life carried on like this until the mid-1980s, when the City found itself in the midst of a huge change in working methods. Out went the cosy arrangements of the past and sleepy stockbrokers who worked from 10 to 4 with three hours for lunch. In came big banks, big money, long hours and a sandwich lunch at your desk, if you were lucky.

In addition, out went the old stock exchange, where the public could watch goings on from a viewing gallery. Now, no actual place as the stock exchange or stock market exists. Everything's traded electronically. All you get to see in a stockbroker's office is an ocean of trading screens covered in a tidal wave of numbers.

But the fundamentals of what makes markets tick haven't changed. And another thing hasn't changed: rising shares are shown on screens in blue; falling ones are in red. These colours are just as they were in the old days when prices were displayed using coloured chalks.

Understanding Shares

A *share* is literally that – a share, or part, of a company. And if you own shares, you have a stake in the fortunes of the firm involved and a say in its control, in proportion to the number of shares you hold.

BT, for example, has over 1 million UK shareholders. All bar around 7,000 hold fewer than 10,000 shares. But although nearly all the shareholders are small, it's the big investors who really control things – in the case of BT, the major investors own about 85 per cent of the company. Most other big companies have an even greater proportion of their ownership concentrated among huge investment organisations.

Never get misty-eyed about your shareholder rights in any big company, such as voting or attending annual meetings. They rarely add up to a row of beans. Still, if the meeting is controversial, you may end up on the TV news.

Shareholder democracy and shareholder power only really work for major investors. Shareholders can put pressure on companies, but don't expect them to do this at a public annual general meeting. They use their influence behind the scenes, sometimes working together to oust directors they consider failures. Major shareholders, who are sometimes called _activists_, buy big slices of a company, usually building up their stakes over a short time. They're not interested in the long-term worth of the company but want to push the directors into a strategy that's good for their owner interests. This isn't always in the best interests of other, less-well-organised shareholders.

Why raise money through shares?

Companies can raise money from banks and other lenders, and most do so. But share capital is what makes most companies tick financially because shares have big advantages. After the share is issued and paid for by the initial investor, that money permanently belongs to the company. The company never has to repay the money and has no obligation to pay for it in terms of dishing out regular payments such as dividends (even if dividends are a good idea). And no interest is charged as it would be on a bank loan.

All _limited companies_ (a legal term meaning the liability of the company is limited to its resources, which leaves shareholders not having to find extra cash if the company hits problems and goes bust) have shares. But only a few companies have shares that are traded on stock markets. They're generally the biggest companies, however, so what happens to their share price day to day is important.

All companies traded on stock markets in the UK are _public limited companies_ (PLCs). But not all PLCs are traded on markets. Some PLCs are really tiny companies trying to look big and tough.

How companies get to the stock market

The process of bringing a company to the stock market is more complicated and vastly more costly than bringing a cow to a cattle market. The process involves lawyers, accountants, investment bankers and public relations specialists. They all take big fees, often adding up to tens of millions of pounds in a big company, because they need to feed their expensive salary habits.

The process of bringing a company to the stock market used to be known as a _flotation_ but now it's more likely an _initial public offering_ (IPO). Effectively, they're one and the same. The IPO is accompanied by a ferocious amount of documentation known as a _prospectus_. It gives you the following:

✔ Details about the company, its past performance and prospects for the future (including profit forecasts).

- A full balance sheet.

- The past records of directors and senior managers (including any disasters they've been involved with).

- Pay packages for the top people and details of any deals between directors and the company.

- The advisers, such as brokers, banks, accountants and lawyers, used by the firm. The quality of these advisers is important. If some or all of them are small or not generally known, or have a past poor reputation, potential investors could criticise the IPO.

Large companies often bring their business to the stock market through a public offering, so anyone can apply. This is how the UK government sold most of the privatisation shares.

Smaller firms often use a device called a *placing*, where they offer large parcels of shares to selected stockbrokers and investment banks, who then distribute them to clients. This method has the disadvantage of locking out other investors but the plus point of a lower cost. If you invest through a collective fund such as a unit or investment trust, you may end up with some of these shares in your portfolio.

Note that some companies list on foreign markets (that includes overseas firms listing in London and UK firms going for overseas market quotes) when they want to extend their shareholder base, because some investors are limited to buying securities traded in their own countries or don't want the inconvenience of dealing with overseas-based equities. This doesn't usually involve existing shareholders, although stock exchange bosses claim that a wider geographical base makes the shares more attractive.

Ways to buy shares

Buying shares through an IPO is usually a good deal – provided you feel the shares have a future. One reason is that they're cheaper, because you have no brokerage fees or stamp duty to pay. In addition, companies like to bring their shares to market at a little less than the amount their advisers consider fair value. They want the headlines to say 'first day big share price advance' because an early gain grabs investor attention. They don't want stories that warn 'overpriced shares going down'. The launch of the IPO should occur at a good time in the company's progress – obviously, no one would invest if the consensus was that the firm was heading for the corporate graveyard.

However, the prospectus, to which you must have access, is full of gloomy stuff that the lawyers and regulators insist upon. Some of this is common sense, such as 'the company cannot predict the future, but here's our best estimate' although sometimes the prospectus includes small-print warnings about the directors' past failures – especially worth looking for if you're investing in a smaller company.

Regardless of all the optimism, an IPO is no guarantee of long-term success. Many fail to match their hype, producing losses for initial investors. Just because a marketing machine is going flat out to convince you doesn't mean you should abandon your critical faculties. And, by the way, watch also for directors and other large shareholders using a flotation to unload millions of shares for cash. If they had faith in the company, they'd want to hold on to as many shares as possible.

Sometimes, huge numbers can benefit from an IPO. Back in the late 1980s, the Abbey National was a building society owned by its members. But at that time, it decided to become a stock-market-quoted company. It gave each of its qualifying members a set number of shares in return for giving up their membership rights. These people received 100 shares worth £1.30 each. The company also sold additional shares at the same price to these investors. These shares are now part of Banco Santander, the Spanish bank that subsequently bought Abbey. Some of those former Abbey savers still have shares in Santander. These are now worth around eight to ten times the initial value.

More recently, the Royal Mail IPO saw many hundreds of thousands applying for shares in what was an extremely well-publicised launch, with commentators saying the 330p price per share during the offer period was a 'steal' (from the taxpayer, who was effectively the owner of the business before it was privatised in autumn 2013). It generated so much enthusiasm, however, that individuals were limited to just 750 shares, and many got none at all. Big investors got millions. Here, the hype was justified because Royal Mail shares posted big gains in days.

Companies can issue more shares later on, offering them to all shareholders through a *rights issue*, which gives every shareholder the right (but not the obligation) to buy shares in a fixed ratio to their present holding, usually at a lower price, or discount, to the then stock-market value. So if a company launches a one-for-four issue, someone with 400 shares can buy up to 100.

If you're attracted then you have to send a cheque for the full value. But if you can't afford them or don't want any more of that company's shares, you have two choices:

- ✔ You can sell your allocation as *nil paid rights*. This works on the basis that although you haven't paid for the shares, you own them until the closing date for the rights offer, so you can sell them in the stock market to someone else who's willing to pay for them.

✔ Sit back and wait for a cheque. If you do nothing then your allocation will be added to all those that aren't taken up and sold in the stock market after the rights issue period finishes. You get per share whatever big investors were prepared to pay. Obviously, the more successful the company and the more attractive the terms of the rights issue, the more you get.

Firms can also issue shares to pay for companies they acquire, so those firms' former owners acquire equity in the new company instead of a cash payment.

The shares most people buy and sell, though, are properly called *ordinary shares*. Some companies have an additional type, known as a *preference share*. Note that ordinary shares are often called *equities*, but they have nothing to do with the UK actors' union Equity! In the United States, shares are usually referred to as *stock* or *common stock*, but the principle behind them is the same.

Companies may offer other investment possibilities, such as bonds or loan stocks, but ordinary shares, or equities, are the most frequently traded. They're also potentially the most profitable and, also, the most at risk.

Equity holders only receive a dividend after other classes of investors – such as bondholders and other stakeholders like banks that have made loans – have been paid. And they're last in line for anything if the company goes bust. They usually get nothing in that event. But equity holders are the legal owners of the company. They get all the earnings of a successful firm after obligatory payments to loan stock and bondholders. Equity holders take the lion's share of the risks, but they get the lion's share of the rewards.

The perks you get when buying ordinary shares

Each ordinary share counts equally. So each one is worth the same amount when it comes to the value quoted in a newspaper or on a screen. (This discussion ignores the higher cost per share of buying and selling a small amount.) And the amount of dividend paid per share is equal.

And there's parity in voting rights. Companies are democratic, but instead of one person getting one vote, one share gets one vote. Shareholders can (but aren't obliged to) vote at annual general meetings (usually called AGMs) for items ranging from directors' remuneration to approving the annual report and accounts, and re-appointing auditors. They may also vote at extraordinary general meetings, often held when the company acquires another company in a takeover or issues a substantial number of new shares.

You can attend both annual and extraordinary meetings no matter how many or how few shares you own, but you're under no obligation to do so. Most shareholders don't attend. That's actually a good thing because finding a venue large enough would be impossible – nowhere in the UK can house even 100,000 investors.

Attendance, however, gives you the right to quiz the directors in public. No matter how unpopular or controversial your views may be to the directors, you have a legal right to be at the meetings. The company can't refuse to admit registered shareholders. You can even sign a form to send someone (known as a *proxy*) in your place.

The ability to buy just one share and have the same rights to speak at annual meetings as investment companies who own millions is good news for environmentalists, consumer activists, those with a political point to make or anyone looking for publicity for their cause. In theory, you can unite with shareholders owning 10 per cent or more of the company and enforce an extraordinary general meeting on a company and maybe unseat a director. In practice, this never happens with small investors unless they can find some big investors to join them in their protest.

Holding one share also gives you the right to an annual report and accounts. Many bigger companies save money by sending out an abridged version that leaves out most of the complicated numbers but often leaves in the pictures of directors smiling or showing off their new corporate helicopter! Know that you have a legal right to the complete version, which companies must supply to all shareholders who ask for one. Serious shareholders should always insist on the full version. You nearly always find a copy of the full accounts online – put the name of the company plus 'corporate' or 'investor' into a search engine to find its website.

Understanding Bonds

Lots of financial bits and pieces are called bonds. Many come from life-insurance companies. Some come from the sometimes febrile minds of the ever-inventive people who work in marketing departments. Others are Premium Bonds, a once-a-month National Savings & Investment flutter. The word *bond* even sounds reliable. The reason is because of all that old stock-market stuff about 'my word being my bond'. But in this book I don't focus on those bits and pieces called bonds. Instead, I cover *bonds* that are loans made to a company or government that you can trade on stock markets.

Governments have raised money from citizens and others through loans called *bonds* for centuries. Now companies increasingly get cash by issuing bonds instead of, or as well as, shares.

A bond promises a regular and fixed interest payment and repayment of the original amount on a set future date. Between the date the bond is acquired and that of its final repayment, the bond's price goes up and down according to circumstances.

Owners of company-issued bonds, usually known as *corporate bonds*, must be paid before equity holders if the company is in a sticky financial situation. However, if the firm goes bust bondholders will probably lose their money.

Chapter 10 deals exclusively with bonds, when you're ready for detailed information on the subject. For the purposes of this discussion, I just want to point out the perks you *don't* get when buying bonds:

- ✔ Bondholders don't get the right to attend annual general or extraordinary general meetings (although most companies don't object) unless the meetings are labelled as specific meetings for bondholders.
- ✔ Bondholders can't legally put questions to directors, although nothing stops them acquiring one share to do so.
- ✔ Bondholders don't receive an annual report as a matter of right.
- ✔ Bondholders can't apply for more shares if the company launches a rights issue.
- ✔ Bondholders generally have no rights when another company tries to acquire the firm via a takeover bid.
- ✔ Bondholders don't receive larger payments when the company does well.

Getting Familiar with the Ups and Downs of the Market

Every day, many newspapers carry hundreds, and sometimes thousands, of share and bond prices. But some papers have given up these lists or have greatly reduced their scope. The Internet is better because it offers access to tens of thousands more, often changing prices not just once a day, like print publications, but as they happen (often with a 15-minute delay, which you can avoid if you subscribe to certain sites). Online you can find quotes from all over the world, often with back-up material such as share price graphs.

Prices go up and down most days, if not most hours. Shares of the biggest companies with the greatest number of shareholders are the ones whose prices move most frequently. These shares are called *liquid* because prices flow easily with buying and selling orders.

Smaller-company shares are less liquid or often illiquid. Dealing is less frequent, but when it happens, the effect is far more pronounced.

Why do prices move? It's the question investors most frequently pose, and it's the most difficult to answer. And even when the answer is obvious, such as a price rise due to the company announcing a juicy new contract or a price fall due to the company losing a juicy old contract, why the price has changed by the percentage it has isn't so obvious.

Not to worry. This section helps you sort out the reasons for market ups and downs.

Why do prices rise and fall?

A market truism is that prices rise because there are more buyers than sellers. Don't take that literally, though, because sometimes there are a few large buyers and thousands of small sellers. But if the number of shares buyers are bidding for exceeds the number holders who want out are offering for sale, the price rises. And vice versa.

This stuff is basic supply-and-demand economics (see the nearby sidebar 'A digression into potato prices' for an example using, well, potatoes). If the demand from buyers is high, the price rises to persuade more holders to sell. This situation continues until buyers believe that the price has risen far enough or, as happens often in markets, too high.

Keep in mind, though, that supply-and-demand trends in stock markets are far from those neat supply-and-demand graphs you see in economics textbooks. Prices often tend to overshoot in one way or another but they do that all over the place – look at oil prices, for instance, where in one recent one-year period they went from $145 a barrel to under $45 and then rose again. Remember that in most financial price turmoil, only a very few are active sellers or buyers – what happens at the margins determines values, not what the majority do, which is usually nothing.

The law of supply and demand, or the balance of buyers and sellers, always exists. What investors must do is calculate the plus and minus factors for any equity or bond.

Looking at specific and systemic risks

A share price is an amalgamation of many factors – some applying to the company you buy into and others applying to the stock market in relation to the general economy and to the firm's business and that of its competitors at the time. Factors that apply to the company itself are called *specific risks*. Factors that apply to the stock market itself (and thus to all shares) are known as *systemic risks* or *market risks*.

A digression into potato prices

Shares are just like anything else where a free, unfettered market reacts to supply and demand. Consider potatoes, for example. If the supply of potatoes falls due to a bad harvest or transport problems, the price goes up. But it doesn't go up forever.

After a time, new sources of potatoes may come on the market because the price has risen to a level where it's worthwhile for foreign firms to ship potatoes to the UK because it's now more profitable than selling the potatoes in their own location. Alternatively, instead of supply rising, demand may fall. Some potato eaters may get fed up paying high prices and move to rice, pasta, polenta, couscous or bread – or just eat less. When a share price gets too high, investors switch to other shares (perhaps they see these as undervalued), or to other assets such as bonds, property or cash.

Back to our chips. When supply exceeds demand, maybe due to a bumper harvest, potato prices fall. Then foreign farmers decide sending produce to the UK isn't worthwhile. But when the price is low enough, those eating rice or pasta may decide to switch back to potatoes, so demand increases again.

Now substitute shares for spuds and you'll see why when a shortage occurs, prices go up and companies consider issuing further shares to soak up investor demand.

Don't forget that risk can be good or bad. All the word means is that prices may go up or down more than you may otherwise expect or be comfortable with. Risk isn't a word of abuse like *dodgy* or *dishonest*.

In fact, professional fund managers can even invest in *volatility* – that's the amount a share or share price index moves either side of a fixed point. If you're interested in how this works, check out the VIX index. High VIX readings mean investors see a significant risk that the market will move sharply, whether downwards or upwards. A low figure indicates steady as you go. Some investors confuse risk with fear, but the VIX can be high because share buyers expect prices to zoom. Risk or volatility is really just another unknown to add into the share price equation.

A share in Real Ale Breweries PLC, for example, (not a real company, obviously, but one I've made up) carries specific positive risks, such as a hot summer pushing up sales, beer becoming more fashionable, more pubs and shops stocking the brewery's products or someone discovering that a pint of beer a day (or more!) is good for your health. The brewery also carries specific negative risks, such as the directors running off with the takings, health warnings on beer, new taxes on alcohol and drinkers switching to wine. But systemic risks also exist, such as unemployment or higher interest rates so that consumers have less to spend on anything and especially anything that's not as essential as shelter or gas and electricity.

Systemic risks are different from specific risks. They take in the market as a whole. When prices are generally rising, and every evening TV news bulletin

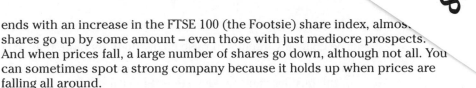
ends with an increase in the FTSE 100 (the Footsie) share index, almos
shares go up by some amount – even those with just mediocre prospects.
And when prices fall, a large number of shares go down, although not all. You
can sometimes spot a strong company because it holds up when prices are
falling all around.

You can never totally isolate the systemic risks from the specific. But if you
buy individual shares, or subscribe to a fund that does so for you, the underlying quality or rubbish status of an equity usually works through eventually. A
top-class company may fall in a collapsing market but less steeply than others.
And when the recovery finally comes, it gains more quickly and more strongly.

Much share analysis is concerned with relative values rather than absolute
gains or losses. A share or fund that falls 10 per cent when the index or average of all funds loses 30 per cent is considered a success, even though you still
lose money. Likewise, a share or fund that goes up 10 per cent when the index
or average gains 30 per cent is considered a flop despite your profits!

Looking at factors that can make share prices rise

Here's a checklist of factors that can cause a share price to rise. Use this list
every time you think about buying into an equity to see how many factors apply.

Nothing ever happens in isolation, so never fixate on one point alone when
considering whether to buy an equity!

- Investors in the company believe that a takeover bid is likely for the
  company whose shares they own.
- The company has a major new contract.
- The company has a big new product.
- Prices for what the company does are going up fast.
- The company has a new dynamic director.
- The company is expected to make record profits – more than previously
  forecasted.
- The company looks more lowly rated on its likely future than rival
  companies.
- The company earns a lot of money from importing, and foreign curren-
  cies have fallen in value against the pound.
- The company earns a lot of money from overseas operations, and
  the pound has fallen against the principal currencies in which it does
  business.
- The company has a lot of bank borrowings, and interest rates have fallen.
- The stock market overall looks like rising, and this share usually goes up
  faster than average shares in the market as a whole.

- ✔ The company is about to win a major legal battle.

- ✔ The company intends to raise its dividend by more than average.

- ✔ The company has plans to cost-cut by shutting down unprofitable parts of the business and sacking superfluous staff.

Looking at factors that can make share prices fall

Many of the factors that cause prices to fall are the reverse of those that make prices rise. Other factors apply only to falling markets. And the last one in the following checklist has a special perversity of its own:

- ✔ Bad publicity is expected. For example, the company is responsible for an environmental disaster, or the accountants have been caught falsifying figures.

- ✔ The stock market is in a bad mood, and this share usually falls faster and further than the average.

- ✔ Figures show that trading is bad in the company's main business area.

- ✔ New government legislation will add to costs or force the company to operate in a different way.

- ✔ The company has launched a takeover bid for a rival company, which could turn into a battle involving an auction set to get out of control.

- ✔ The company, to raise money, is issuing millions of new shares at less than the present price. This will 'dilute' your holdings.

- ✔ The company's product range has been criticised as being out of date or technologically inept.

- ✔ The company's credit rating falls with international bond assessment agencies.

- ✔ The company issues a profits warning.

- ✔ A takeover rumour turns out to be wrong or a takeover approach collapses.

- ✔ The company is seen as sound but unfashionable, so the hot money moves to hot (and often over-heated) sectors.

- ✔ The company says that it will cut the dividend or not pay at all.

- ✔ News is absent and/or investors perceive the company as being boring or forget all about it and divert their investment money to rival firms.

Can anyone predict these moves?

Billions of pounds a year are spent on stock-market analysis. Extremely highly paid people examine every nook and cranny of bigger companies, consider the economic wider picture and look at any other factors they consider relevant. And that's *before* fund managers enter the scene. (*Fund managers* are professionals who buy and sell shares on behalf of clients and big financial institutions. They focus their efforts on pension funds and unit trusts, so they have their take on what they think is going on.)

Some market analysts get it right more often than they get it wrong, but many have a lower than 50 per cent success record. This outcome sounds like they don't earn their money, and to be truthful, some don't deserve what they get. The difficulty all analysts face is that what moves markets is a sense of surprise – happenings, either good or bad, that haven't yet been factored into the equation. All they can do is to point out what they know. They know unknowns exist! And they're also aware of the unknown unknowns and the totally unknowables!

Stock-market operators are remarkably good at reacting to news. The share price often changes in seconds. But after an 'event', when the market adjusts either up or down, it's too late for smaller investors. It may even be too late for major shareholders thanks to *high-frequency trading*, computerised programs that carry out thousands of transactions in micro-seconds.

After news is revealed, whatever facts are revealed are referred to as 'in the market' or 'in the price' (both phrases mean much the same), and the share value may have changed to take account of it.

Take a look at the checklists of factors that can cause prices to rise and fall (located in the previous section). At any one time, some or all of those factors are the subject of comment or a news release. It's only when these factors change for the better or the worse that prices move – going nowhere or coming in exactly as predicted leaves a share price static. Of course, this is about specific risk – systemic or market risk is far more down to big economic factors. So when banks were going bust in late 2008, prices fell across the board.

One way to predict market moves is to have enough information sources so you can spot a trend before others do, and especially before the company has to reveal it.

What smart investors do

Keeping up with the market means being ahead of the curve. Smart investors look for new products and scour the trade press and Internet sites to find details of potential new contracts, and, on the negative side, they try to spot early signs of consumer discontent. Knowledge is what makes markets tick, so you need to try to spot trends and act accordingly.

One way to spot changes before they're officially announced is to get inside information from someone working for the company, a practice known as *insider trading*. It's illegal as soon as an investor tries to profit from it. The illegality applies whether the investor works for the company or simply knows a source of factual material.

Information, disinformation and downright rubbish

Bank of America is one of the biggest companies in the world. Its shares are traded every minute of the day on one stock exchange or another across the globe. It's exceptionally well governed, and the company must put any information it intends to publish through layers of lawyers and ranks of regulators before release. It does everything feasible – and beyond – to prevent information leakage. In this way, it acts like all responsible companies in the markets of whatever country.

None of this stops those who claim to have inside information trying to make a fast buck. Recently, investors have received a spate of emails and unsolicited phone calls from those who say they know something about Bank of America that would be profitable if you acted on it. At other times, the target company has been Amazon or Exxon or Pfizer – the company is usually American and is always big.

People love secrets – that's why they buy showbiz gossip magazines. But just as the content of those periodicals comes from publicists who have their motives, those who spread so-called inside news of major companies also have their motives. They mix information that's out in the market – say Bank of America has told the world that it's lending more to US businesses now than three months ago – with disinformation that's what they want you to think. The information has no connection with reality but always sounds plausible because those pushing it out know how to make anything sound believable. And because the news is painted as 'inside' information, effectively from the bank's innermost vaults, recipients are tempted to put their trust in it. Some of the information is downright rubbish, but unless you're an expert, you won't know the difference – banks are very complex creations, as are most very large concerns. A veneer of truth can hide a whole load of nonsense.

An old stock market saying goes: 'Where there's a tip, there's a tap.' This means that people offering you secret information, the tip, have a bucketload of shares to sell – they need to turn on the tap. If you think about it, obviously if I had secret information that could be profitable, I wouldn't share it with you. Why would I? If the information was accurate, I'd risk insider trading charges. I'd want to buy or sell the shares and then exit the market with as little noise as possible.

The authorities have rarely been successful in prosecuting insider trading, although they're getting tougher, with more high-profile arrests. These may not lead to successful prosecutions but they're warning shots designed to curb others' wrong-doings. Getting a conviction is always difficult. Insider traders hide their tracks through offshore companies in exotic locations where little, if any, regulation exits. Plus the authorities struggle to prove insider trading in a market where so much rumour and tittle-tattle exists, ranging from the totally accurate to the downright and intentionally misleading.

'But I don't have time to do all the stuff professionals do!'

You have a number of disadvantages compared with professional investors, including an almost certain lack of time and resources. Unless you give up your day job (definitely not advised!) or are retired (then only invest money in shares you can afford to go without!), you won't be able to spend hours on end looking at share movements and company announcements. And if you can afford the battery of screens the professionals use then you're too advanced and too wealthy to need this book.

You also won't have access to all those big ticket brokers trying to sell you services by offering research into markets and individual shares. Nor will you be able to call on in-house analysts and economists.

But don't worry. No evidence exists that all that material actually helps professional investors with the right calls. Instead, all that material acts as a prop and an excuse when things go wrong, as they inevitably do at one time or another.

As a small investor with your own horizons, you have the advantage of seeing the wood and not being confused by all those trees. These days, with the availability of the Internet, any investor can know what's happening with a given share or market almost as soon as the professionals with their batteries of screens. Online services offer information for free with a 15-minute delay, or instantaneously for a fee. And with online dealing, you can respond almost as quickly.

Don't feel disadvantaged if your reaction time is slower than the professionals. They're paid to deal quickly and often, and if they don't move shares around all the time, their bosses start to question whether they're worth their big pay cheques and even bigger bonuses. And when they deal, they're probably only buying or selling a small amount of their total holding in a company, whereas you're likely to be selling all you hold. There's also no one, other than yourself and your responsibilities, overshadowing what you do.

You also have the advantage of distance. You can look at shares and the companies behind them in a different way from professional investors. You're able to take a more reasoned and rounded view, away from stock-market gossip; you're not part of the herd of professionals all heading the same way for fear of being out on a limb and you don't have to respond instantly to anything.

 You can't definitively predict market moves. But neither can the professionals. You have the advantage, though, of being able to set your own investment agenda. This could include your ability to simply ride out price falls. After all, you don't have to worry about three-monthly reviews or the chances of being sacked as a fund manager.

Understanding the Mechanics of the Stock Market

Most small investors stand well back from the day-to-day, hour-to-hour and minute-to-minute goings on in the stock market. They do just as well, if not better, following this course. But short-term movements can sometimes add up to a long-term trend, and understanding basic UK stock-market mechanics helps you make sense of those newspaper and online columns that discuss daily ups and downs.

Most markets are made up of four levels: the producers and the product, the middleman, the retailer, and the consumer. In the vegetable market, for example, the producer is the farmer; the middleman is the wholesaler at one of the big central markets, such as New Covent Garden in London; the retailers are greengrocers or supermarkets; and the consumer is you.

Stocks and shares are no different. The product is the tiny part of the company represented by each share, the middleman is the market maker, the retailer is the stockbroker and the ultimate consumer is you.

The pivot in markets is the middleman, and the stock-market middleman is the *market maker*, a market professional who assesses second-by-second the weight of buy and sell pressures and adjusts prices accordingly. This activity determines what the brokers charge you or give you when you sell – adjusted, of course, for their fees.

Market makers always try to find a price level where both buyers and sellers are satisfied at any one moment. This practice is called *balancing the book*. If more buyers than sellers exist, market makers are *short of stock*. They don't have the shares to satisfy demand. So they increase their prices to bring out sellers so they can achieve balance.

Equally, when more sellers than buyers exist, market makers are *long of stock*. Prices are marked down to entice new buyers. Market makers are no different from vegetable wholesalers who mark up prices when demand is high and mark down prices when buyers are scarce.

Buyers pay more than sellers receive. The gap between the bid (or the buying or asking) price and the offer (or selling) price is called the *spread*. The bigger the company and the more often its shares are traded, the narrower this spread is. A major company such as Vodafone or Lloyds Banking Group may only have 1p or 2p or so between the bid and offer prices. But smaller companies can have larger amounts. Note that the prices shown in newspapers and on websites are mid-prices – halfway between the bid and offer.

Knowing just how much a share would have to rise for you to get your money back is always vital. The price you see in a newspaper isn't the price you pay. You have 0.5 per cent stamp duty and commission. And on top of that is the spread (or *touch*), which is how the market makers earn their living. The way it works is that your share has to rise more in percentage terms if it's priced in pennies than if it's priced in pounds.

Market makers make their spread in pence or part of a penny, not in a percentage. A very lowly priced share could have a spread of one penny, but that would be a very large percentage. A share that the newspaper quotes at 5p could have a 1p spread. You'd then pay 5.5p to buy it but get 4.5p if you sell it. The price would have to go up 1p to a mid 6p (or 20 per cent more) before you could get out at the 5.5p you originally paid; that's because a mid 6p implies you'll get 5.5p when you sell (you'd have to pay 6.5p if you were buying). A big company share priced at 500p with a 2p spread would only need a 0.4 per cent uplift before you were back to the starting point. You'd pay 502p for each share, so when it goes up 4p to a mid 504p you'd be able to get out at 502p (the mid price less the spread that goes to market makers). These figures ignore broker fees and stamp duty, which make the real increase needed to get back to square one even larger.

Market makers have to quote prices in the bigger companies. Often, several market makers exist, so the competition between them should narrow the spreads. That means less for market makers, but it's good news for investors.

How big money moves big money

Around 85 per cent of the value of the London stock market is owned by big investors such as pension funds, insurance companies, unit trusts and investment trusts. They don't really own it, of course, because they're merely working for the real owners – you and me and millions of others who've entrusted savings to them. Or, in the case of *sovereign wealth funds*, huge investment funds that act for the governments of nations from Saudi Arabia to Norway, they're acting for those countries and their inhabitants.

Nevertheless, all these big investors act as though it's their money, and they're the people whose influence moves share prices most readily. They have more effect on big companies because they trade shares in these major corporations more often. Many smaller companies may have their share register dominated by the firm's directors and private investors.

You can find a daily list of trading volume in large company shares online or in the *Financial Times*. This list gives figures for the amount of shares changing hands on any day. You must divide the figure, in thousands, by two because each share is traded twice – once as a buy and once as a sell. Every fully quoted share can be traded every day, but volume can vary from zero (rarely) to hundreds of millions.

High volume (jargon for 'lots of trading') in a share often occurs just after a statement from the company. But if you can't see an obvious reason that shares in a company are heavily traded, make some more enquiries, especially if the price changes substantially. Look through newspaper market reports and scour Internet sites. They won't always give you the reason, but high volume should always alert investors in those shares. It could be good news if prices are higher on high volume but bad news if the opposite!

Smaller companies whose shares aren't actively traded may not always have a market maker. Instead, shares are bought and sold through *matched bargains* posted on an electronic bulletin board. Think in terms of the Wanted and For Sale columns in your local newspaper. If you want to buy 500 shares in TeenyWeeny PLC, your broker posts your requirement on the bulletin board and the price you're willing to pay. Eventually, someone posts a sell order at a price that's suitable, and if it's for 500 shares or more, the deal is done. Matched bargains can sometimes take days or even weeks.

You may have previously heard the term 'market movers'. Don't confuse market movers with market makers. A *market mover* is anyone with enough influence to shift investor thinking. Market movers include certain newspaper columns, big-fund managers, major stockbroking houses, economists and analysts – and legendary individuals, such as George Soros and Warren Buffet. Watch to see how prices change after a comment from any particular source to see who's just hot air and who can really influence share values.

Knowing How Companies Leave the Market

Companies disappear from the stock-market lists for all sorts of reasons.

Some (hopefully not many!) go bust. Northern Rock was an example of this sad departure.

A second group of companies gets taken over, but investors can end up with shares in the firm that bought their company as an alternative to a cheque. For example, the Abbey National shareholders I mention earlier on in this chapter now have a stake in Banco Santander, the Spanish bank that took it over, instead. Of course, nothing stops shareholders in companies receiving a mix of shares and cash.

Many others *go private*. Going private and hence dodging the scrutiny of regular stock-market reporting used to be the preserve of small companies. Now very large companies including Boots, the high-street chemist, and BAA, which runs big UK airports, have been taken off the stock market by *private equity* companies. You can't generally get involved in this because private equity is very private indeed. With private equity, a handful of banks and entrepreneurs get together, buy out the shareholders and run the company as their personal property. They hope to get a lot more money out than they put in by using clever strategies known as *financial engineering*.

However, some investment trusts and other funds open to all investors sometimes put money into private equity ventures, so it can be useful to have a basic idea of what happens. Private equity firms try to buy companies cheaply with cheap finance from the banks. Then they sell off what they can and get rid of as many employees as possible before trying to find a new buyer or re-launching the concern on the stock market. Things don't always go to plan, though. Rising interest rates for starters can knock the projections for six, and some private equity entrepreneurs find that the reason the firm was cheap in the first place is because its finances and business models are huge black holes.

But if you're a shareholder with no emotional capital in the company, whether the takeover comes from another quoted company or from a private equity setup makes little difference. The cash is what counts.

Now the shareholders have to decide what to do with their money! So, they could be heading back to this book's basics.

Chapter 7

Taking the Catwalk Route to Investment Success

··

In This Chapter

▶ Looking at fashions and styles in investing

▶ Getting to know the UK stock market

▶ Weighing up big and small companies

▶ Taking a secret peep at how fund managers make decisions

··

*O*ne stock-market theory advises investors to watch the hemlines of women's skirts. When they go up then folk are optimistic and share prices will rise. But when they go down, it's a sign that harder times are coming and that share values will fall.

It sounds a load of nonsense. However, it makes some sense to link fashion to finance. Short skirts often mean free-and-easy living, which comes from optimism – the roaring '20s and the late 1960s are good examples. Long skirts mean the opposite – they indicate life getting more difficult. And of course, they're useful in cold climates.

Well, that's the theory, for what it's worth. But the fact is that investment styles go in and out of fashion just like the clothes you wear. And it takes a brave person to flout fashion altogether.

Equally, what goes around, comes around. When it comes to investment theories, nothing new under the sun exists because ideas go stale and then get reinvented.

This chapter looks at investment styles. And just like short skirts versus long skirts, it suggests a number of opposites. But the important thing – just like clothes – is to end up with something you feel comfortable with.

Exploring Common Investor Styles

You may think of yourself as an investor, out to maximise your money, but the investment industry likes to pigeon-hole people a little more. It divides the world into 'growth' and 'value' stock-picking styles, which I explore here. A third style also exists – the momentum investor with a shorter-term time-frame. There are other ways of looking at investment choice, which I shall look at later on in this chapter, but they still depend on these three basics. I introduce you to top down and bottom up. They are interesting styles but investors still have to know whether they are looking for value, growth or momentum.

No one style is better than another, so pick one that you feel comfortable with. And then stick to it until it no longer produces what you want.

Looking at performance: Growth investors

Both growth and value investors (see the following section) want their share portfolios to grow by above-average percentages. The difference is in how they get to their goal.

Growth investors look for the past to continue into the future. They search for companies that have impressed investors with previous growth – or at least the promise of it. Now, these shares don't come cheap. They're already highly rated by other investors due to their solid history of regular earnings improvements.

This means the *price/earnings ratio* or p/e – a key indicator to how investors see a company; the higher the number, the higher the expectation – is already soaring into the high teens or even the early 20s. And that's certainly above average. The p/e ratio is the earnings per share divided into the share price. It can be either historic (based on the last set of figures) or prospective (based on what investors expect in the future). A high p/e is said to be forward looking.

Why aren't investors put off by already tough-to-live-up-to ratings? Simple. They expect these companies to continue to grow at an above-average rate. They believe the growth story is sustainable over the next one to five years. And that, they hope, will pull in other investors, whose purchases will drive the share price even higher.

What do growth investors look for? High growth in the past combined with analysts forecasting growth, for starters. They want surprises – good ones, of course. They need to know that the demand for the firm's products and services will continue to outstrip the economy. And they look to see whether the managers and directors are confident enough to put more of their own money into the shares. Of course, if the investors get it wrong, the downside here is that the share price could well tumble by more than they may expect.

Growth investing is a fashion. Some would never 'wear' anything else!

Spotting what others have missed: Value investors

Value investors take the view that companies exist out there that investors have overlooked. That's usually because these companies have previously disappointed investors by failing to live up to expectations. Others have simply been ignored – maybe they're too small for most professional investors or they're in a sector that's totally out of fashion.

Now, smoking is very bad for you, but tobacco shares have been great for investors. Cigarette companies were totally out of fashion some years ago. They had a product that was being squeezed by regulations including advertising bans, and it was one for which there'd likely never be a technological breakthrough. Cigarette companies weren't exciting.

The result was that the shares languished on low p/e ratios. A few investors realised, however, that all those negatives were positives. All the rules meant no new company would ever want to enter the market in developed countries. But in less-developed countries, which had a free-and-easy attitude to cigarettes, a huge untapped market existed of young people who see Western cigarettes as aspirational. And the lack of product progress? Great news, because it prevented costly research programmes that could end in expensive disasters. Plus tobacco firms don't need to worry too much about their advertising budget – publicity is banned altogether in many countries.

These investors took the contrarian approach. Value investors believe the rest of the market has missed a trick or three. The low p/e ratios eventually go higher.

Like growth investors, value investors reckon the share price will outstrip the current p/e rating. They have to factor in, however, that the merry-go-round will stop sometime. Timing the exit is crucial for value investors – knowing when to let go and leave the growth to someone else is just as vital as knowing when to buy in the first place.

Living for the moment: Momentum investors

Momentum investors are the big followers of fashion. They look for the trends, ride them as long as they're the latest big thing and hope to jump onto the next big idea as soon as the current fashion starts to fray a bit at the edges. They buy the fastest-moving shares (in the fastest-moving sector) in the belief that they'll continue to soar. The trick is knowing when to jump to the next fashion. Momentum investing is really for the screen watcher. These investors are looking for big changes over a short period – a sudden emergence from being a wallflower to being the hottest item on the dance floor. They track trading ranges and short-term growth forecasts.

Of course, momentum is great when prices are rising. But when gravity takes over, prices can plummet. However, now so many ways to make money out of falling shares exist – such as spread bets, futures and options – that the thought of share price declines does nothing to deter the momentum investor. (I explain spread bets and similar devices in Chapter 20.)

Opting for slow and steady: Income investors

Income investors look for shares paying high dividends that they hope will be secure, although they realise this isn't guaranteed. The idea is that although they don't expect the capital value of their shares to grow at a great rate (they'd be more than happy with the average), they foresee that the dividends will add that much each year and, over time, their investment will grow to a big gain, especially if they reinvest the dividends into more shares.

This is a long-term concept. Even if the shares go nowhere fast, five years of 5 per cent dividend returns gives a good gain – around 28 per cent with compound interest. But these shares can disappoint. When times are hard, companies can slash dividends and a cut payout nearly always equals a falling share price. So these investors would suffer twice over.

Mixing and matching your way to investment sophistication with GARP

Just as with what you wear, no law prevents you mixing and matching a little – provided your styles don't clash too much for your taste. A new style around is called 'growth at a reasonable price'. And because investors love initials, they shorten it to GARP.

This approach combines features of growth, value and income investing styles. What happens is that you take the p/e ratio and then divide it by the annual percentage growth. So if Company A has a p/e of 15 and the annual growth is 15 per cent, then the result is 1. Company B has a p/e of 12 and annual growth of 24 per cent, which gives 0.5. Company C has a p/e of 24 and an annual growth estimate of 12 per cent, which results in a GARP of 2. Company A is on course to be average; Company B has a rating that's failed to keep up with its potential; but Company C is obviously well past its prime – the market hasn't yet come to terms with its more mundane future and so it's riding for a fall.

All very technical, I agree. And although some high-profile professional investors swear that GARP is the route to riches, many others dismiss it as a fad that's passed.

Taking it from the top, or building it from the bottom

Back in the early 1990s a popular idea was *chaos theory*. It was supposed to make sense of the seemingly random patterns of the world in all sorts of areas, from finance to the weather. After a brief flurry of popularity and big book sales, chaos theory returned to the academics who invented it. But one poignant image remains for me: butterflies flap in Beijing; hurricanes happen in Haiti. (In other words, a butterfly flapping its wings over Asia can cause a storm over Africa or Latin America.) The idea is that a small and unexpected movement in one place can have a larger knock-on effect somewhere else. Take this on a few times more, with each move growing in size and significance, and you eventually get to something dramatic, which leads to the purpose of this section.

Yikes! Investing styles in opposition

Although I think that the easier investing approach for most people is to take the top-down view, both the top-down and bottom-up styles of investing have their own benefits and drawbacks. Take a look at the following key points in favour of each investing style (when the opposite occurs, you get the disadvantages):

- Top down triumphs in times of stability and economic prosperity. When everything is progressing smoothly, investors are more willing to treat all shares and all equity markets in a similar way.

- Bottom up triumphs when life is uncertain. Picking winners in troubled times means you have to look at individual circumstances.

- Top down triumphs because it takes less effort. You're only looking at markets and their indexes, not the thousands of stocks that make them up.

- Bottom up triumphs because there'll always be winners and losers if you look closely enough. The smart investor hopes more of the former exist!

- Top down triumphs because you can concentrate on the big picture and go for the 'best in class'. You think getting into oil stocks is the greatest idea around? Then just put all your money into a vehicle such as an exchange-traded fund investing in oil companies.

- Bottom up triumphs because the micro view gets you looking through all those nooks and crannies to come up with tiny or otherwise overlooked firms that will grow.

Consider these last two contrasting investment styles:

✔ **Top down** says that you start with the big events, the big companies and the world view. Top down is like looking for the hurricane first and then searching for the ensuing damage.

✔ **Bottom up** says that you should construct your investment portfolio starting with companies you like, irrespective of the wider context. Bottom up is like looking for the butterfly flapping its wings.

For investors, chaos theory demonstrates that the trees make up the woods – that everything small counts toward the whole. But it also suggests that nothing happens in isolation. What occurs in one country has an effect elsewhere. So even if you never invest outside the UK, you still need to be aware of what goes on elsewhere. While one market suffers, another may prosper. Money is very mobile – it moves at the touch of a screen.

Getting Up Close and Personal with the UK Stock Market

Buyers of UK shares have approximately 3,000 companies to choose from. The value of the biggest 20 of these by market capitalisation is worth more than the rest put together. The names of these big beasts change, but this percentage (okay, admittedly not down to decimal points) doesn't vary.

Understanding market cap

A huge and seemingly perennial debate rages in the fashion press about zero-size models (they're the skinny ones) versus plus-size (they're the more endowed women). But that's nothing as plus-sized as the continuing style debate among investors that pitches big companies against little companies – with some rooting for the middle way.

Investors measure the size of a company by its *market capitalisation* (market cap for short). It's an easy figure to calculate. You just multiply the share price by the number of shares in issue or, if you don't want to do the maths, you can find it on any online company share page.

What's large, mid-sized, small or even micro cap depends on market conditions. You can't put numbers on it. But generally, the shares that are in the FTSE 100 Index – that's the Footsie that's quoted all the time in news broadcasts and newspapers – are considered large cap. That's because the rule for Footsie inclusion is based on market cap. Large companies are usually considered to be more stable (although that didn't stop some banks from crashing to zero or little better in 2008–2009).

The next 250 shares by size are in the Mid Cap index – the FTSE 250. And the rest, well, some are the Tiddlers in the small-cap world and some are the virtual-invisibles of the micro-cap universe.

Obviously, if you work for or run or own shares in one of these companies then the micro cap is important for you. But in the big picture, these firms really don't matter. It's not that big investors think they're all rubbish. It's the sheer cost of researching and then their inability to pick up more than a few thousand pounds' worth of shares that counts against their investing. Yes, someone will one day trumpet he found a company worth £1 million that's now valued at £10 billion. That's the needle in the haystack. No one boasts that he found a £1 million company that's still worth £1 million. Or less.

The FTSE 100 (the Footsie)

The UK stock market's main health measure is the FTSE 100 index, usually known as the *Footsie*. The Footsie is recalculated every second, so any up or down movement in prices from trading in any of its constituent stocks automatically changes the index for good or bad. Most no-cost Internet services quote the figure (as well as share prices of individual companies) with a 15-minute delay. Services that you pay for, including some services offered by stockbrokers as part of an overall package, offer the numbers in real time.

The Footsie contains the 100 biggest UK-quoted companies by market value. The list is revised once per quarter. Companies whose capitalisations have shrunk are replaced by those who've grown larger. There's a relegation zone and a list of companies that may be promoted from among the biggest just outside the Footsie. Arrangements are also in place for immediate substitute companies if an index member drops out either because of a takeover or, less often, from going bust.

Being in the top 100 brings prestige. It also ensures a lot of buying interest from fund managers. Some funds, obviously including index-tracker funds that buy all the index constituents in their right proportions, only buy Footsie stocks. Others have to keep a substantial proportion of their investment money in the top company shares, because the rules of their fund say they have to and a mainstream fund ignoring all the most important companies wouldn't make much sense.

Falling out of the Footsie brings a sharp drop in prestige. All the good points from the previous paragraph go into reverse. Dropout companies are often sliding down the table anyway, and expulsion adds to their woes. Nothing stops a company bouncing back to the list in the next set of ups and downs, of course. A few companies have behaved like yo-yos in this respect!

Investors who look regularly at market values can often work out the likely promotions and relegations ahead of the official announcement from the Footsie folks. You just look at the capitalisations and take it from there. The advantage? You're ahead of the game, beating those fund managers, such as those running index-tracker funds who buy all the shares in an index in their correct proportions so their fund looks like a replica of the index, going up and down in line with the publicly available calculations. (Index-tracker fund rules say that managers can only buy shares after a company is firmly in the index and must sell shares only after they've been properly thrown out.) In any case, the Footsie folk make official announcements of changes some days before they take effect.

Is Footsie feeble?

The Footsie is quoted all day long on news programmes as a measure of the health of the UK stock market and, by extension, of the UK economy. It's not perfect, however. The Footsie can fail to represent, or underplay, whole sections of the UK economy, and over-represent other sectors. Many have little or nothing to do with the UK, such as overseas mining and energy firms. They're in the index because they've chosen to list their shares in London for legal, regulatory and prestige reasons.

Footsie facts and figures

Here's a hodgepodge of Footsie information that you may find helpful (or at least interesting). It's all based on easy-to-find, publicly available information.

- ✔ The total value of the Footsie is around £1,750 billion, making the average firm worth £17.5 billion. The biggest – HSBC and Shell – weigh in at about £135 billion. The smallest (probably on its way out of the index) is worth less than £1 billion.

- ✔ The stocks from the top ten companies account for more than 40 per cent of the total value of the index. So a move in the price of any share in this leading part counts for far more than a change in the lower ranks. The top 20 listings are nearly two-thirds the value of the index.

- ✔ Oil and mining companies dominate the index. Banks used to be very important – until they started to have their problems a few years ago – but they're still big players. A bad day for the oil or mining sector means a bad day for the index – and for the UK, even though their UK interests are often tiny. A good day for the oil or mining sector brings loads of investor smiles because these companies tend to move in big jumps, so their gains perk up the overall index.

- ✔ Few companies with any engineering interests are on the list.

- ✔ Few companies in the top 100 are largely or totally UK-focused. Those that are largely represent high-street retailers. Some index constituents are in mining overseas so they have few, if any, UK interests.

> ✔ Over the past few years, a number of well-known companies such as Abbey National, BAA (the airports company), Boots and Cadbury, plus a whole load of gas and electricity companies, have left the list because they've been either taken over by foreign companies or have become private, non-stock-market companies.

The FTSE 250: The Mid Caps

Mid Caps is stock-market jargon for companies with a medium-sized market capitalisation. They're too small for the Footsie but too significant to be considered Tiddlers (see the following section for what Tiddlers are). Their measure is the FTSE 250, or the Mid Cap. As its name suggests, it's an index covering the next 250 shares after the Footsie. It contains many of the activities that are missing or under-represented in the Footsie, such as house building, entertainments and engineering. A handful of specialist unit and investment trusts focus on this medium-sized company area.

Beyond the FTSE 250: The Tiddlers

The Tiddlers are the small companies beyond the largest 100 and the next 250 that appear in the Footsie and the Mid Cap lists. Approximately 2,000 of these small-quoted companies exist, and their combined market value is smaller than the biggest Footsie company on its own. Some are former large companies down on their luck; others are companies that came to the stock market on a wave of enthusiasm that quickly ran out of steam; and a third group consists of firms with a hoped-for glittering future – well, a future one day.

Tiddler shares are unlikely to be traded on a regular basis. Sometimes it takes days or even weeks for a buyer or seller to come forward, so just one purchase or disposal order can send prices shooting upward or spinning downward. But a number of specialist funds concentrate on small-company shares, arguing that small companies can outperform the big companies because the people running these concerns are nimble enough to come up with ideas that will turn out to be tomorrow's winners.

Smaller than tiddliest Tiddler: AIM

AIM, or the Alternative Investment Market, is a market regulated by the London Stock Exchange but with easier entry requirements and less demanding rules than the LSE demands. It's a bit like a golf club that lets in players with lower abilities – provided that they don't use the greens at weekends.

Small can be beautiful

For many years, small companies as a group outperformed their bigger brothers. But although that outperformance was real enough on paper, investors had to be very lucky to capture it for themselves.

Just a few front runners existed among the few thousand small companies. Their share prices doubled, tripled or even sextupled in a year. But if investors' portfolios missed out on them, the investors received nothing very special. Investors made a fortune out of small companies only if they were lucky or very well informed.

Since the late 1990s, the small company outperformance effect has been even harder to detect. Big funds and major stockbrokers have been unwilling to research small companies. They argue that seriously researching one small company can take as much, if not more, person power than looking at HSBC, Britain's biggest company at the time of this writing. Devoting loads of expensive research effort to a company worth £10 million at best compared with one valued at billions isn't worthwhile, they argue.

If you invest in small companies, you'll find few mentions in newspapers or from online sources. But they're the life blood of tipsheets (high cost, low circulation publications that purport to tell you what shares are about to go up), newspaper share-advice columns and a number of specialist services from stockbrokers. But remember to take care, here, as people with an existing interest in a share often write how wonderful these companies are! If you're lucky, you may find a small-print disclaimer.

AIM-quoted companies vary in stock-market value from more than £200 million to under £500,000. At the top end, they could easily graduate to the main market if they wanted to. Doing so would enable them to increase their attraction to big investment managers who often can't buy AIM stocks because their fund's rules put up a bar to their investing in shares that aren't quoted on the London Stock Exchange itself.

At the bottom of the AIM list are companies worth less than a modest house in London. Most of these companies have shares whose values have plunged to 1p or even less. What these companies do is often unclear, sometimes even to their directors and shareholders.

Shares quoted on AIM vary immensely in quality. In general, they haven't performed as well as the promoters of this market once claimed. Over a typical five-year period, AIM shares in the AIM index (remember this excludes the real rubbish) perform much in line with the big companies in the Footsie. But to get there, the ups and downs are far more pronounced – and the chance of a dividend from an AIM company is lower. To be brutal, AIM no longer has the style cachet it once had.

Some AIM stocks have been associated with stockbrokers who've been fined and forced out of business by City watchdog the Financial Conduct Authority. An AIM listing isn't a quality mark.

Just because a stock is listed on AIM doesn't make it a good idea. Some really bad-quality companies have gone on to AIM – some designed to grab as much investor money as they can before disappearing into the blue yonder. A number have been sold by overseas *boiler rooms* (illegal offshore sales pushers) or by UK-based and UK-regulated *bucket shops*, which are like boiler rooms except that they have a veneer of respectability. No sure things exist in investing. Expect that investing in rubbish or companies with too-good-to-possibly-be-true stories will lose you money.

Here are various AIM-related titbits to be aware of:

✔ AIM shares are exempt from stamp duty on purchase so that makes them 0.5 per cent cheaper. And according to HM Revenue and Customs, AIM shares are unquoted. That can count as an advantage for some inheritance tax calculations.

✔ More than 1,000 companies are listed on AIM. But that's substantially down on the near 1,700 in 2007.

✔ One advantage of AIM for people building up their own companies is that they don't have to sell many shares to outsiders to achieve an AIM listing. That way, they can keep control. Whether that's good for investors is another matter. A danger is that directors will continue to see the company as their own personal toy rather than run it in the best interests of all shareholders.

✔ AIM companies are unlikely to be researched. Some brokers send out material on companies in which they or their existing clients hold a major slice of the stock, but this is hardly unbiased research!

✔ The gap between the quoted buying and selling prices from market makers can be huge in percentage terms, especially for very low-priced shares. (A *market maker* is a professional who assesses second by second the weight of buy and sell pressures and adjusts prices accordingly. This activity determines what the brokers charge you or give you when you sell – adjusted, of course, for their commission fees.) A company with a newspaper price of 2.5p per share may cost you 3p to buy, but you'll get only 2p if you sell. So your purchase may have to soar before you can sell for the price you paid in the first place. You're running fast to stand still.

The markets you need a microscope to find

Believe it or not, a market exists for companies that are too tiny or too infrequently traded to warrant even an AIM listing. Sort of – because attempts over the years to set up facilities to buy and sell shares beyond AIM have so far failed to grab the interest of stock market fashionistas. Instead, market after market has been left on the sales rail. And not even the abolition of the 0.5 per cent stamp duty on purchases has done anything to ensure attendance at this fashion parade.

For the love of penny shares

Small companies with a full quote, such as those on AIM and those on ISDX, may fall into the penny share category. Originally, a *penny share* was a share whose price was below one shilling in old money (that's 5p now) and so priced only in pence. With decimal currency, the term was first stretched to 10p or double figures, and then to 50p. Many of the original penny shares were in speculative 'products of Empire', such as tea and rubber plantations in Malaya (now Malaysia), or gold mines in South Africa or Australia. Now they're just speculative.

Despite their very high risk, the penny share has a special place in share-buying mythology.

UK investors love, for some unexplained reason, to own a large number of lowly priced shares (as opposed to investors in the United States and most other places, who prize a high share price). The UK dislike of heavy prices is so great that large companies often subdivide their shares after they reach £10. Somehow, to UK investors, owning 1 million shares worth 10p each is better than owning 1,000 shares worth £100 each.

The theory of the penny share is that even a small 1p rise is proportionately huge. A 1p gain on a 10p price is 10 per cent. On a £10 price, it's 0.1 per cent. The maths works in theory. But nothing else does in practice. For example, the opposite also applies! In addition, most penny stocks are from companies down on their luck, or where Lady Luck has yet to appear – and that's usually for a reason.

Some investors put money into these fallen stocks for no better reason than 'What was once up and then fell will always rise again' (or 'What hasn't yet risen will surely do so some day'). But while day follows night, no certainty exists that a stock-market up will follow a down or a never-got-off-the-ground.

The latest incarnation of this ever-so-junior market goes by the initials ISDX, standing for ICAP Securities and Derivatives Exchange. (Don't ask about what ICAP stands for – that's lost in the mists of time.) This is the latest incarnation of the old PLUS market, which specialised in micro-Tiddlers. ICAP bought PLUS for £500,000. And PLUS, in turn, had replaced OFEX (which stood for Off Exchange). Firms listed on ISDX include football team Arsenal, brewers Adnams and Shepherd Neame, and Newbury Racecourse.

Within ISDX is a main board, a secondary market and a growth market. In all, more than 100 companies are listed on ISDX – although the number leaving is greater than those joining.

Just to confuse matters even further, the Social Stock Exchange was established in 2013. Its stated mission is:

> '. . . actively recruiting member companies who are delivering a positive impact with their business. Having a single venue where a comprehensive range of both debt and equity instruments can be showcased is seen as being instrumental in promoting impact investment as a mainstream proposition.'

Currently, 11 companies are listed, ranging in value from £325 million to less than half a million.

Finally, more than 200 smaller companies are currently on the PLUS-quoted market. These companies include long-established family-controlled breweries where few shares ever change hands, some football clubs and new companies in technology. But to be brutal, the PLUS market has never had much of a fashion-approval rating.

Assessing How Fund Managers Mark Their Styles

I've taken a secret peep at some internal fund manager documents. They're stamped 'not to be distributed to the public'. But I think they give such a good idea of how so many of the professionals go about their business that I have to share them with you.

They start out with three big top-down categories – shares, bonds and themes.

- ✔ **Shares** are subdivided by geography – United States, Europe, Japan, emerging markets and the UK.

- ✔ **Bonds** are classified by risk – government bonds, investment-grade bonds from companies, high yield (that means dodgy) and debt from emerging markets.

- ✔ **Themes** include areas such as property, gold, commodities, medical matters and technology. Themes can be important – all those I've just mentioned have had their moment in the spotlight (and in the investment trash can!) over the last decade or so.

Now, the professionals split each of these categories into tactical and strategic. *Tactical* is what they expect over the next three to six months and *strategic* looks farther out. The idea is to see which is likely to gain, fall or stay the same. If both tactical and strategic point up, that's a firm vote in favour. And if both are trending down then it's 'don't touch with a bargepole'.

Perhaps even worse – and this is a trap many investors fall into – is to mistake the short-term tactical trend for the long term. That way, you could easily get suckered into a tactical upswing that leads to a strategic disaster, or miss out on a tactical downturn that becomes a strategic success. England's football failure in World and European cups is bad news tactically for pubs and stores hoping to sell merchandise. But they get over it strategically.

Doing all this clarifies the asset allocation decision – how much of your fortune or fund to put into the various investment classes that you started out defining.

Now, the fund managers put some flesh on these bare bones. They explain why they've made these decisions and how they'll implement them in their buying and selling.

- ✔ Tactical decisions include short-term factors such as *volatility* (how the market is bouncing around) and economic data due to be published over the coming weeks. A lot of this is market noise that can hide the big picture.

- ✔ Strategic moves are based on looking ahead a year or two. Will the economy prosper or go into recession? What will the long-term outlook for currencies be? And can they learn anything from the history of the markets?

Did my secret source get it right? Only time will tell – so come back here in five to ten years' time! But doing this sort of hard grind has to be better than investing either on the back of what you overheard on a crowded commuter train or the sort of advice you so often get from financial advisers whose sole purpose is to sell the latest launched fund that carries a big commission for them.

Shares that don't behave as they should

When markets move up or down, it's usual for most shares to follow the trend. Those who watch stock-market screens talk of a 'sea of red' when prices are falling or an 'ocean of blue' when they're on the way up. But a few always defy the trend.

- ✔ Interest rates go up? This means inflation and higher prices. And, believe it or not, supermarkets actually welcome that (although they won't admit to it). If prices start to rise, they can adjust the stickers on the shelves even faster and further in the knowledge that few will notice it. That way, they increase profits and benefit shareholders.

- ✔ Higher VAT? Again, no problem for supermarkets because so much of what they sell – well over half – is VAT free.

- ✔ A really bad winter that hits everything that moves (or rather, doesn't move!)? Bad for all sorts of shares including transport, high-street stores and insurance companies, but great for drug companies, which will sell a lot more cold cures.

- ✔ Market hit by a fall in the value of sterling? Don't worry. Companies that do loads of business abroad using other currencies will shine out from the gloom.

- ✔ Share prices pushed up by really good news? Don't expect that to extend to water and power companies, where prices are subject to regulation. In any case, although you may celebrate good economic data with a bottle of champagne, you never toast happy statistics by leaving more lights on!

Deciphering the Greek alphabet

Fund managers and serious investors sometimes start talking in Greek. But don't worry. Their knowledge rarely goes past the first two letters of the Greek alphabet – alpha and beta.

✔ **Alpha:** A high alpha is good. It shows that the fund manager or the big investor has managed to outperform a passive or index-tracking fund. It's the difference between the actual rate of return and the expected rate.

Alpha is important because otherwise fund managers can collect fees for really doing very little. But you have to look at a high alpha to check whether it's sustainable into the future and not just chancy tactics that won't last long.

✔ **Beta:** This is a measure of how risky a share or other asset may be compared with the average for similar assets. For example, an investor would compare a share in the UK's FTSE 100 index for risk and volatility against the index itself. Some individual shares gyrate more wildly than the index and some less so. Investors may compare the beta of a collective fund against the average of all similar funds, or an index or whatever else is meaningful for their purpose.

A beta value higher than 1 indicates a higher-risk investment that should be compensated by higher rewards. A low beta – a figure under 1 – means lower risk. A beta score of zero is cash in a safe bank account.

Fund managers who come up with a low beta but a high alpha really earn their fees.

By the way, gamma and delta, the next two Greek letters, are for complex option plays.

Chapter 8

Investing in Markets

* *

* *

Do you ever look through those newspaper columns headed Recent Wills? I admit I do. And I bet I'm not alone.

One of the interests is seeing how much money the newly deceased but dearly beloved left behind and whether it all went to the local home for stray moggies. But the real fascination, for me at least, is trying to imagine how people who feature in the wills sections made their money. A substantial number of people made theirs from shares, often doing little more than just buying mainstream equities when they could afford them and leaving them to grow. It was a policy of benign neglect.

Trading ten times a day (or ten times a month) is bad for your financial health. The typical share purchased by an individual must go up in price around 6 to 8 per cent before you can sell it for the money you first paid for it.

These days, very few people put their entire portfolios into individual shares. Despite all the campaigns by governments and stockbrokers to increase private share ownership, private investors now own only 10 per cent of the stock market directly, and that's the lowest ever (although the figure may be a little higher because some personal holdings are owned through trusts and other vehicles). However you count, 10 per cent is well down on the 20 per cent at the start of 1990 when privatisation mania was at its height. So what's happened? Well, an awful lot of privatisation shares were taken over and out of the stock market. In most cases this was because rivals, often from overseas, bought the companies. For whatever reason, most investors never reinvested the cash they got for their shares into the stock market. Others simply cashed in.

How easy making a million really is

American automobile manufacturer Henry Ford famously said that history is bunk. And I say that you can't ever rely on the past to prove the future in the investment world. But we can both be wrong sometimes.

If you have £25,000 now and are prepared to be patient, you can end up with £1 million. All you have to do is invest in the UK stock-market index, put all your dividends and other payments back into your fund, sit back and wait. You don't have to be a stock-market genius or even spend time looking at companies. All you have to do is buy a basket of shares in the constituent companies of a widely available share price index and let the power of equities do the rest. Or at least, that's one lesson from stock-market history. Now let's have a close look at the figures to back this up.

Research from Barclays Bank shows how equities have the power to make you rich, provided that you're not tempted to spend your gains. Using the timeframe of 1919 to 1985, the researchers worked out how long it would take for £25,000 to become £1 million. (They reduced the starting amount by inflation.) The researchers invested the starting £25,000 (or

equivalent) into the FTSE All Share Index or an earlier equivalent. This is a measure of the share prices of some 750 UK companies ranging from the massive to the miniscule.

The researchers found that the quickest journey to millionaire status was 14 years – achieved by those who invested just after the First World War and also by those who were brave enough to put money in after the stock market hit a low point in early 1975. For the majority of the investments, however, the magic million came in 20 years or less. In only seven instances (starting-point years), reaching the magic million took 25 or more years. The investments that took the longest to reach £1 million included those that were started around the time of the 1929 market crash, which was followed by a huge economic slump; the Second World War; and the mid to late 1950s.

However you cut this one, you can see that getting big money over your lifetime isn't impossible, but only if you reinvest the dividends rather than spending them. For even during the stock-market doldrums of the first decade of this century, investors who reinvested dividends did see substantial growth.

Investors with long memories also recall how they suffered in the dotcom boom at the end of the 1990s. But the figures don't mean people have ceased to invest in shares. The majority simply now do so via collective investments and low-cost methods such as exchange-traded funds.

This chapter provides some helpful tips and titbits as you begin investing in the stock market – so you can someday impress people – although I hope you can do this a long time before the curious read about it in Recent Wills. In this chapter, I show you routes into the market, explain the benefits of keeping an eye on the long-term trend, share a couple of industry secrets and focus you on some big-picture items to *always* keep in mind.

Looking at Where the Stock Market Entry Routes Are

Three routes into the stock market exist. Traditionally, you could either hold collective funds or buy shares in individual companies. Now there's a third way into longer-term investing – the exchange-traded fund or ETF. (A later section, 'The advantages of exchange-traded funds', gives full details.) And, of course, no rule prevents you travelling two or three of these routes at the same time.

With collective funds you have fees to pay. Here a company takes money from many small investors, pools it to give buying power plus research capability, and then entrusts it to a manager who decides what to buy and sell. Fund managers earn fees for this service. The main collective fund categories are investment and unit trusts (most are now officially renamed as open-ended investment companies or OEICs).

The concerns you must consider with a collective fund are selecting the market and then choosing a good fund manager. You can own several funds and/or invest in a fund of funds that puts your cash into the funds its own managers choose. (Part III of this book looks at collective funds in detail, when you're ready for the full lowdown.)

Buying into individual companies is both simple and complex. It's easy because all you have to do is buy a share and then it's yours. You don't have to pay anyone to do anything between the day you buy and the day you sell. It's difficult because you really have to make some tough choices to decide where to put your cash.

The advantage of having your own shares is that you're in control, and you don't have to pay yourself an annual fee for looking after them. Don't forget that although 1.5 per cent a year may not sound much, it adds up to a big sum over 10 to 20 years. This is especially true for pension funds, where some people can invest for 40 years or even more.

You can also consider passive investment (more on this in the later section 'The passive versus active path to profits'), where you simply choose a vehicle such as UK or US stocks and then buy into a package of shares that reflect the indexes for these markets. You can do this via a collective fund or an ETF.

Knowing the Trend Is Your Friend

A share may only seem to be a bit of paper (or a record in an electronic file if you've got rid of old-fashioned certificates for the joy of dematerialisation). But that bit of paper represents something very real. It shows that you own part, albeit a very small part, of a real live company. And as long as that company continues doing well then so will you.

The likelihood, of course, is that you'll own shares in more than one company – either directly through your own portfolio, so that you build up your diversification and spread your risk, or through a fund, such as a unit or an investment trust, where you pay someone else to do all the research, diversification and risk spreading for you.

Now if your idea of a portfolio is a collection full of super-speculative penny stocks and no-hopers, you can skip the rest of this chapter. But the rest of you need to see how trends are your friends:

- ✔ What do you know about wages? They tend to go up.
- ✔ What do you know about prices? They tend to go up.
- ✔ What do you know about prosperity in general? It tends to go up.

Okay, the first and third points have been absent recently in the UK. But I'm talking long-term trends. Adding all these things together, you know that the profitability trend in companies in general should be upward over the long term. Wages and prosperity have suffered but company profits have worked better. When profits rise, the payments from shares, known as *dividends*, should go up. And so should the share price.

 Only a share can give you a direct interest in rising prosperity. Okay, the first decade of the 21st century was generally a disaster zone for shares, but over the past 100 years equities have given an annual return of nearly 10 per cent. Bonds have averaged just over 5 per cent, not far off half. The gap gets wider the longer you hold shares. This extra return from shares is called the *equity risk premium*. It's what you get for taking a greater chance with your money. The trick is to gain the premium but reduce risks. This chapter has some fascinating pointers.

Identifying Two Top Investment Trade Tricks

In this section, I let you in on two stock-market secrets. The first one, which is about the benefits of the passive-investment path to profits, is actually just classified material, so it's really not super-secret. But the second one, which is about the benefits of exchange-traded funds, is top secret and for your eyes only, requiring the highest degree of confidentiality.

The passive versus active path to profits

One stock-market secret is that the long-term investor can do well by buying all the shares in companies that appear in an index such as Footsie, the Eurostoxx or the US's Standard & Poor's. Naturally, you'd do better if you could just spot the best 10 per cent. Try, though, and you're in danger of getting the worst 10 per cent!

You can't buy all the shares in an index yourself unless you're very wealthy and prepared to monitor your holdings constantly. You need a specialist fund (backed by a well-programmed computer) to do this for you. Specialist fund types include index trackers and exchange-traded funds.

Buying all the shares of companies in an index in their same proportions as the index compilers use, irrespective of what anyone may think about their individual prospects, is called *passive investment*. Footsie trackers are popular. A *tracker* is a fund that aims to replicate the ups and downs of an index (here the FTSE 100 or Footsie) by buying all the constituent shares.

The opposite approach is called *active investment*, where you take a view on each company and only buy those that you think will do best. The problem is, as mentioned at the beginning of this section, you may end up buying the worst 10 per cent and losing a great deal of money!

Active versus passive investment is a very big debate. Most of the material published tends to come from those with prior positions and commercial interests on either side, so it tends to develop more heat than light. This dispute goes on whatever is happening to stock markets. Even when shares go down, the two sides quarrel as to which approach is less harmful.

The pros of the passive approach

Here are the benefits of the passive-investment approach:

- ✔ The only thinking you need to do is deciding which index to follow, when to buy and ultimately when to sell.

- ✔ The computer works out which shares to buy and in what proportions.

- ✔ No index has ever gone down all the way to zero, so you'll never lose all your money. Bust and failing companies come out of indexes and are replaced by the shares of healthier firms.

✔ Following the ups and downs is easy. The index is published in newspapers and online.

✔ You're not wasting money on analysts and researchers, who often contradict each other. When some are saying sell and some are hollering buy, they can't all be right, can they?

✔ The charges are usually lower than other forms of investment. The typical tracker charges 0.3 to 0.5 per cent a year in management fees. Anything more is pure robbery because you're not getting any extra value. But active funds hit you for 1.5 per cent and sometimes more. All those yearly 0.5 to 1 per cent cuts in annual management charges plus lower entry costs add up to a big amount of money over 10 to 20 years.

✔ Over long periods, tracker funds usually come in at around the 35th to 40th percentile in fund performance tables. A percentile is a 100th of the table, so in a table of 500 funds, each percentile would be five funds deep. A third of the way down would be the 33rd percentile; halfway is the 50th percentile. This means, trackers come somewhere just outside the top third in performance tables. Few active funds manage this on a consistent basis, and many never succeed in getting into the top third.

✔ You can use passivity for a *core and satellite* approach to investing. The passive fund is the core for your holdings, so you put 80 per cent or so of your money there. The satellites are your other holdings, where you back your hunches.

The pros of the active approach

Here are the benefits of the active-investment approach:

✔ You don't get landed with dud stocks. Index trackers have to keep failing shares heading to the knacker's yard until they're expelled from the index.

✔ You can buy into shares when they're still cheap or little known. The way indexes usually work is that companies are put on the list only when their value reaches a certain level, which may be too late for growth.

✔ You're not forced to change your portfolio just because an index compiler says to do so.

✔ You can pick defensive shares that will do better in falling markets and go for aggressive stocks in rising markets.

✔ You can buy shares in the proportion you want. You don't get landed with too many or too few in any particular company.

✔ You can avoid shares in dodgy or unethical industries, or if you really want to, you can opt instead for a basket of *sin stocks*, such as stocks from gambling, tobacco and armaments companies.

✔ You can pick shares to suit the level of dividend income you want to generate.

✔ You don't waste money in tracking error. Tracking error comes from all the costs a fund hits its customers with and the expenses it has to lay out. It also comes from being unable to replicate each movement in the underlying shares at precisely the right moment.

✔ Some indexes, such as the Japanese Nikkei, are difficult to track.

The advantages of exchange-traded funds

The usual route into the tracker concept is via a unit trust. But here's another stock-market secret for you: check out the exchange-traded fund or ETF. Some professional financial advisers won't invest in anything else – they say their clients do best with a mix of ETFs, trackers and cash in the bank because it's low cost, it's flexible and it works.

Why look at ETFs? The problem is, unit trusts have drawbacks as trackers. For example, most unit trusts only allow dealing once or, at most, twice a day and at times to suit the managers. So that's not much use if you spot a sudden buying chance. An index can move 3 per cent or more within a day. That's a lot of money if you get the wrong side of it. ETFs, by contrast, are traded continually.

Unit trusts have a further disadvantage. Every time you buy into the fund, you have to pay stamp duty one way or another. (It's more hidden in a unit-trust purchase than when you buy a share and the stamp duty is on the paperwork, but it exists all the same.) Call it crazy, but you pay no stamp duty on ETFs.

So if the answer to these difficulties is an exchange-traded fund (ETF), how do you get one? You can buy this type of fund through a stockbroker, just like any other share. However, unlike other shares on the stockbroker's list, an ETF doesn't give you a stake in one company. Don't get scared, but the ETF is a sort of artificial stock-market creation, a piece of financial engineering from the guys who would be rocket scientists if they weren't so keen on money-making. Here the rocket science is called 'derivative trading'.

How this works would fill this book and a half, believe me (and that's genuine understatement!). But what the ETF does is dead simple. The ETF does what it says on the tin. For example, the Footsie ETF would move up and down exactly in line with the Footsie index, second by second, 100th of a point by 100th of a point. It's always spot on. And you can get regular dividend payments just as with a normal tracker fund.

You can save money as well. Don't forget that derivatives including ETFs don't attract UK government stamp duty, which takes 0.5 per cent up front from your other shares' investment money. Otherwise, charges are similar to those imposed at the low end of the unit-trust trackers' fee range.

You can use derivatives for all sorts of complicated strategies. The easiest is *shorting*, meaning that you can sell the ETF if you think the index is due to fall and then buy it back later at a lower price. The gap between the two is your profit (or loss).

ETFs are big business in the United States and increasingly in Europe as well. When they get better known, they'll be big in the UK as well. Currently, you can buy into the Footsie, the Eurostoxx and the Standard & Poor's 500 via UK-quoted ETFs. But you don't have to stop there. If you want, you can find an ETF to invest in international pharmaceutical companies, the price of wheat or even one that finds shares in agricultural machinery firms. This means that you can access a portfolio of shares in an industry or country that may otherwise be difficult to invest in. Where a demand exists, either real or foreseen, some investment bank or another comes up with an ETF.

So although once ETFs limited themselves to the big pictures such as the US, Japanese or UK stock markets, now you can get literally hundreds of them. Some can be really esoteric. Take the ETF that invests in companies making farming implements, for example. It's a great, low-cost way to buy into an agricultural price boom because farmers replace their tractors more often when they see they're getting more for their crops. Or fancy the fortunes of gold-mining companies but haven't the first idea which shares to buy? Don't worry, there's an ETF for you. And another that just tracks the gold price (rumour has it that it's backed by a big warehouse full of bullion). Likewise, drugs companies, oil firms – in fact almost anything you can think of.

Investment banks create ETFs. Banks can go bust. The danger always exists, even though tiny, that the bank may not be able to meet its liabilities. Avoid *synthetic ETFs* that aren't backed by physical shares or bonds in one shape or another. Some are fine, but they're controversial and you could back a winning strategy with a losing ETF.

Check on the fund's costs before buying – anything over 0.5 per cent a year should ring alarm bells. And always check on the names of the manager, trustee and custodian. Do these ring true and do you know who they are, or is the ETF run by a group of 20-year-olds in the back streets of a Latin American shanty town? Also steer clear of funds where all these functions are in different countries. None of this means they're run by crooks. But it does mean that if anything goes wrong or if markets start to zoom down, the structure is more likely to fracture.

Knowing What to Consider When Buying Individual Shares

You need to know this fact up front: you can buy great shares that slump and equities in crummy companies that go up. In other words, stock markets are fickle creatures that have no permanent rules.

When you play or watch a game of football, you know that there are two halves and that each, ignoring injury time, should last for 45 minutes. You know what the object of the game is, and at the end each team has a result: win, draw or lose.

But stock markets are different. In particular, no fixed timeframes and no clear goals exist. Shares go on until a company ceases to exist. This could be tomorrow or in a hundred years' time. Quality will carry the day eventually, but no one knows when that *eventually* will be or even whether the company will change directions for the better or worse in the meantime.

What you have to do is look at the big-picture items, such as the economy or interest rates, that have the power to push the great to mediocrity (or worse) or the very average to a nice little earner. And you have to keep in mind that markets swing very easily and very speedily between feast and famine.

Knowing the psychological impact of the economy

How do you feel when you get out of bed in the morning? Do you feel (Mondays not counted) confident of your job or your pension; that you can make ends meet; that you can cope with the credit card bills; and that the mortgage isn't overwhelming? Or do you worry about your job; fear for your pension payments; fret about being able to afford a holiday this year; know your credit card is ruining you; and have no idea how you're going to pay the mortgage this month?

The likelihood, of course, is that you're somewhere between the euphoria of the first description and the misery of the second. But wherever you are on the scale of being happy or sad about your money prospects, the reason is likely because of the economy. People who prosper in good times have problems when the economy turns sour, even though they continue to work as hard and budget in the same way.

Investor psychology drives markets. When most people are happy, they have the confidence to buy shares, so shares go up in value.

Knowing the power of interest rates

The most important single factor in the modern economy is the interest rate. In the UK, the base rate (which sets the tone for all other interest rates) is fixed at noon on the first Thursday of each month by the Bank of England. This base rate dictates the interest level at which banks and very large companies can borrow money. In turn, it gives the cue to banks, building societies and loan companies in calculating the interest levels they charge to consumers for credit in stores, homebuyers for mortgages and smaller firms for the finance their businesses need. Everyone else pays more than the base rate, of course.

Over the course of the 2008–2009 financial crisis, official interest rates collapsed to an all-time low of 0.5 per cent. They were still there five years later. The low rates were intended to stimulate the economy by making it less costly to borrow. Did it work? No one knows, because you can't divide an economy in half to test one economic concept against another as you could with the trial of a new drug.

Interest rates also set the tone for share prices because

- ✔ **Most companies borrow.** Finance directors calculate that borrowing is fine if the company can use that cash to produce a greater return than the interest bill. Suppose, for example, that a company borrows £1 million at 5 per cent per year. So the company will pay £50,000 in interest. It uses the money to buy a machine or open a new outlet that produces £70,000 per year in profits. The company is now £20,000 per year better off. If interest rates fall to 3 per cent, the cost of the bank loan falls to £30,000, so now the company gets £40,000 per year in profits. But what if interest rates rise to 10 per cent? The company is now spending £100,000 per year on the money borrowed, which produces £70,000. So it's losing money at the rate of £30,000 per year. Higher interest rates mean higher costs of borrowing. If you pay more to borrow the same amount of money, your profits will drop – and vice versa if interest rates fall.

  Companies that borrow the most in relation to their size benefit the most from falling interest rates. This is called *gearing.* Many now use the US term *leverage* instead. Whatever you call it, these firms that profit from low cost loans because they have borrowed lots suffer from the opposite effect when interest rates rise.

- ✔ **Most individuals borrow to buy pricey consumer goods.** Companies have to sell products or services either directly to consumers or to other concerns who provide items for stores and services that deal with the ultimate consumer. When interest rates fall, consumers have more money in their pockets (called *disposable income* by economists) because they don't need to spend as much on mortgages and credit-card loan costs. If rates rise, shoppers have less scope to buy goods. So higher interest rates dissuade people from borrowing, and fewer goods are sold and companies make lower profits. This is all bad for shares.

✔ **Company payouts look better when interest rates fall.** Say that you bought a share for £1 that (ignoring tax) pays 5p a year in dividends. At the time you bought, a cash account paid 5 per cent, or 5p, for every £1. Now, say that interest rates drop to 4 per cent. The dividend stays at 5 per cent, but the cash account rate falls to 4 per cent. Share dividends are now more attractive, so investors will buy the shares themselves, pushing up the price.

✔ **Falling interest rates mean the next time a company needs money, it won't have to pay the bank so much.** Therefore, it will be able to carry out its expansion, making the firm bigger and more valuable.

That said, interest rates are a blunt instrument, and they hit companies in different ways. Here's a list of sectors that are bludgeoned the most by rising rates:

✔ **House builders:** They're usually big borrowers in comparison to their size. They nearly always sell what they build to consumers who also need loans.

✔ **Retailers:** When rates rise, their customers have less cash because they're paying more for mortgages. Consumers are less likely to use credit cards. Most big purchases are non-essential and can be put off. But for how long? The new three-piece suite can nearly always wait; the new generation 3D television is far from necessary; and the replacement for the clapped-out fridge can usually be put on hold for longer.

✔ **Fund managers and life-insurance companies:** Firms that make their living out of the stock market hate rising interest rates, which scare people off equities. Customers put new money into savings accounts, so the fees these people get from investing other people's money fall.

✔ **Exporters:** Higher interest rates can often push up the value of your currency on foreign exchange markets. This is bad for exporters who get less when their foreign earnings are turned back into their home currency.

✔ **Banks:** Surprisingly perhaps, banks do badly when interest rates go up. They do charge more for loans, but not as many people want to borrow. Worse, banks can't hit customers with as big a gap (technically known as the *margin*) between what they give to savers and the amount they charge to borrowers.

And here are some stock-market areas that should do better than average when rates are rising:

✔ **Food retailers:** People have to eat! In tough times, people still need a few shopping-therapy-style treats, and these are more likely to be a bottle of wine or a box of chocolates than new clothes or the latest electronic goodies.

✔ **Discount shops:** Stores where nothing costs more than £1 or where you can buy a complete outfit with change from £50 are obvious winners in harder times.

✔ **Companies with cash:** Not all companies borrow. Some have big balances at the bank, so they profit if rates rise.

✔ **Tobacco companies and breweries:** People tend to smoke and drink more when they're miserable, whatever the health effects. And because they spend little on product development, these companies tend not to borrow and have lots of cash.

✔ **Importers:** Higher rates can mean a stronger currency so importers can buy their goods overseas with a smaller amount of their home currency.

Knowing the long-term trend

Ever heard that story in the Bible about seven good years followed by seven lean years? Thousands of years later, life hasn't changed that much, except now people call it the *economic cycle.* The good years are when interest rates are falling and people are happier. But interest rates can't keep falling for ever, and one day they must go up, leading to a period of belt tightening.

Governments, investment banks and big businesses spend a fortune trying to predict where the big economic wheel is, how fast it's going and in what direction. They don't have a great deal of success. But here's a secret: most of those earning a crust by giving forecasts of future economic conditions just follow the trend. If you follow what happened yesterday (or last week or last month) and repeat it today (this week or this month), you're statistically more likely to be right than wrong.

In any case, you don't have to follow the so-called experts' forecasts. You couldn't buy fully into their research and guesstimates even if you could afford to buy their material. It's not usually for sale because it's reserved for pension and other funds controlling billions, which give the researchers and their bosses huge volumes of business.

But don't worry. As the long-term manager of your own money, you can do as well if not better than those highly paid City types in many ways.

Enjoying the Payments and Perks of Owning Shares

Shareholding has its plus points including, in some cases, the chance to pick up a bargain when you go shopping or away for a break. These plus points can lighten the down moments and help your finances when the shares themselves are looking miserable.

A few companies offer shareholders discounts on their products, such as lower hotel prices from leisure companies or cut-rate telephones from BT. But nice as they are, these never add up to a reason for investing.

Most companies send you a twice-a-year share payment (occasionally four times a year), called a *dividend*. It's the various companies' way of saying thank you for your cash and loyalty in hanging in there through thick and thin.

The first dividend of the year is called the interim payment, and the second is called the final payment. Sometimes, though, the final dividend is called the second interim. A few legal reasons exist for this, but the name makes no difference to investors. The company usually announces the interim payment with the six-monthly figures halfway through the firm's financial year, and announces the final dividend with the preliminary results, or prelims, of the financial year, so called because they're revealed before the official annual report. Some companies now pay out four times a year – usually those based overseas or listed on the New York stock exchange. Quarterly dividends are normal in the United States.

Shareholders get to vote on the amount that the company will pay out as a final dividend for the year at the annual general meeting, although you can count the instances of investors turning down money on the fingers of one hand. This usually happens as a form of protest against either the company itself, an activity of that company or some of the directors.

When the company announces a dividend, it sets a date on which it'll pay the dividend to those on the shareholder register at that time. Investors who buy from that date onward must wait until the next time (probably in six months or so) for their first payment.

Most companies send a dividend cheque, even for a small amount. You could even end up with a cheque worth less than the stamp on the envelope used to send it.

Most companies will also arrange for your dividend payment to be sent straight to your bank account. This arrangement has advantages for the company because it's cheaper than issuing cheques, and it has advantages for you because you get the money immediately instead of having to trust the post, deposit the cheque in the bank and wait for it to clear. If they credit your cash automatically, the company still sends you a notice detailing the dividend payment and any tax deduction. You can often opt for the company to send these notices by email. Don't throw this paperwork away because HM Revenue & Customs insists you keep all records for 22 months after the end of the tax year in which you received the dividend.

Another option, offered by many big companies and virtually all funds, is *automatic dividend reinvestment* (sometimes called DRIP, for Dividend Re-Investment Plan). Your money is used to buy new shares in the company at the price ruling on the day the dividend is announced. Of course, it's unlikely that your dividend payment buys an exact number of shares, so usually some change are carried over to the next dividend payment and then added to your dividend. Note that you must pay UK government stamp duty at 0.5 per cent on these purchases, but generally any stockbroker fees are minimal. This is a great way to build up a holding over time without needing much out-of-pocket financing! And you don't have to worry about brokerage fees or timing. Again, your paperwork shows the dividend your holding earned.

Reinvesting dividends makes sense if you don't need to spend the money. The Barclays Bank Equity Gilt Study figures show that much of the advantage of shares is lost otherwise.

An investor with £10,000 at the end of 1979 would have shares worth £101,537 after 30 years, at the end of 2009 (ignoring costs and tax). Putting the dividends back into shares would have turned that same £10,000 into £250,772. Even making allowances for tax and costs, reinvesting dividends gives a huge, long-term uplift to your investments. It also has the advantage that you continue buying shares when prices are low, so you can enjoy any eventual bounce upwards. And which period you choose doesn't matter – the result always favours those who re-invest.

And now for some bad news: you may have to pay more tax on your dividends. But you can't reclaim the amount the firm's already paid even if you don't pay tax yourself.

If you pay no tax or, as most do, pay at the basic rate, you *probably* have no more tax to pay. Why probably? Adding your dividends into your other earnings could just nudge you into a higher tax-rate band. You may also think that you're a basic-rate taxpayer and then get a big pay rise or bonus that takes you into the next level. The starting point for the 40 and 45 per cent higher tax bands changes every year in the budget, but if all your earnings including dividends and interest payments top the £45,000 mark then you'll probably be a 40 per cent taxpayer. To pay at 45 per cent, you need to be earning at least £150,000 a year.

Now about that document you receive with your dividend payment: it's very important, which is why many companies put an 'HMRC: *KEEP THIS*' label on it. This means what it says. HM Revenue & Customs rules say that you must keep dividend notice forms for 22 months after the end of the tax year in which you received the dividend payment, even if you don't have any tax to pay. If your dividend was paid in May 2016, the tax year ended on 5 April 2017. You must send your self-assessment tax return, essential if any dividend payment brings you into the top tax band or you're already there, by 31 January 2018. You must then keep all your returns until 31 January 2019, or longer if the tax inspector queries your assessment. HMRC has up to six years to challenge your return but must start this process within the above time period if it relates to dividends or interest payments.

Chapter 9 looks at dividends in more detail, if you're interested. It explains what investors can understand from their payment levels, increases and reductions. This stuff can be a good guide to future prospects.

Chapter 9

Analysing Stock-Market-Quoted Companies

In This Chapter

▶ Understanding what company profits are all about

▶ Getting familiar with the price/earnings ratio

▶ Understanding that dividend declaration you get from the company

▶ Deciding whether you can trust forecasts

▶ Working through company takeovers

▶ Deciphering share price charts

*B*eing a successful share investor involves looking at numbers and understanding them. But don't worry. You don't need a PhD in mathematics or rocket-science physics. Much of the figure work involves nothing more complicated than looking to see whether something is going up or down. And most of the rest involves the simple task of comparing figures from one company with those from another.

The most difficult maths task is working out percentage sums, which you can do on a calculator costing a fiver or so – and you've probably got one on your phone for free. Many investment decisions depend on knowing how a figure compares with the previous year and with expectations of the future.

That's what this chapter is all about – being a successful share investor by looking at numbers from stock-market-quoted companies and then understanding what those numbers mean.

Of course, if you've decided you don't want to invest in individual shares but stick to collectives then you could skip this chapter. But even if you leave it up to fund managers, knowing about these basic analysis tools is still useful.

Comparing Apples with Apples: The Gospel According to the Market

Stock markets don't have set rules or timescales like a game of football. So whatever figures you come up with during your investment number crunching, you must compare them with other numbers that are around at the same time.

For example, you may calculate or hear that profits at a company have increased by 10 per cent. Well, that's obviously better than profits going down – or even going up by just 9 per cent. But you can only see how important that 10 per cent gain is by referring to the market as a whole and to companies that compete with the company you're looking at.

If the market average gain is 15 per cent, your company is in house building and rival construction companies have gained 20 per cent, then your share is doing very badly! The converse also applies, of course. A 10 per cent profits advance when most other comparable firms are struggling to make any gains is really good news!

Lots of people get basic percentage sums wrong because they input the numbers on their calculator in the wrong order or divide when they should multiply. The task is made more difficult because some calculators use different keys for percentage calculations. The thing is, getting it wrong can be very costly. So practise with sums that have answers you can easily check in your head. For example, a firm that earns £1.5 million this year is 50 per cent ahead of last year's £1 million and has gained 50 per cent. Going down from £1 million to £750,000 is a 25 per cent fall. A decrease can't be more than 100 per cent!

Identifying the Basic Building Blocks of Companies: Profits

Investors in shares have one concern that overrides all else. They need to know how much profit (or loss) the company will make in the future. Nothing else counts. The past is more than a foreign country; it's a nowhere place.

But future profits are the great unknown, although investors try to estimate what they'll be and how they'll compare with other companies. Share values adjust to these expectations, and investors then compare their hopes or fears with the reality when it's announced.

When stock-market experts forecast a 20 per cent profit increase at a company, they factor that expectation into the share price. They calculate whether 20 per cent is above, below or in line with competitor companies and with the market as a whole. They also look to see how that compares with previous figures and expectations from the company. And outside the direct orbit of these experts and the firms they work for, other market participants also consider the forecasters' credibility. A forecast from an analyst known to have a good record and close contacts with the company counts for more than a forecast from a largely unknown source.

But the real test is the actual profit number when the company officially releases it. If the reality is 30 per cent, the share price will gain on the news. But if the gain fails to reach 20 per cent or only scrapes by that figure, disappointed investors will sell, so the shares may fall unless some other positive news emerges. Targets in the stock market are there to beat, not just to equal. Otherwise, it's 'all in the price' – a phrase meaning investors have weighed up what the expectations were and have adjusted the share value accordingly.

Quoted UK companies must publish a five-year record of their profitability or loss-making in their annual report and accounts. These figures are also easily available on a number of company information websites.

Looking at profits from an accountant's point of view

If you buy a car for £1,000, repair it and sell it for £2,000, you've made a £1,000 profit. Or have you? Although you have £1,000 more in your bank account, you need to count a lot of costs, including materials to repair the car, your time and advertising the vehicle. And don't forget the cost of the £1,000. You either had to borrow the money, which cost you interest, or had to raid your savings account, losing out on interest. Go a bit further and you have the rent on the garage you kept it in (or the amount you lost by not letting out that space to others) and the expense of the tools you needed.

If you were a big company, you'd go a lot further again, employing teams of accountants who can either make your profits look impressive for investors or minimise them for the tax inspector.

If you had to account for your car-repairing venture, the £1,000 would be the *gross* profit and just the start of the process. The actual gain is less.

Examining a company's profit-and-loss account

Look at a company's annual report and its profit-and-loss (known as the *p & l*) account. It lists lots of different sorts of profit. You need to find the right one to see whether the company is going forward or backward, but you also need to understand the others to see the message they give out.

Most company accounts are called *consolidated* because they bring together all the various subsidiaries that big firms have. You can ignore subsidiary profit-and-loss accounts. If you want to see them, they're filed at Companies House and you can get a copy if you want. You really don't need to, though.

All UK companies have to produce detailed accounts once a year. Quoted concerns also issue half-yearly statements to show their progress. And a growing minority comes up with figures every three months. In the US, quarterly reporting is the rule for most companies, so UK firms with substantial US interests tend to produce figures every three months. All these figures are the key to what's going on. Most sets of figures in the UK follow an established pattern, which starts with the biggest number at the top of the page and keeps taking away the farther down you go. So the top line may be billions, but the bottom may be pennies. (When you look at a company's account, note that accountants don't use minus signs. Instead, they use brackets to indicate items to subtract. Likewise, if a company makes a loss, the account shows that figure in brackets.)

Here's a breakdown of what you'll see on a sample company's account – from the top to the bottom, with some figures and what they tell you. Note that most accounts show sums in millions. Note, too, that this stuff is technical, even though I'm not explaining the most complicated versions. The latter are really impossible to follow unless you have a postgraduate qualification in company accounts. The most complex come from oil and insurance companies.

- ✔ **Turnover (£100 million):** This is the very biggest figure. It lists the amount people spend with the company. For a high-street store, it's the amount that came in through the tills. For a bank, it largely consists of the income from interest on loans and investment gains on big deals.

- ✔ **Cost of sales (£80 million):** This is the amount the company has spent on raw materials as well as manufactured items it bought to sell to customers. It's high at a retailer, low at a management consultancy.

- ✔ **Gross profit (£20 million):** This is what's left after taking the cost of sales away from the sales themselves. It's the biggest profit figure, but you can take a lot away from it.

- ✔ **Operating expenses (£15 million):** This is the cost of running the company, including staff salaries and rent on premises. The pay that directors get is listed in notes to the accounts, the small print where quite a bit of the detail is hidden.

- ✔ **Operating profit (£5 million):** This is what the company would make if it operated in a vacuum! If there were no tax to pay or interest on bank loans to count, this would be the actual profit. It's a good indicator of a company's management efficiency. If two competitor firms both sell £100 million, the one with an operating profit of £5 million is running itself better than the one with an operating profit of £4 million.

✔ **Exceptional items ($500,000):** These are one-off items that really have nothing to do with the day-to-day running of the business – things like profits made from selling off a piece of spare land or the expenses of relocating the firm. They can be positive or negative. Firms often don't have any of these items.

✔ **Profit on ordinary activities before interest ($4.5 million):** This tells you how much the company made before paying for bank loans. It's a useful indicator of progress because it doesn't involve a major external such as interest, over which the company itself has no control whatsoever. Don't worry. This section is a fair way along the road but there's still an accounting hurdle or two to go.

✔ **Net interest payable ($500,000):** This is the cost of bank and other loans needed to run the business less any interest earned on bank deposits. Occasionally, companies may have earned more interest than they spent. This is an important figure because it tells you how susceptible the company is to interest-rate changes. Here, the interest charge is 10 per cent of the operating profit. Compare this with previous years and with competitor firms.

✔ **Profit before tax ($4 million):** This is the big headline figure and the profit definition used in most media reports.

✔ **Tax ($400,000):** Everyone has to pay taxes, but companies have ways and means of keeping the figure low. These can be controversial, with sales diverted to low-tax nations.

✔ **Profit after tax ($3.6 million):** This is the amount the company has for ploughing back into the business and for paying out dividends. This amount is entirely at the control of the directors.

✔ **Minority interests and preference dividends ($200,000):** These are amounts companies must pay to special groups of investors before paying their own shareholders. Many companies don't have this item.

✔ **Profit attributable to ordinary shareholders ($3.4 million):** This is what you and all the other equity holders have to share out.

✔ **Dividends ($1.9 million):** This is the cost of the payments made to shareholders.

✔ **Retained profit for the year ($1.5 million):** This is what's left to plough back into the company after taxes and dividends; it's used for future expansion and research.

✔ **Earnings per share (17p):** This is the profit attributable to ordinary shareholders ($3.4 million) divided by the number of shares in issue – in this case 20 million. It comes at the end, but it's a key figure for working out how well your investment is doing.

Understanding what company profits and losses actually mean

The ideal scenario is for a company to make record profit gains every year and beat the expectations of the experts by a huge margin. Don't ever bank on this happening, though. If such a paragon of virtue company existed, its shares would be really expensive because such amazing expectations would already have been 'discounted by the market' (that's another way of saying 'it's all in the price').

The 99.99 per cent probability is that companies whose shares you buy have variable profits records, doing better in some periods than in others, compared to competitors and to the overall economy. Your job is to understand what the figures mean.

Profits may not always be quite as real or as rosy as a company's investor and media relations teams like to make out. And although no one wants to make a loss, getting into the red may not always be a disaster or even a danger signal.

So headline profit figures may not be what they seem. Following are some key profit moves to look for and assess. And don't forget that many companies are great at creative accounting, which is the stock-market equivalent of turning a sow's ear into a silk purse. Creative accounting, or window dressing, can go much too far, as in the cases of bust US power company Enron, bank Lehman Brothers or the downright fraudulent Ponzi scheme from now jailed fund chief Bernie Madoff. Here are some examples of creative accounting to watch out for:

- ✔ **Rising profits year on year:** These sound really good. In most cases, they are. These are just the sort of companies investors love. But look out for comparisons with rival companies that may be doing even better; whether the company is doing anything more than just keeping up with rising prices in its product area; tricks such as massaging the profits upward with accounting devices; and whether the rising profits are due to the company buying other firms and incorporating their earnings into its own.

- ✔ **Profits reported each year but sometimes up and sometimes down:** This is a normal pattern, especially if firms can't rely on rising prices year after year to give paper profits. Check that the ups are as good as, if not better than, competitor firms. Look at the reasons for the setbacks. Could they have been avoided? Did rivals do better? Did the company warn shareholders adequately that problems may occur?

- ✔ **Making neither a profit nor a loss:** Not a good sign, but if the company is in a healthy business with a good reputation, this status may say something about the failings of the management. Good companies with poor people at the top tend to end up with a takeover bid: good news for shareholders. Don't forget that breaking even when others are losing loads of cash *is* doing well.

Check that directors aren't overpaying themselves. A fair balance must exist between boardroom pay, including bonuses, and what shareholders, who take the ultimate risks, receive.

✔ **Losing money:** Acceptable reasons include heavy research and development costs, a company starting up and needing to spend heavily before establishing itself, and economic slumps. Find out what the company is doing to turn itself around. If no reason exists and you see no light at the end of the deficit tunnel, run a mile from this company. Don't forget, it's your money the company's losing, so you have to get some gain after your pain.

Published company figures are two to four months out of date when they're released. Circumstances by then may have changed. Companies take different times to add up the figures. High-street stores and banks tend to be quick. Firms with lots of different overseas offshoots and smaller companies are usually slower.

Bad figures take longer to add up than good ones. That's not literally true, but companies that delay releasing figures or are late compared with previous years are usually in financial trouble. Treat any postponement as a danger signal.

Knowing What to Look at First: Earnings Per Share

You may only have one share in a company that's issued 1 billion. But that *earnings-per-share (eps)* figure at the end of the company's profit-and-loss account is your share (literally!) of the profit. And even if it's at the very bottom of the page, it's where in-the-know investors look first. Don't confuse this with the dividend, which is usually a lower figure.

You can use the eps figure rather than the headline profit to see whether the company is really moving ahead. It may have issued millions more shares to acquire other firms, which could result in the profit it brings in boosting the pre-tax profits figure, but after it's divided up among more shares, the end result could be down. For example, say that Company A has £10 million profits attributable to shareholders who have 10 million shares between them. So each earns £1 per share. Then Company A buys Company B by issuing 10 million shares. Profits go up to £15 million, but each share now only has 75p in earnings because the company must divide £15 million out 20 million ways. The takeover has been bad (or to put it in jargon, *non-earning enhancing*). It may work out better later on, of course. Or even worse.

Owners of shares in companies that are bought tend to fare better than those who own shares in companies that are doing the acquiring. This may say something about the quality of those in the top executive suite – sometimes, they may buy a company for a short-term profits boost that gives a long-term increase to their pay package.

The eps figure is also honest because it's after tax. It measures what's really yours and not a slice the tax authority will grab.

Understanding the price/earnings ratio

The earnings-per-share figure lets you compare one year with the next at the same company. But it's pretty useless if you want to rate one firm against another. Whether your earnings are high or low depends on the share price.

A 20p eps sounds twice as good as a 10p eps. But it's not necessarily so. It all depends on the share price. Dividing the earnings into the share price gives a magic figure called the *p/e*, which stands for *price/earnings ratio*, and it's widely used in working out whether a share is good value. It tells you how many years of earnings at the last published level you'd need to equal the share price.

Loss-making companies can't have a price/earnings ratio because they have no earnings. That's why the p/e column in newspaper listings sometimes shows a dash. Some investors calculate the loss/earnings ratio, though, and it can be useful to compare two loss-making companies.

If two companies have identical prospects, the one with the lower p/e number is the better deal. If both companies are going to earn, say, 10p per share, the one with the p/e of 12, equalling a 120p share price, is more attractive than the share on a 15 times p/e, because then you pay 150p for the same thing. Of course, a good reason may exist for this particular rating so doing some digging for the real reasons is worthwhile. Numbers rarely exist on their own. You should look at them in as wide a context as you can.

What a prospective price/earnings ratio tells you

The p/e is a great comparative tool. It's widely quoted in newspaper reports, and it's carried in many share listings both on- and offline. It goes up when share prices rise and down when they fall. But it has one big weakness. The figure you see, called the *historical p/e*, is based on the most recent accounts, and the company is unlikely to make the same profits again. It may make more or less.

The way around this weakness is the *prospective p/e*, which is based on what the stock market thinks the company is going to make in the current financial year and sometimes in the year or two after that. For example, a company with earnings last year of 10p and a current share price of 100p has a p/e of 10. The forecast is for earnings of 20p per share, so the prospective p/e falls to 5 (100p divided by 20p). If the forecast were for earnings of 4p per share, the prospective p/e would rise to 25.

Take prospective figures with a pinch of salt. They're educated guesses with a bit of help from the company itself, which steers or guides stockbroker analysts in the right direction, or should do. Some investors prefer consensus figures that average the guesstimates of all published analysts. You can find these online.

How to use the price/earnings ratio

So what can you really do with the price/earnings ratio? Well, you can use it to

- Compare the share prices of companies that appear to have similar prospects.

- Pick out companies that the market thinks will grow. Growth companies have higher p/e ratios.

- Check whether you've spotted a growing company early on. If the p/e starts to climb after you buy, congratulate yourself.

- Determine whether to sell. Some investors sell shares if their p/e goes a certain percentage above the average. Remember that a high p/e means the market is expecting more growth, but if the p/e is too high, the company could fall short of the target. In any case, you could sell high p/e companies and look for those that are still low.

- See which shares are in or out of fashion. A low figure suggests that other investors are ignoring the company. They may be right, but their information may be out of date. Or this particular company may be beyond the risk appetite of most major investors.

- Provide a framework. Ask questions if a p/e is much higher or lower than similar shares.

Beware of shares with astronomic p/e ratios that imply you'd have to wait 100 or more years to get your share price back if earnings stayed the same. Mega ratios usually come with shares with more hype than hope, more faith than a fair future. Or they may simply be figures based on a previous year when earnings were much higher.

Knowing What Dividends Really Mean

Would you like a twice-per-year cheque from your share investments that you can spend or save or plough back into the stock market? Or are you happy to just rely on whatever your shares fetch on the day you decide to sell? Most UK investors opt for the first choice.

Companies pay out *dividends*, or share payments, usually around every six months, some quarterly, of so many pence per share. That price is multiplied by the number of shares you have, and you get a cheque or a bank transfer for the amount to the nearest penny.

Some companies offer reinvestment schemes, so you can use your dividend to buy more shares. Because your dividend probably won't buy an exact number of shares, any leftover amount is carried over to the next dividend payment. (You can only buy whole shares, unlike units in unit-trust funds, which subdivide each unit by 100.)

Dividends represent your share of the profits. And they're a major part of the UK share scene. But not all companies pay dividends. Exceptions are new companies, where investors expect the company to plough all the profits into the business, as well as companies making losses, which can't afford to spare the cash. However, when companies are in the position where they can afford the payments, they're expected to do so. Holding back without an explanation is viewed with grave suspicion and reaps a fast-falling share price!

Understanding what dividends say about the company

Because the dividend is seen as a vital part of the share make-up in the UK (less so in quite a few other countries), analysts look at its level as a vital sign of that firm's financial health or perhaps lack of health.

The essential figure is the *dividend yield*, a figure that requires an investor to add up all the dividends in a year. Some firms pay more than twice a year, and payments are rarely equal. Companies with seasonal businesses, such as package holiday firms, may pay only a token amount at one payment and nearly everything in the other payout. That's because the cash flowing in and out of the company is uneven.

Working out the dividend yield means working out a percentage sum. You need to divide the dividend in pence by the share price in pence and multiply by 100 (or press the percentage key). So a 50p share price paying a 1p dividend gives a 2 per cent yield. And a 100p share price paying a 10p dividend gives a 10 per cent dividend yield.

Dividends and dividend yields are based on the past. These may not provide any indication of the future. For instance, the dividend yield in a company that's failing could look very attractive. But a strong likelihood exists of a dividend cut (or getting rid of it altogether), so the yield here is fictional. A 20p dividend on a 100p share price looks a bargain, but it's not if the dividend is cut to 2p in the coming year.

The price/earnings ratio rises with share prices. But the dividend as a ratio falls when shares go up.

Looking at dividends, like everything else in the investment world, is comparison work. No absolute levels exist. For example, many companies that paid a 10 per cent dividend yield in the inflationary 1970s now pay around 2 to 3 per cent. Always compare like with like.

You need to be concerned with two dividend yield figures. The current rate is the one you use for analysis. But the rate worked out for the price you paid for the share can also be important because it gives you an idea of what another investment would need to produce to give you the same amount of spendable cash. If the current share price at 300p offers you a 10 per cent yield, you'd have a 30 per cent yield on your cash if you bought the shares at 100p.

To look at dividends, you need benchmarks:

- ✔ **The average yield on the FTSE All Share Index:** See whether your share comes up with a higher or lower number. The higher the figure, the less the stock market thinks of the share's future growth prospects. Many newspapers and websites carry this statistic.

- ✔ **The sector average:** This looks at companies in similar businesses to your own, such as breweries or software companies. This figure is also published in some newspapers and is available online.

- ✔ **The yield on a basket of UK government stocks, or *gilts*:** This helps tell you what you'd get for your money in the safest UK investment. If the dividend yield is lower than the one for gilts, then hope for future share price growth to compensate. Otherwise, taking the risk of equity purchase is pointless. When the yield on a share is lower than on government stocks, it's known as the *equity risk premium*.

Most shares yield less than gilts because they have growth possibilities; gilts can never return more than their face value. The greater the difference (known technically as the *reverse yield gap*), the more growth orientated your stock is. Shares with yields higher than gilts can be suspect! Look to see why such a big payout isn't rewarded with a higher share price. Remember, high yield equals high alert! The dividend could be in danger.

Deciphering the signs that dividends provide

Comparing a dividend yield or return with its benchmark, such as a sector average, and the amount paid in previous years gives a list of possibilities for investors looking for pointers to a company's future health. All the ideas here offer clues to the company and how other investors see it.

Rising dividend payments

Rising dividend payments are what investors expect. The ideal share increases the payment each year to reflect growing profits. But this increase should be gradual because investors want payouts that can be sustained, rather than go up and down in a volatile fashion.

But investors would be worried if payments went up faster than earnings because that would show that the company isn't investing in its own future. Instead, it's trying to buy stock-market favour, perhaps to ward off an expected takeover bid. The exception is when a company has a lot of cash and has announced that it thinks shareholders can make better use of it than the company management. You could get a *special dividend* – a one-off return of cash that won't be replicated in the future.

Static dividend payments

Generally, static dividend payments are viewed as bad news because the company isn't growing its profits. Static dividend payments are viewed as even worse news if the company has to dip into its bank account to pay the dividend. Firms shouldn't borrow to pay dividends. Doing this is generally seen as a danger signal.

Falling or no dividend payments

Falling dividend payments or no dividend payments are really bad news, but companies often prepare investors for this situation ahead of the announcement because it's even worse if the decision to reduce or cut out payments comes as a surprise.

A company that surprises the market by saying it's forced to halve its dividend will see its share price rise steeply over a relatively short period. Investors are more forgiving if they can see light at the end of this tunnel in the shape of a return to dividend growth in the future. Remember, companies aren't supposed to drop bombshells.

Very high dividend payments

When you see very high dividends, do a reality check. Can this continue? Or is it an attempt to buy investor favour?

Dividend yields shown in newspapers are historic because they're based on the most recent payouts. The company may have announced a reduction or complete cancellation of its next dividend, so check websites and other news sources before relying on this yield figure.

Even if the company has said nothing publicly, investors can often put two and two together and find out whether the company is going to have to cut dividends. If the company is about to cut or abandon (technically called *passing*) the dividend then investors tend to sell.

Looking at the dividend cover

Dividing the dividend per share into the earnings per share gives something called the *cover*. For example, an earnings per share of 20p with a dividend of 5p gives a four times cover. This figure is the number of times the dividend could have been paid out from after-tax earnings. In this case, the 5p dividend could have been paid four times over, so the cover number is four.

Too low a number, especially less than one, tells you the company is pulling out all the stops and all the cash from wherever it can to avoid the indignity of a dividend cut. Companies can only get away with this if they have a really good excuse and a promise that they'll go back to a higher cover in the future.

There's also the danger of running near to empty. A company paying out most or all of its earnings in dividends has nothing to fall back on if times become harder and profits fall.

But too high a cover, perhaps more than four or five times, suggests that the company is hoarding cash. Nothing's wrong if you can see the reason, so find out whether its research, development and other expansion requirements really need it to be quite so mean to shareholders.

Deciding Whether Forecasts Are Reliable Sources or a Lot of Hot Air

Stockbrokers and investment-fund management firms spend a fortune on highly paid analysts who are supposed to predict the future. Some firms employ people to research just one or two stock-market sectors, although smaller broking outfits expect staff to look more widely.

Some of this research is available to small investors. A number of investment magazines print extracts from broker recommendations, and many stockbrokers dealing with private clients send out material. As a rule, big firms of stockbrokers tend to cover the biggest companies, leaving the Tiddlers to the brokers who specialise in individual investors. (Check out Chapter 7 for details on who the Tiddlers are.)

Most stockbroker notes list the share price when the research was finalised; essential ratios, such as the price/earnings and the dividend yield; the share's high and low points over the past year; past earnings; and – most crucially – what the analyst expects the company to report as a profit for the next full year or perhaps even the year past that. Obviously, the farther the figures point into the future, the less reliable they are.

The notes should also contain some detail on where the company is going, ranging from 100 words to 100 pages. In addition, good material then compares the profits forecast to the present share price and decides whether that price fairly reflects the prospects.

You should also see a recommendation, such as buy, sell or hold. You'd think a rough equality would exist between the buys and the sells. After all, most investors don't have limitless money, so they want some guidance on what to sell so they can purchase something with brighter prospects. But very few broker notes these days are headed *Sell*.

The reason, cynics say (and they're probably right), is that too many brokers get their information on where a company is going from the company directors themselves in special briefing sessions. Some analysts don't want to bite the hand that feeds them! Broking firms may also have a special relationship with a company in which they represent the company in the stock market. In this type of arrangement, the broking firm is known as the *house* broker, and the firm may not want to jeopardise this arrangement with negative comments.

But due to scandals – especially in the US, where some analysts were putting out company views as their own because they had a vested financial interest in puffing up the company – analysts are now likely to have a clean act and stress how independent they are. Some no longer use terms like *buy* or *sell* but come up with targets for their expectations of profits or the share price and then leave investors to make up their own minds. This is an improvement.

Looking at past records is the only way to check on whether your source of stockbroker information is any good. If the recommendations produce a bit more than the average or the fund invested in the stock market index then you've hit on a good research analyst. Don't let go of him! You'll never get 100 per cent accuracy, so better than average is a winning proposition.

Much of what you read in newspapers comes from analysts. They don't always get name checks. Some don't want the wider publicity of media appearances, but talking up shares their clients already hold may suit them.

Looking at Takeovers: Good, Bad or Ugly?

Takeovers occur when one company wants to buy another stock-market-quoted company lock, stock and barrel. They get headlines that can be emotive, as when a foreign company bids for a 'much loved, iconic company', or exciting, as when a bid battle occurs with rival companies bidding auction-style for the target. Whatever the reaction, takeovers involve all shareholders because, whatever the company directors recommend, the real power lies with those owning the equity.

Takeovers happen because:

- The company making the acquisition thinks it can squeeze more profits out of the target company, and so it's worth paying for.

- The target company has profitable patents or products that the acquiring company wants.

- The target company is a rival, and a successful takeover bid would mean less competition. (Note that this scenario may have to pass UK Competition and Markets Authority hurdles if the result would place too much power into the hands of one company.)

- The target company has lots of assets, such as property, that can be bought for less than their true worth and then sold for a profit – a practice that can lead to *asset stripping*. This is frowned upon, but it still happens.

- The acquiring company is running out of steam and ideas, so it wants to bring in a smaller, more successful firm to rejuvenate it. This scenario is called a *reverse takeover* because the smaller firm ends up in charge. The smaller firm may not be listed on the stock market, but don't fret because its advisers will find a workaround.

Whatever the reason for them, takeovers usually generate big share price gains for the target company. Takeovers are supposed to be top secret before the official announcement, but leaks and rumours are common even though they're covered by legislation banning insider trading.

In the past, most takeovers came from competitor firms (for instance, when one supermarket buys another supermarket). Now, many come from *private equity companies* that borrow money to buy existing shareholders. Private equity companies use financial techniques to squeeze value out of their purchases. As far as investors are concerned, though, private equity money is as good as cash from competitors.

At least ten takeover rumours exist for every real bid. So don't believe every one you see mentioned in newspapers and elsewhere.

The share price of the target company goes up for the usual reason of supply and demand. In this case, there's demand for every share from the bidder, so the value naturally goes up.

The company making the bid hopes that the directors of the target company will recommend the bid to their own shareholders. But the shareholders want to see a second bidder, counter-bidder or rejection from the target company because it should send the price up even further. Investors with shares in the target company always benefit from an auction between two or more determined bidders.

Holders in the target company may be offered cash or shares (or a mix of the two) in the acquiring company. With cash you know what you're getting; shares go up and down over short periods. A *loan stock option* is an alternative to cash. It's a device whereby the company keeps your takeover cash and pays you regular interest on the amount. The purpose is to help investors cut down on capital gains tax bills by cashing their loan options in instalments each year rather than the whole lot in one go.

Bids come with timetables and complicated rules. Shareholders in the target company must choose between accepting the bid, hanging on for a better offer or ignoring the deal by siding with the current directors. Sometimes, selling immediately in the stock market during a contested takeover can be the best idea. Bids fail, and the target's share price could fall. It's a bird-in-the-hand decision.

Takeovers are mostly good for shareholders in the target companies. Many academic studies show that takeovers are less advantageous for acquiring firms. Shares in the bidding firm commonly fall when it announces a takeover.

Perhaps the worst example ever was Royal Bank of Scotland's controversial takeover of Dutch bank ABN Amro. This move was criticised at the time, but the RBS board still went ahead. The takeover quickly proved disastrous for RBS, helping to bring about near ruin, a share price collapse and a massive taxpayer rescue.

Discussing Technical Analysis: The Arcane World of Share Price Charts

Warning here: what I discuss in this section is so technical that it's called *technical analysis.* It involves looking at share price charts to make decisions rather than other factors such as earnings expectations or the future of the market where the firm operates. Cynics say technical analysts, or *chartists*, can make decisions without even knowing what business the firm's in. So technical analysis isn't everyone's cup of tea. But those who use it swear by it, and fans include a number of stock-market movers and shakers.

Technical analysis is a way of making investment decisions that goes in and out of fashion. So you need to know about technical analysis, even if you dismiss it as mumbo-jumbo.

Most people look at the fundamentals of shares. The fundamentals include the general economic situation, industry-specific trends, interest rates and foreign currency exchange rates, how the company you're looking at is seen to be doing, balance sheet strengths and weaknesses, the company's products, the company's management, and a host of other financial and business factors.

But a minority of investors reckon that looking at the fundamentals is a waste of time. So these investors go back to square one – sometimes so far back that they don't even care about the name of the share, bond, currency or commodity they're looking at. Instead, they revert to one of the very early lessons investors have to take in: that you can't always explain what's going on except by saying that prices rise when buyers outnumber sellers and that prices go down when sellers outnumber buyers. So instead of looking at fundamental factors, they do technical analysis: draw up charts of prices, log the ups and downs, and look for patterns. It's the ultimate version of supply and demand.

The theory of technical analysis is that markets move on expectations and sentiment rather than cold facts. Fans of price charts say that all the publicly revealed facts are, by definition, already known and so they are included in the share price. What you need in addition is the *psychology* of market participants to get a real picture. And the only way you can get this psychology is via a chart showing the forces of buying and selling. Technical analysts believe that price charts show human emotions present in investors – emotions such as greed and fear, panic and elation – and that these sentiments are often only revealed by understanding the flow of money in and out of shares.

Share price chart fans say they can often spot big movements before they happen by picking up unusual patterns. They say they can see through the 'noise' coming from companies, including attempts to make bad events look good, and that they don't need to read company statements or work out whether a denial of a story such as a takeover bid is true or not.

Discovering Dow Theory

The Dow Theory on stock price movements is the granddaddy of technical analysis. It was derived from the writings of Charles H. Dow (1851–1902), the first editor of the *Wall Street Journal,* but Dow himself never used it! His theory works on the premise that history repeats itself and that market prices for shares and other assets take everything into account, including investor psychology.

It's based on these concepts:

✔ The market has three movements or swings: main (or long term), which lasts anything from a year to several years; medium, which lasts a few weeks to several months; and short, which could be just a few hours.

✔ Stock prices change in line with new information. As soon as news is out in the market – and these days, you can measure that in milliseconds – prices adjust to take these facts into account. Here, Dow Theory mirrors one of the major points of the efficient market hypothesis.

✔ Growth in one sector should be reflected elsewhere. For example, when factories prosper they'll be better bank customers, so banks will do well and their staff will earn more, so retail firms will be able to increase trade.

✔ Volumes confirm price trends. One of the most useful facets of Dow and other chart theories is to look at how many shares are traded. The more that change hands, the more significant the move.

So is studying this theory worthwhile? The academics are divided, as they are on other forms of technical analysis. But if it works for you then it's a good idea.

Technical analysts, or *chartists,* produce all sorts of patterns. Some charts cover a very brief time, and others look at decades. They attempt to read the future by evaluating the past. Here are some patterns and what they mean:

✔ **The moving average:** This is a line that smoothes out short-term fluctuations by averaging prices over the past (usually 100 or 200 trading days). The trick is to compare this line with the actual day-to-day ups and downs. The idea is to see whether the longer-term trend is moving up or down.

✔ **New highs and new lows:** This isn't a chart at all, but a list based on new tops and bottoms for a share over a period, usually a year. Some newspapers print the number of shares that have made new high or new low points for the year. They may also print their names. As the numbers of new highs or new lows increase, the likelihood is that prices are due to reverse. This isn't surprising. At the very top of a share market with lots of new highs, people panic to get in, so share values zoom up. At the bottom of a falling market with lots of new lows, people rush to get out, so a record number of shares hit new bottoms.

✔ **Head and shoulders:** This is one of many body-part patterns used in share price charts. The first shoulder is formed by a line as the price is ticking along. Then the line shoots up to form the top of the head as the price increases. If the line then comes down to form a new shoulder, the outlook is poor because the price has decreased. Chartists reckon that the head represents excitement from buyers, which has now ended.

- ✔ **Reverse head and shoulders:** This is the head-and-shoulders pattern turned upside down. If the head-and-shoulders pattern points to lower prices then a reverse head and shoulders must look to better values.

- ✔ **Double bottom:** This isn't a body-part pattern! If a share hits a low point twice in a period, but the second low point isn't as bad as the first, then chartists take it as a positive sign.

- ✔ **Double top:** This is the opposite of the double-bottom pattern and hence a bad sign. Nothing to do with darts.

- ✔ **Support level:** Chartists use a variety of statistical methods to put a line on the chart that shows where buyers are likely to come in. This level can put a floor under the share price. But it's not solid and recalculating the support level can create a new floor.

- ✔ **Resistance level:** This shows where sellers are likely to overpower buyers, so when a price reaches this level it's likely to go no further and will probably succumb to selling pressure. It's a ceiling, but just like the support level, it's not set in stone.

If a method works for you, enabling you to spot more winners than losers, that's all you need. Whether you look for a reverse head and shoulders in a price chart, examine Japanese shooting stars (see the nearby sidebar for info on them) or concentrate on companies at the end of the alphabet (a theory from one investor – that no one looks at these companies until it's too late because most methodical share researchers start with A instead of Z), the aim is to make more money. Never apologise if you manage this, even if the method you use sounds daft!

Burning the candle at both ends – the Japanese way

Three hundred years ago, Japanese rice traders wanted to have a better idea of how supply and demand was affecting the price of this staple food. But they didn't want rivals to know how they were thinking. So they came up with a charting method where the price action was disguised as a candlestick, complete with candle, wick and shadow. People still use these disguises today.

These patterns have great names, like *shaven head* and *spinning tops*. In addition, when several candlesticks are put together, they form *hammers* (where the market is hammering out a bottom prior to a recovery). And the *hanging man* warns investors that they may soon lose their financial lives when the execution trapdoor opens. There are *shooting stars, morning stars* and *evening stars* as well.

Does this method work? Fans say that it's lasted 300 years, so it must have something going for it. Others say it's a delusion, and you may as well read tea leaves instead.

Chapter 10

Banking on Bonds

· ·

In This Chapter

▶ Understanding bonds and their role in your investments

▶ Getting inside the risks

▶ Looking at different types of bonds

▶ Working through the figures

▶ Comparing individual bonds with bond funds

· ·

During the 1970s, 1980s and most of the 1990s, bonds were boring. Worse, they were guaranteed losers. They were no-hope purchases for no-hope purchasers. The only sensible investments during this time were equities. Shares in quoted companies made real gains even after the high inflation of much of this period. Even mediocre shares in boring companies earned their keep. It all had to do with something called the cult of the equity. Pension-fund managers, who controlled more and more of the stock market during the second half of the 20th century, bought shares with their members' money. Their counterparts in the United States and Europe continued to buy bonds, but their performance didn't compare with that of the UK management firms. Equities ruled.

But then something strange happened that caught all the equity folks by surprise, even though they should have seen it a million miles off. The members of those pension funds got older and the number of fresh employees joining fell dramatically as scheme after scheme was barred to new entrants, or totally closed. Fund managers no longer had to deal with a collection of 30-somethings who didn't worry much about pensions, but retired or almost retired folks who wanted the security of regular payments. And the only way they could get those monthly payments with any degree of security was through bonds. Shares, with their big ups and downs, just aren't suited to regular pay cheques.

Over the past 15 years or so, bonds have come full circle. They were out of fashion when equities boomed, came back in fashion when equities slumped and just when they reached the top of the popularity charts, equities or shares came back into favour again. But with an ageing population looking for some security for life savings, bond salespeople, bond issuers, bond purchasers and bond traders aren't likely to find themselves on the redundancy scrapheap anytime soon. Leaving aside whether they can beat equities or property or not, bonds do have a role. And even if you don't want to buy bonds or you just think they're ever so boring, you need to know about them because their prices can determine other parts of the financial mix.

This chapter gives you the savvy about bonds so that you too can be a fashionable investor.

Getting Down to the Bottom Line on Bonds

Bond is one of those words that the financial services industry uses all over the place. Industry folks like it because it inspires confidence. In this chapter, though, I'm referring to the technical meaning of the word. At its basic level, a *bond* is a loan made by investors to a company, national government or international body. In return, the company, government or international body offers to pay the holder a set sum of interest on set dates and promises to repay a pre-established amount on a set date in the future. Because of all this certainty, bonds are often called *fixed-interest* or *fixed-income investments*.

Cash is the lowest-risk investment idea around. Bonds are one step up from the security of cash in an established bank. The returns are a little higher, but you have to take a little more risk on board for the privilege. Of course, I'm talking about real bonds issued by genuine governments and classy companies here – not the highly complex 'bonds' sold by financial advisers, which are based on some very tricky financial engineering or investing in some totally weird asset. These can be disastrous for you, although profitable for those selling them.

Here's the simplest bond deal: a company, a government or a non-governmental organisation needs money, and issues a new bond to raise £100 million. You buy £10,000 of that. The issuer promises to pay you 5 per cent interest (£500 a year) divided into six-monthly instalments, so you get £250 (less tax) twice a year. The company also promises to repay your £10,000 on a fixed future date – say 31 January 2025. The face value of £10,000 is known as the *principal* or *nominal amount*.

This sounds very much like a fixed-rate mortgage where you promise to pay a set sum of interest at regular intervals and repay the capital borrowed sometime in the future at a date laid down in the home-loan paperwork. For the organisation borrowing the money, that's a true assessment.

However, substantial differences exist. You may not have paid £10,000 for the certificate with that sum printed on it. You may have paid more or less, even if you purchased it on the day of issue.

Bonds are usually quoted as something for each £100 of principal value. If the issuer needs to pay a little more than 5 per cent, then it prices the bond at, perhaps, £98, so that each dividend payment (or *coupon*, to use the technical term) is worth a touch over the stated percentage. Likewise, if the issuer prices bonds at £103 for each £100 then the return would be less than 5 per cent. Bond buyers do the maths, down to several decimal points.

Bonds are traded on stock markets. Although the cost to issuers, such as companies or governments, doesn't change during the bond's life, the value to the holder can change all the time. The price goes up and down with economic variables, most importantly interest rates, although also the perception of the issuer's credit rating. But the amount the company has to pay when the bond reaches its payback, or *maturity*, date doesn't vary (except for a few *index-linked bonds* – bonds whose values mirror rising prices).

If the certificate says £10,000 then £10,000 is what the holder gets back on maturity, regardless of the price that person paid. I consider what the bond is worth between your purchase and its final maturity (or redemption) date in 'Identifying What Makes Bond Prices Go Up and Down', later in this chapter.

'Do I need bonds?'

You need bonds if you think they'll outperform equities and other investments, such as property or cash. But you also need them if

- ✔ You're a cautious investor who wouldn't be happy with share price ups and downs.

- ✔ You have a defined aim for your money, such as you must pay education fees on fixed dates or you want to give a set sum to a child on graduation or reaching a certain age.

- ✔ You have investment funds for your retirement years, and you're within five to ten years of stopping work. Some plans allow you to move gradually into bonds from shares. This arrangement, known as *lifestyling*, helps prevent your pension from being hit by a sudden fall in share values. Chapter 14 on investing your pension has more on this.

- ✔ You've retired and need certainty of income from your savings.

'Tell me the big differences between bonds and shares'

Companies that need to raise cash can issue equities – or *shares* as they're better known. They can also issue bonds (called *corporate bonds* to differentiate them from those put out by governments) and get the same amount. So what's the difference?

- **Permanence:** Shares are permanent. After issue, they carry on until the company ceases to exist, either because it goes bust, is absorbed by another company or buys in its own shares to cancel them. Equally, investors have no time limit on their equity holdings (except for a few specialised investment trusts). Bonds usually (although a handful of exceptions exist) have a fixed life, which is shown on the paperwork you get. You know when they'll stop paying you a regular amount and give back the original cash instead.

- **Pay:** Shares pay dividends, which can go down as well as up. Sometimes the company misses dividend payments altogether. The rate of dividend depends on the profits of the company and what it needs to do with the cash it generates. Bonds pay interest (known as the *coupon* because old bond certificates used to contain small squares that holders had to cut out every six months to claim the payment; from *couper*, the French word for *cut*). This interest is fixed whether the company is doing well or not. A company must pay bond interest before issuing share dividends.

- **Say:** Shares give holders a say in the company proportional to their holding. Shareholders are the legal owners of the company, and they get to attend an annual general meeting where they can quiz the board. Bondholders, in most circumstances, have no ownership or annual meeting voting rights. Bondholders are only active when the bond issuer (company or government) is in financial trouble.

- **Variance:** Share prices can be very volatile. Bond prices vary less from day to day.

- **Concerns:** Shareholders have to worry about how well the company is doing. Share prices depend on profits. Bondholders have to worry more about credit risk – the chance that a company will do so badly that it will default on loan repayment or on an interest payment. Some companies have different classes of bonds, some of which go to the front of the queue if the company goes bust.

Looking at UK Government Bonds: All That's Gilt Isn't Gold

Understanding the basics of bonds is most easily achieved by looking at *gilts*, which are UK government bonds. In case you're interested, they're known as gilts or gilt-edged because the certificates used to have gold-coloured borders. That titbit aside, gilts are one of the ways the government pays for state spending other than by raising taxes. (It also borrows through National Savings.)

Gilts are super-safe. You don't have to worry about the issuing company going bust. Think about it: if the UK government fails to pay its legal obligations then many more problems will exist than just some angry investors!

Gilts also appeal to cautious UK investors because they're in sterling. You can buy bonds in dollars, euros or several other currencies, but you'll have to worry about currency exchange rate risks as well.

When the government decides to issue a new gilt, it advertises

- ✔ **The amount it intends to raise (often £1 billion or more):** This info fascinates economists, but it's not very useful for investors.

- ✔ **The name:** Most gilts are now called *Treasury* or *Exchequer*, but no difference exists between the two. Older gilts may have other names, such as *Funding* or *Conversion*, but they don't mean much of anything either. The figures are what matters. So in a title such as *Treasury 6% 2020*, look at the numbers, not the letters.

- ✔ **The coupon:** This is the headline rate of interest that forms part of the gilt's title. So in a title such as *Treasury 6% 2020*, the headline rate of interest is 6 per cent.

- ✔ **The redemption date:** This is the final date after which the government will repay the gilt. The date is typically 5 to 30 or more years in the future. It's also part of the title, so in a title such as *Treasury 6% 2030*, the redemption date is the year 2030. On the paperwork you see the exact day.

- ✔ **An indication of price:** This is the tricky bit. Everything in bonds is based on the nominal value of £100 (or $100 or €100). But what you pay when the bond is launched and at any stage afterward may be more or less than the nominal sum. When launching a gilt issue, the UK government usually sets a fixed amount per £100 nominal for small investors. Big investors with millions may have to enter an auction and may end up paying a different price for the same bond at the same time. That price may not look that different, but if you're dealing with hundreds of millions, if not billions, then tiny fractions of a penny add up.

Gilts (and all other bonds) can go up and down in value. But the shorter the remaining life of a bond, the more you can be sure of it. Government bonds react to interest rates above all. If your bond has only a few months before redemption, a big interest-rate change isn't likely. If it has 20 years to go then what will happen is anyone's guess.

After you buy a gilt, either directly from the government at the very start of its life or in the stock market, you're on your own. You can't force the government to take it back until its final redemption date, which could be a few weeks to several decades from your purchase date. But you can sell it in the stock market through a stockbroker – just like a share.

Also note that no one can force the government to come up with new bonds, so if the government isn't currently issuing gilts but you or other investors want one, you'll have to buy already issued bonds through a broker at whatever price is on offer at the time. Remember that when a lack of new stock meets high demand, the price rises.

The gilt price you see in a newspaper or on an Internet site is the middle price. You get a little less if you sell and pay a bit more if you're a purchaser. You have to pay commission for the sale or purchase. But, hey, the government can sometimes be generous: you don't have to pay stamp duty when dealing in gilts (and many other forms of bonds), which saves £5 for every £1,000, or 0.5 per cent.

Identifying What Makes Bond Prices Go Up and Down

Put your £1,000 savings in the bank, and your money stays at £1,000. What you generally don't know, though, is how much interest you'll get. Most bank accounts have variable rates. Put the same money into a gilt or other bond, and your £1,000 could be worth more or less the next day. But you know how much interest you'll get. With a bond, your interest is fixed, but your capital value is variable, except on redemption, of course.

Like everything else in stock markets, bond prices are driven by supply and demand. When people want to buy, the price rises. And vice versa.

Working out why people want to buy or sell shares is complicated. So many factors hit the average company that it's a real juggling act to get them all in the air and then make some sense out of them when they land. But bonds are simpler. Investors look at three main factors:

- ✔ Interest rates in the economy
- ✔ Credit risks or the chances of the bond issuer defaulting on obligations
- ✔ The remaining life of the bond

The interest-rate gamble

Investors buy bonds to provide interest payments. Purchasing bonds is only worthwhile if all the following points apply:

- ✔ The rate of interest together with any gain you make between the buying price and maturity is better than the rate you're likely to get from a bank or building society over the life of the bond. The interest rate has to be higher because of the uncertainty to your savings. Additionally, buying and selling a bond costs money in stockbroker fees.

- ✔ You have confidence in the bond issuer. Bonds can go bust. There's always the danger that the issuer will go bankrupt or have financial troubles that stop short of total disaster. This can happen with governments as well as companies. No government-backed rescue scheme exists if it all goes wrong. And even if you're happy about the name on the bond, the longer a bond has to run, the greater the chance that interest rates will change or something totally unforeseen will happen.

✔ You know what will happen if you hold the bond to maturity. You may receive more for your bond than you paid for it, so making a profit. Or you could receive less if you paid *over par* – more than £100 for each £100 on the certificate. (See the sidebar later in this chapter on guaranteed losses.)

✔ You're happy that inflation will be moderate or non-existent. Rising prices erode the real value of your savings. You'll get the face value of your bond on redemption even if the £100 of the future will only buy a fraction of what it buys now. Know that 3 per cent inflation doubles prices every 24 years.

Bonds offer fixed interest and a fixed repayment of the nominal capital on a future date. But although they're a lower-risk investment, they aren't risk free. Assuming everyone is happy about the quality of the bond issuer and its ability to hold to its side of the bargain, bonds are a balance between their capital value and the interest rate. When interest rates fall, bond prices go up. When interest rates rise, bond values fall. This scenario is like a seesaw, where both ends can't rise or fall at the same time.

When interest rates fall

Suppose that interest rates are 10 per cent and you buy a bond offering a 10 per cent coupon for £100. You get £5 twice a year, or £10 in all.

Now suppose that interest rates fall to 5 per cent. Bond values go up when interest rates fall, so the value of your bond to new investors would be twice as much, or £200. They'd continue to get the same £10 per year interest, but it would only work out at £2.50 every six months, or £5 a year, for each £100 they spent on the bond. You're getting twice the amount of interest compared with new investors who get the going rate.

Now you have a choice. You can continue to enjoy your larger fixed-interest cheque every six months, getting more than you'd get as a new bond purchaser. Or you can cash in on your good luck. A new investor would pay £200 for your bond and get the fixed £10 per year. You can collect a £100 profit to reinvest elsewhere.

When interest rates rise

Suppose that rates rise from the 10 per cent at which you bought the bond to 20 per cent. No investor would pay £100 for your bond because they could invest that money elsewhere to earn £20 per year. So because the interest rate has doubled, your bond is only worth half as much. You have the tough choice of taking a loss on the capital value or accepting that you'll get far less interest than a new investor.

A time when bonds were a disaster

Bonds were an investment disaster in the UK during the second half of the 20th century. A person who invested £100 into UK gilts at the end of the Second World War and reinvested all the income without paying any tax would have had £3,668 55 years later, according to figures from Barclays Bank. Inflation reduced the real value by 85 per cent, resulting in investor misery.

The same money put into equities would have produced £65,440, or £2,689 after you count price rises. That's a gain of nearly 27 times.

Sometimes, bonds bounce back. Changing investment patterns ensured they were one of the best investment classes during the first years of the present century, when equities were largely a disaster. But over long periods, equities should always beat bonds. You get 'paid' for taking on the extra risks associated with shares. This is known as the *equity-risk premium.* The difficulty with the equity-risk premium is knowing just how long you have to hold for it to work in your favour.

I've simplified these examples to make the point. In real life, you must consider other factors including how much of the bond's life remains until redemption and the market's view of future interest-rate levels.

Interest rates often go up because the inflation index that measures rising prices increases. When you have high interest rates and high inflation, the paper value of your bond goes down. You're given a double hit:

- ✔ Interest levels rise, so the capital value falls on the seesaw principle.

- ✔ The real value of each fixed payment and the final redemption amount drops in purchasing terms because each currency unit (such as the pound, dollar or euro) buys less at the shops.

The way around the interest-rate gamble

Rising prices are bad news for bonds. The £100 they pay back for each £100 shown on the certificate isn't worth as much as when the bond was issued. A 5 per cent inflation rate halves the real value of money every 14 years or so

And how do governments react to inflation? They try to control it with rising interest rates, also really bad news for bondholders. Or they let inflation rip so they can repay debts in devalued currency. That's bad news as well.

Still, investors who fear that rising prices will wreck their bond calculations have a way around this problem. It's called the *index-linked gilt.* It's like an ordinary gilt because it pays income every six months and has a set future date for repayment – anything from a year or two to more than a quarter of a century. But that's where the similarity stops because each half-yearly coupon and the final repayment are linked to inflation using the government's retail prices index (RPI) as a measure.

Here's a simplified example (it ignores compounding and the eight-month delay between the RPI figure's publication and its effect on your money): you put £10,000 into an index-linked gilt with a 10-year life with a 2.5 per cent pay on day one. Your first year's interest works out at £250 before tax. After the 10 years of 7 per cent annual inflation, prices have doubled. Your final dividend is £500 per year, and you get back £20,000. And in the last year, you get 2.5 per cent of £20,000, which gives you a dividend equal to £500.

Sounds like magic, so what's the catch? You start off with a far lower interest rate than on a conventional bond, so it could take years of rising prices to catch up. And if price rises drop to nothing or go in reverse, you lose out.

The UK government has replaced the RPI measurement with the consumer prices index (CPI), which is used widely in Europe for many purposes and is rated as more accurate. CPI ignores housing and mortgages and has generally resulted in lower headline figures. But the Office of National Statistics will continue to calculate the RPI for many years to come, and RPI-linked government bonds will carry on using the RPI for calculations.

The credit-rating conundrum

If only life for bond purchasers was as simple as second-guessing where interest rates and prices are due to go over the life of the bond. But, alas, life for bond purchasers isn't that simple. And that's why armies of highly paid analysts look over each bond with superpower spreadsheets.

Besides interest rates in the economy, a big factor for bond investors is whether the bond issuer will pay out the money on time or even at all. Bonds are issued by all sorts of organisations, from the US Treasury to biotech or dotcom companies with a 1 in 20 chance of survival beyond a year or two.

A bond is only as good as its issuer. No guarantees exist that you can call on. In the past, bonds issued by big nations such as Germany, Russia and Argentina have all failed. They became worth as much as wallpaper, except for a few attractive-looking certificates sold to collectors who framed and displayed them. (I have a Russian bond certificate from 1916, which I bought for £1. The frame cost more.) More recently, the 2010 financial crisis in Europe started when international investors feared that Greece couldn't repay its bonds.

Alphabet soup: Looking at credit-rating codes

You can get some help with working out which bonds have higher or lower credit ratings. Agencies such as Standard & Poor's, Moody's and Fitch look at each bond issuer and the terms offered, and then come up with a risk-rating code.

The code isn't difficult to decipher. You just follow the alphabet. The highest level is AAA (or triple-A), followed by AA, A, BAA, BA, BBB, BB, B, with plenty more points all the way down to D. Plus and minus signs are used as well, showing whether a bond's been upgraded recently and is now less risky, or whether it's been downgraded into a higher-peril situation. Each rating agency has its own little quirks, but the higher the letter in the alphabet and the more letters used, the lower the risk should be of something going wrong.

Triple-A means a minimal risk. The US and UK governments and the biggest and best-financed companies used to pick up AAA, but the financial crisis has dented almost all issuers so very few AAA bonds are around. But all the A grades are good, and some of the Bs are acceptable as well. Lots of bond investors draw the line at BBB, which, they say, is the lowest level of investment-grade bonds.

All the rest of the bonds, many bond investors say, are undependable rubbish. With C grades, you run a reasonable risk of problems, and with D grades or ungraded bonds, you're gambling. You may miss a payment or two, or you may never see your money back on the redemption date. But note that bond experts don't call these bonds rubbish or garbage. Instead, they unofficially call them junk bonds (or, more politely, *high-yield* bonds).

Can you trust these ratings? They're as fallible as anything else in investment that tries to look forward. And the ratings agencies picked up some really bad publicity during the 2008 bank crisis when too many of the complex instruments that came with high ratings turned out to be junk or worse. But they're all anyone can hold on to – and their much-talked-about failures were in bonds so complex that each would need a whole volume of *Investing For Dummies* to explain. As long as you stick to plain vanilla bonds (and that's as far as this book goes) then the ratings agencies should be fine.

If the big players find agencies credible then most people have faith in their ratings. But should they have doubts, alphabet soup is off the menu. Their failures in 2008 mean their powers to move markets have taken a notable tumble. Downgrades are no longer the catastrophe investors once feared them to be.

Over the past few years, the United States, France and the United Kingdom have all seen ratings reduced by one or more (they don't always agree) of the major rating agencies. The reason for this is that government bond markets have been manipulated by central banks with programmes such as quantitative easing (or printing money). This non-stop flow of cash substantially outweighs the thinking of what many big investment firms now see as largely unreliable rating agencies.

The higher the rating, the lower the interest rate. Investors want something extra to make up for the dangers of a poor credit rating but are willing to give up interest for the security of a top rating, such as triple-A or AAB. The rating looks at how long the bond has to pay out. A government or company may be good for a year or two, but will it still be paying out in 20 or 30 years' time? Agencies regularly revise risk ratings. What starts out at AAA can fall to junk levels, and rubbish can rehabilitate itself and move up the scale. Many investors have made a major re-assessment of debt from emerging market countries such as China, India and Brazil: their stock is not as scary as it once was.

Junk bonds: Where there's muck, there's brass (maybe!)

Why invest in junk bonds when the rating agencies say they're below investment grade? The obvious answer is the risk/reward equation. Junk-bond investors hope to spot bonds that are due for an upward re-rating that should push prices up.

Issuers of junk bonds pay higher interest rates to make up for the risk. And you can often buy the bonds at far below their face value. You pay, say, £30 for a £100 face-value bond from a company or a country that may or may not live long enough to repay investors as it should. If the issuer survives, you've made £70 plus bigger interest payments all the way along the line. If it fails completely, you've lost your £30, but if you've had a few years of above-average payments along the way then your loss doesn't look so bad. It may even work out that you've received your £30 back and more.

One junk bond may be a recipe for disaster. But put together a diversified collection in your portfolio, and you've a good chance that some winners will more than make up for the losers.

Look at the following example portfolio to see how a diversified collection can sometimes work out in your favour. Assume that all the bonds have five years left to run and that you've invested £1,000 face value in each. The examples ignore tax and compounding of reinvested income.

- ✔ Bond A costs £60 for each £100 (£600). It pays 8 per cent nominal and survives intact. After five years, you have interest totalling £400 (£80 × 5) plus a £400 profit (£1,000 that you get less the £600 you paid). *You make £800 in all.*

- ✔ Bond B costs £25 for each £100 (£250). It pays 4 per cent nominal and lasts for three years before going bust. You collect £120 in interest but lose your £250 capital. *You lose £130 overall.*

- ✔ Bond C costs £50 for each £100 (£500). It pays 6 per cent nominal. But the issuer gets into trouble and never pays you a penny. The bondholders form a committee and force the firm into early repayment of the bonds at £75. You receive £750. *You make £250.*

- ✔ Bond D costs £70 for each £100 (£700). It pays 5 per cent nominal. The credit agencies decide to take the bond issuer off the junk list because it has new management, and the agencies put it on the quality list. The 5 per cent is about right for the market, so the price shoots up to £95. You sell and take a profit. *You make £175.*

- ✔ Bond E costs £10 for each £100 (£100). It pays nothing and goes bust within weeks. *You lose £100.*

TECHNICAL STUFF

How low can you go?

At the top end of the quality scale, credit ratings are only for the ultra-nervous. The gap between AAA and AA or A isn't really that crucial for most bond buyers. But anything below BBB is speculative. Investors have to pay more attention to junk-bond ratings because the risk of loss is real. So how low can you go?

✔ BB is probably still fine, but investors have long-term fears over the issuing company or government. The company is more likely to be a bit late with the cash rather than not pay out at all.

✔ B should be okay as well, but if the economy or the business turns down, you may face problems. No guarantees exist, but you should get your payments. You can expect to get around 3 per cent per year extra on these bonds compared with AAA.

✔ CCC, CC and C stand for caution. A problem exists currently in the business or country issuing these bonds. An improvement on what you see now needs to occur before you can rest easier. You can expect around 4 to 7 per cent extra per year on these bonds.

✔ DDD, DD and D stand for distress, disaster and default. Default is the bond dealer's shorthand for anything going wrong. The bond issuer is already in severe trouble, has missed out on payments and may be heading towards an early death. D-style bonds are only worthwhile buying if you're prepared to take a big gamble. Aim for at least 10 to 15 per cent per year more here, to make up for the ultra-risky rating.

Some winners, some losers.

In some cases, bondholders faced with a collapsing company or a country that defaults on its bond obligations form a committee (you have to be a big investor to help form one but any bondholder can join) to negotiate something out of the mess. This something can often be a *debt for equity swap*. Here you give up your almost worthless bonds and swap them for shares in the company or a new version of it. Bondholders hope that one day the shares will be worth something, so selling them will help claw back some of their losses.

How can bondholders do this? Well, they often have rights somewhere in the legal small print that mean they can prevent a company or government reorganising itself to avoid complete meltdown. Bond legalities are often complex, and a great source of revenue for law firms.

TIP

Credit ratings apply to bonds from countries as well as companies. Countries can go bust or have problems repaying interest or debts. But some countries, such as former parts of the Soviet Union or nations in Africa, are young and don't have much of a credit record, so they get low marks. Always remember, bond buyers are naturally cautious. If they weren't, they'd be buying something racier.

The redemption calculation

Assuming that you're happy with the credit rating and the interest rate, you need to look at the redemption date of the bond. That's the day on which you'll receive, say, £100 for each £100 nominal on your bond certificate. It doesn't matter what you paid; you get £100.

The redemption date may be anywhere from days to decades away. Bonds fit into three main categories according to their final date:

- **Shorts or short-dated:** Anything up to 5 years.
- **Mediums:** From 5 to 15 years.
- **Longs:** From 15 years upward.

With the passage of time, a long becomes a medium and then a short. The US is different (natch!). Over in New York, a long bond is called a long bond from day one all the way to the date it's finally repaid.

The date matters because the longer away it is, the greater the risk of either a default (the issuer missing a payment or not being able to repay) or an interest or credit rating change. Not much will happen over the next 30 days, so a very short-dated bond is unlikely to change much in price. The next 30 years, however, is a different matter. Bonds with a very long date can be very volatile, although that's only by bond standards! Shares can and do move up or down 10 per cent, 20 per cent or more in a day. Bond moves are small by comparison, but bond investors, more used to fractions of a percentage point, don't think so.

Longer-dated bonds should pay more interest to reflect the greater risks. This arrangement is called the *yield curve*, and the pay rate should go higher the further a bond has to run. Investors often look at why they're buying bonds and choose a life to fit. Someone with a 12-year-old child looking to fund educational fees may opt for a 10-year bond because it should coincide with a hoped-for university graduation and the need for funding in the big, bad world.

I want to briefly share one more thing related to this whole redemption calculation business. Bonds have two interest rates:

- **The running yield:** This is the amount you receive on your bond divided into the price you paid. So someone paying £90 for a £100 nominal value bond and earning £9 a year in interest would get a 10 per cent running yield.
- **The yield to redemption:** This one takes the running yield and then adjusts it for the gain or loss you make on final repayment. If you buy at over £100, your yield to redemption will be lower than your running yield; and if you buy at under £100, the redemption yield will be higher (assuming the bond won't go into default). A complicated formula exists for working out the yield to redemption, but most mortals just believe the figures they see in newspaper and online bond listings.

'What's this? I don't see a date for repayment!'

Some UK government bonds don't have a date for repayment. That's because the government never has to pay them back – ever! These bonds have wonderful names, such as *Consols* or *Treasury After '61,* but the best known is *War Loan,* which was raised to help pay for the costs of the First World War.

If you buy these types of bonds, you should get the same return forever. Their prices go up and down according to interest rates at the time. But although the UK government guarantees

your interest, it makes no promises to repay your bond in the future. However, if interest rates fall so low that the government is paying out more than it has to then it may repay the bond. The small print says it can.

War Loan was a disastrous investment for the patriots who bought to help out the inter-war government. But the big interest-rate falls of the past two decades made big money for those bold enough to take a plunge. Some investors tripled their money.

Taxpayers are better off with gains on maturity than high running yields. That's because UK government bonds that are under £100 should give a tax-free capital gain on redemption when they're paid back at £100. Other bonds, such as those issued by foreign governments or UK or overseas companies, are liable for capital gains tax. Income is always taxed whatever its source unless it's in an Individual Savings Account (ISA).

Knowing Which Way to Buy Your Bonds

Two main routes are available for buying bonds:

- ✔ **Purchase individual bonds through a stockbroker.** You pay the normal commission. Alternatively, if you're buying UK government bonds, special facilities are available through the UK Debt Management Office service, which is designed for small investors. Commission costs start at £35 for deals of up to £5,000 – see www.dmo.gov.uk for more details. If you buy gilts at a debt-management-office auction when a government stock is first announced, you must apply for at least £1,000 (nominal).

- ✔ **Purchase bonds through a fund.** Hundreds of unit trusts specialise in bonds. They range from gilt funds, where the yield is low, to speculative junk bonds and bust-country bond funds. You buy these through independent financial advisers – don't go directly to fund companies because you'll end up paying more.

Bonds bound to lose you money

Would you buy an investment for £120 that guarantees to repay you £100 – no more, no less? The answer would appear to be a no-brainer: *No way!* But that's exactly what investment professionals do all the time, and they do it with your money and play with your financial future.

Here's an example. A UK government bond with the enticing title of *Treasury 4.25% 2032* cost £120.73 for £100 of nominal stock. This means investors will get £100 back in 2032. They'll lose £20.73 – and due to inflation, the £100 they get back will likely buy less than now.

What's the point of that? No one consciously goes into investment to lose money deliberately. The clue is in the 4.25 per cent, or £4.25 a year, from each £100 of nominal investment. That's a lot more than anyone could have got at that moment by sticking the cash in the bank. And it's guaranteed to be consistent up to 2032.

That certainty is attractive if you're running a pension fund – or organising payments to retired people. As long as you know what comes in and what goes out, the security of that long-term assured cash flow is essential for your planning. Pension fund managers have to think well beyond 2032 – retirement incomes can be in payment for 30, 40 or even more years.

The fund looks at the yield to redemption, the figure that takes in the running yield (4.25 per cent) and then adjusts it for any loss or profit made when the bond is finally repaid. In this case, the yield to redemption is 2.77 per cent. It's able to fund more retirement cash from now until 2032 than it would otherwise be able to do. And because it knows it's bound to lose in 2032, it can plan for that as well.

The choice is yours. To help you make an informed decision, here are the pros and cons of the two options:

- **Conditions:** Individual bonds come with set conditions. You know the payments you'll get as long as no defaults occur. This setup makes them ideal for paying items such as educational fees, where you have a start date and an end date. Unit trusts offer less certainty. Even if all the bonds survive, you're never promised your original cash back. The price of the units depends on market levels when you buy and sell.

- **Charge:** Individual bonds have one charge when you buy them through a broker. You pay no charges for bonds bought when they're issued, nor annual fees. Unit trusts charge an initial fee of around 5 per cent, and between 0.5 and 1.5 per cent as annual fees after that.

- **Management:** Individual bonds mean you're on your own, unless you can persuade a broker to help you for a fee. When the bonds are repaid on maturity, you have to think afresh about what you're going to do with the cash. Unit trusts offer management, so you don't have to be so involved.

> ✔ **Interest:** Individual bonds send you interest on fixed dates. Unit trusts offer a choice of interest on fixed dates or rolling the money into new units if you don't want to spend it at that time. And some trusts offer monthly facilities, so you get a regular income.

Bond funds can be one of the most worthwhile components in an Individual Savings Account (ISA) plan. You sidestep the tax on all income and capital gains – saving 20 per cent if you're a basic-rate payer, 40 per cent if you're a higher-rate payer and 45 per cent if you hit the super-rich tax band. You can invest up to £15,000 per year into an ISA from April 2015.

Some funds have both bonds and equities. Bond ISAs have better tax breaks than equity ISAs. Where a mix exists, the taxman gives a trust a bond-fund label if 60 per cent of its value consists of bonds. On top of this, the interest on most bond funds is greater than the dividends on equity funds. So you get a bigger ISA bang for your investment bucks.

Chapter 11

Conquering Commodities and Getting into Gold

・・

In This Chapter

▶ Understanding the commodities basics

▶ Getting into the mindset of a commodity investor

▶ Considering types of commodities

▶ Investing in different ways

▶ Avoiding the scam brokers

・・

*I*n the beginning, there were commodities. Thousands of years before stocks, shares or currency markets, our distant ancestors were involved in *commodities* – raw materials like grains, cotton and gold. It's in the Bible – the need to store the surplus from abundant harvests to help people tide over during the bad years. And, amazingly, seven good years followed by seven lean years remains a workable concept for understanding commodity investment. Many up-and-down cycles of around seven years exist. Why? Because farmers take time to adjust to supply and demand.

All this matters to investors. For starters, the price of a commodity such as oil can have a big effect on some companies and on the economy at large. Investors in food manufacturers need to know the price of ingredients such as sugar or cocoa. Going one step further, you can invest for yourself in commodities ranging from frozen orange juice to aluminium. You might want to look at commodities as part of the big picture or as an asset class in their own right, perhaps as a diversification from shares, bonds or other assets. It's your choice.

Understanding the Basics of Commodities

Commodities are the basic elements of life – raw materials such as grains, sugar, cocoa, coffee, cotton, wool, copper, zinc, aluminium, oil and gold, to name but a few. All these can be turned into goods via manufacturing and other processes, but without them the factories and the food shops fail to function.

Commodities are priced in fixed amounts. Copper, zinc and many other metals are valued per tonne, rubber and wool by the kilo and gold by the ounce. And when they're traded on markets (London and Chicago are the most important centres in the world) they're also in fixed amounts. Cocoa, for instance, is traded in 10-tonne lots, wheat in 50-tonne lots and metals – other than precious ones such as silver or platinum – by the tonne. Commodities that you can eat or are otherwise affected by natural forces such as the weather are called *soft* commodities.

Whether the gold comes from Australia or Canada, or whether the coffee is grown in Colombia or Rwanda doesn't matter. Providing the commodity comes up to pre-set standards, the country of provenance is immaterial.

Although most traders sell what they buy to the next party along the line, someone eventually has to take delivery of the commodity. Markets don't care whether the final purchaser of that 10-tonne lot of cocoa is a big chocolate factory or an individual investor. Unlike stocks and shares, where you end up with a certificate or, more likely, an entry on an electronic register, with commodities you get what you buy. You could arrive home to find your front door blocked with tonnes of sugar or coffee or lead.

Getting a Grip on Supply and Demand

Centuries BC, our ancestors understood the basics of supply and demand. Those rules haven't changed and they dominate commodity markets. If demand for copper rises – people are building new houses and need the metal for pipes and cables – then the price of copper goes up. If demand falls – fewer new buildings, or the substitution of plastic for copper pipes, or growing use of wireless technology – then the price of copper falls.

But the story doesn't end there because the supply of copper – or any other commodity – can change as well. When prices go up, new copper mines come on stream, and some re-open as higher values make them more viable. The same happens if demand for coffee increases – farmers eventually grow more and perhaps turn their land over to the beans from other crops. But whether a field or a mine is involved, gearing up or down takes time because you can't turn the supply on or off like a tap.

Eventually, however, all this new capacity brings supply and demand back into balance. When prices rise, you may also get substitution. If copper goes up, more pipes sold are made of plastic. If the price of potatoes rises, consumers turn to rice or pasta or noodles or bread. This then brings prices back down, so the whole cycle can start again. This can drive innovation – for example, gas-guzzling cars are replaced by new motors with more economical engines.

The reverse happens if demand falls. Mines shut and farmers cut back on growing certain crops until a new balance exists. But when prices fall, substitution happens again – so if potatoes become cheap, many people buy them instead of rice or pasta. Eventually, that effect helps potato prices recover.

Knowing How Commodity Investors Think

Commodity investors can equally bet on future prices rising (going long) and prices falling (going short). They have to weigh up all the factors than can affect the supply and demand equation. But one – and for some the most important – attraction of commodities is that they're not *correlated* with other assets (see the nearby sidebar 'Contextualising correlation').

Bonds and equities are related – their prices can move with each other. A correlation also exists between property and bonds, and bonds and currencies. But commodities are generally out there on their own. Yes, the price of cocoa or coffee or wheat affects food companies, yet this is just one among many factors that decide their profitability.

Most big manufacturers would purchase, say, soya beans or sugar in such a big and organised manner that they ride out commodity ups and downs. They do this by *buying forward*, which locks in their price for the hundreds of tonnes they buy at a time. A cake maker wants certainty of supply and certainty of price for wheat, sugar, cocoa and other ingredients – and pays to avoid the rollercoaster of day-to-day price variations, even when prices may be falling.

When stocks and shares were in the doldrums following the 2008 bank crash, commodities did amazingly well – they became the 'must-have' asset. That golden period didn't last forever, naturally (and I use that word for all its meanings!). But having part of a portfolio exposed to natural resources – another name for commodities – increases diversification by reducing the risks of having all your eggs in one basket via one asset class. Rough patches in one asset are compensated by smooth running in others.

Contextualising correlation

When two assets move up and down together, this is known as *correlation*. You get a number to indicate the degree. Exactly 1.0 means that two items are in perfect harmony. Imagine a lift and the person inside it. They move up and down the building together – they have no other choice.

Now look at what happens in a department store to the lift and a person shopping on a floor. They have no relationship with each other – the shopper ignores the lift, so this is a correlation of zero.

Go one step further and imagine the escalators in the same store. If Joan is riding upwards from the ground to the first floor and Tom is making the same journey in the downwards direction, they have a correlation of –1.0 (minus one) because they're totally opposite.

The past is rarely a perfect guide to the future, but history suggests that commodities (and particularly commodity futures) have generally been negatively correlated to both stocks and bonds. So they're somewhere between the shopper and the lift (zero) and the two people riding the escalators in reverse directions (minus one).

Commodity prices tend to be highly geared – gearing is when the price goes up or down more substantially than the change in supply or demand. If demand increases by 10 per cent (and assuming supply remains constant), the price will likely rise by substantially more than 10 per cent – an increase of 50 to 100 per cent is possible. Of course, a fall in demand will translate into a disproportionate collapse in prices, although they can't go to nothing or below!

Commodity traders look for bad harvests or gluts – like their biblical predecessors – because they know they'll have a major effect on prices. A combination of bad harvests, rising populations and changing tastes saw wheat prices soaring crazily upwards around 2009. Some people made a lot of money; others lost a fortune. Eventually, a combination of more planting, better harvests and changing consumption patterns meant wheat prices trended back. For what goes up can come down. By summer 2011, the price of gold touched $1,900 an ounce. Then it fell back to around $1,200 over the next two or so years. I consider the special case of gold later on in this chapter (see the section 'Going for gold').

In commodity trading, you take a view on what prices will be in the future – three, six, nine months or a year's time. Traders can go long or short, deciding the price will rise or fall. Going long – assuming the harvest will fail – is more attractive because potential profits are limitless. If a tonne of sugar costs £1,000, a future shortage could drive it up to £2,000 – that's a profit of £1,000. But if a sugar glut pushes the price down, it can't go as low as zero to produce the same £1,000.

Additionally, shortages tend to produce more negatives than surpluses. Well-documented effects include scary media headlines, panic buying and the hoarding of goods from shops, so the price goes up even faster. You don't get the same when a surplus exists – few consumers buy huge amounts of coffee beans when the price falls.

Looking at Popular Commodities for Investment

Here I look at the two main classes in the commodity markets. The first, *softs*, includes foodstuffs and textiles such as cotton or wool. They are literally 'soft'. Confusingly, the second category is not known as 'hards' even though the metals traded are very hard. Instead, investors call them *metals*. Be aware that this class does not include gold, platinum and silver as these precious metals are generally traded on different exchanges.

Sizing up soft commodities

The attraction to traders of soft commodities is their volatility. Soft commodities mainly comprise cocoa, coffee, corn, rice, wheat, soybeans, vegetable (soybean) oil, frozen orange juice, wool and cotton. Because so many short term, and often unpredictable, factors can hit their prices, their ups and downs tend to be sharper and speedier than with metals (see the next section).

These unknowables include the weather, which affects both harvests and what farmers plant, and consumer demand, which can be elastic. People have to eat, but they choose what they eat – hence they can substitute rice for potatoes and cut down or cut out sugar consumption and substitute other sweeteners.

All price changes are 'at the margin', so a £1 move in the price of a tonne of a commodity – say, sugar – costing £1,000 isn't 0.1 per cent but can be much more on a futures contract (see the later section 'Getting a feeling for futures'). It all depends on how *geared* the contract is. If the sugar contract costs £10 per tonne then a £1 gain or loss is significant, to the tune of 10 per cent. Gearing is when a price moves far more than the underlying change in supply and demand.

Making a mint from metals

Prices in metals tend to move more slowly than those in soft commodities. They're usually less volatile. Seeing why isn't hard. Opening a new lead mine takes much longer (and far more capital) than planting an extra field with wheat or rice. Demand, or the lack of it, is easier to predict. Chinese factories need copper for electronics. When the Chinese economy is on the up, copper prices rise. When it's deemed to be falling, the price of copper takes a dive.

Unlike the weather, investors can better see these events coming and plan for them. Surprise events can occur, but these are far less likely in metals than in soft commodities.

The main industrial metals traded are copper, lead, zinc, tin, aluminium, nickel, cobalt and molybdenum. There's also a market in scrap steel in Rotterdam. Additionally, there are specialist markets for precious metals, most importantly gold which is often an asset on its own, as well as silver and platinum.

Savvy investors keep on an eye on the cost of production of a mine or group of mines. Gold is a good example. An ounce of gold in Mine A may cost $500 to extract, Mine B works out at $1,000 and Mine C is very high cost at $1,500. If gold trades at $1,200 an ounce then working the first two mines is worthwhile, but not the third. But if gold rises to $2,000 then Mine C will be taken out of mothballs and brought back into production because its gold is profitable. Equally, if the price falls to $900, only Mine A continues – the other two are shut up (although the owner carries out some minimum maintenance to keep the mine safe and dry in the hope it may be brought back into production in the future). The same goes for copper and other metals where mine owners need to compare the cost of digging up the ore and refining it against the market price.

The following sections focus on trading in gold and other precious metals.

Going for gold

Shakespeare's 'All that glisters is not gold' is a good saying for anyone tempted to invest in gold. You can buy physical gold in the shape of ingots, or coins such as sovereigns or krugerrands, and leave them in a safe, or you can access the gold market via a variety of other methods (see the later section 'Choosing Which Way to Invest').

But however you buy gold, for the vast majority of the past four decades (it's only been a traded commodity since the mid-1970s) gold has been a poor investment. This isn't surprising. Gold can be considered an asset class, along with bonds or equities or property. But unlike these, gold produces no income. Investors receive no dividends, so they're purely playing on the price rising or falling.

Take a look at the long-term gold price chart. At the end of the 1970s, it traded at $520 an ounce. Ten years later, it was around $420, and at the end of the last century it was $290. Over 20 years, it had almost halved. The next decade was better, with gold moving up to nearly $1,100. It had taken 30 years before the price more than doubled, lagging behind most other investment assets and failing to keep up with inflation. And because gold is priced in dollars, if your own currency strengthened the result was even more miserable (although the opposite also applies!). Then gold had a few good years from 2009 to 2011, when it soared to nearly $1,900. But it soon went back again to around $1,250.

When tulips were more than just a springtime flower

Commodity prices can be vital for some economies – South Africa and Australia, for instance, have a lot riding on their metals mines. But sometimes they go mad, and change the long-term history of the world. Arguably, the people of New York may now be speaking Dutch, not English, and living in a city called New Amsterdam had it not been for the effect of the great tulip mania that hit the Netherlands in the mid-1630s.

A virus that hit tulip bulbs created blooms in rare colours in the 1620s and early 1630s. Their price began to rise. And each increase only made them more desirable, so the next person was willing to pay even more. When that trend became obvious, other investors joined in, all helping to push up the value of certain tulip bulbs.

At the height of the mania – in the autumn, winter and early spring of 1636–7 – some bulbs were changing hands up to ten times a day, such was the speculation that one bulb would buy the equivalent of 500 kilograms of cheese, or a four-poster bed, or several oxen. Supposedly, tulips were traded in lots of 40 – and that was more than enough to buy a grand house in Amsterdam, Rotterdam or any other of that country's wealthy cities.

The mania was fuelled by a form of futures contract where you could buy tulip bulbs on margin – often 3.5 per cent of their value. Speculators would put up 35 guilders to buy 1,000 guilders' worth of bulbs. If the price went up to 1,105, they didn't make 11 per cent but tripled their money – the 35 guilders turned into 105. They did this again and again.

Eventually, like all insane bubbles, the mania had to end. It lasted around six months. The market for tulip bulbs had run out of 'greater fools' – those willing to pay more than the last person.

Prices then collapsed even faster than they had risen. A whole section of the Dutch middle to upper class lost fortunes. But even more important, the mania is said to have ended Dutch ideas of European domination and colonial expansion – it destroyed their view of themselves and their self-confidence. So although the Dutch had a major role in creating what we now call New York, it eventually became an English colony.

Gold has shone for just a few periods in the past 40 years. So what's all the fuss about? Why is the gold price quoted so widely when it's been a poor investment? Well, gold is

- ✔ **Beautiful:** A romance and allure is attached to a metal that's so rare and so expensive to process that all the gold ever mined in the world since history began could be stored in a 20-metre cube – effectively a couple of large warehouses – with plenty of space over for years to come.

- ✔ **Easy to buy and sell:** Most high streets have one or more shops, such as a jeweller's or pawnbroker's, that deal in gold. You don't need any special permits or have to join any compulsory watchdog scheme to purchase and market gold. Nor do investors require any complex accounts. You just take your gold in, have it weighed and walk out with the money.

✔ **A hot topic of conversation:** A whole 'gold bug' industry, including some in the gold-mining world, continually talks up the price of gold. Back in the early 1980s, a couple of Costa Rican sisters made it their business to publish subscription newsletters predicting that gold would soon hit $3,500 an ounce. In the ensuing 30 years, it's never been anywhere near that – only rarely has it even traded at half that value. A quick trawl online throws up plenty of 'analysts' who claim that gold will reach $5,000 an ounce in the next few years. These 'analysts' are usually unnamed and work for organisations in the gold business. But never say never in investing. Anything is possible.

✔ **Anonymous:** You don't need passbooks or accounts or computers. In some cultures, people, especially women, wear the family's wealth as gold bangles or other jewellery. Gold does have some industrial and dentistry uses, but most gold ends up as rings or bracelets or necklaces.

✔ **Portable:** A kilo of gold is worth around $50,000 (roughly £30,000) so carrying a very large amount and hiding it is easy. Some families use gold that isn't recorded anywhere as a method of passing wealth down the generations without worrying about inheritance taxes or other death duties. Although this is against tax laws and punishable by fines and penalties, demand for concealed gold helps to maintain the price.

✔ **Unaffected by bank or currency or bond collapses:** Gold does well when banks are in trouble; for instance, during the few years following the 2008 financial crash. It's also seen as proof against currency degradation – especially by those conspiracy theorists who believe that central banks are involved in a massive plot to devalue currencies as part of an even bigger plan involving the United Nations and world government. Most see these views as bizarre, but all investment price changes are driven by the marginal buyer or seller, the last person who dealt. If even a few hold this view, they drive up the price of gold, leading to others piling in simply because of the direction in which its value is travelling.

✔ **The ultimate safe-haven holding for the nervous and fretful:** Around for 10,000 years and more, it's the final retreat for the investor who trusts nothing other than his own ability to store the metal. When the fear factor is high, gold does well. When economies and markets are stable or gaining, gold becomes out of favour. Investors see gold as a perfect insurance policy against unexpected and unwanted events.

The easiest way to buy and hold gold is the physical metal in ingots or coins – investment coins carry no VAT in the UK. If you do this, you may need to arrange secure storage and pay for insurance against theft and other perils. Don't buy jewellery – the mark-up on the value of the gold used is enormous.

Speculative investors work differently. They're hoping they can predict the direction the price travels in, so they take geared or leveraged positions whereby a $1 change in the quoted value has a very large effect on their fortunes. You can buy gold through futures and options – the former come with potentially unlimited losses or gains. You can go long (bet the price will rise) or short (when you expect the price to fall). You can also gain exposure through exchange-traded funds and specialist unit trusts. Read on to find out about all these ways to invest.

Silver, platinum and other precious substances

Investment markets exist for silver, platinum and some other priccy metals. These have clearer industrial uses than gold, and although valuable they behave much like other metals. Some investors look at the ratio of the price of gold to silver (which is cheaper) and then to the relationship between gold and platinum. When these fall outside certain parameters, they take this as a buy or sell signal. They say silver is cheap when it comes below a long-term historical ratio – some suggest that an ounce of gold should tend to be around 45 times the price of an ounce of silver. Both platinum and silver tend to be more volatile than gold.

Choosing Which Way to Invest

The traditional way to invest in commodities is via *futures contracts*. These are agreements to buy or sell, in the future, a specific quantity of a commodity at a specific price. Futures are available on commodities such as crude oil, gold and natural gas, as well as agricultural products such as cattle or corn.

Getting a feeling for futures

Many participants in the futures markets are commercial or institutional users of the commodities traded, such as manufacturers. They use the market to *hedge*, taking a position to fix the price of the raw materials they need to cut the risk of loss should prices move against them. Depending on the commodity and their industrial requirements, hedgers may want to fix the price for three or more months into the future. Some contracts can last for two years.

It takes two (at least!) to make a market, so on the other side of the hedge deals are speculators who expect to gain from changes in price. The speculators bet against the hedgers, so creating a viable and liquid exchange. Speculators don't want to take delivery of the copper or coffee beans, so they *close out* (jargon for terminate) the position before the contract expires.

Futures is largely a market for professionals, but you can open a commodities account with a specialist broker. The rules for each commodity are different – they can also vary between exchanges, such as the London Metals Exchange and New York. In general, each contract has a fixed minimum deposit so speculators buy a geared version. That means putting up, perhaps, 5 per cent of the price.

As with all geared investments, if you get it right, the gains are great; but if you get it wrong, you can lose all your money. With futures, you can also lose more than your money, but other mechanisms, such as options, allow you to limit losses. If your investment looks down, brokers ask you for more – known as *margin money* – or close your position immediately with losses.

Taking a trusting view of commodities

The most common route into gold and other metal markets for UK investors is via unit trusts specialising in the mining sectors. These buy shares in companies that operate mines, usually very large international concerns such as Rio Tinto or Anglo-American. Some trusts concentrate on gold mines, a few on platinum or silver, and others focus on copper or other less precious substances. They may, of course, offer a wide variety of mines. The trust's factsheet tells you what you get (although this changes as fund managers adjust their holdings). You can also buy shares in mining companies directly through a stockbroker.

Whether in a trust or held individually, mining shares tend to be more volatile than the metals they dig out of the ground. This arises from an element of gearing that exaggerates gains or losses. Investors aren't taking a direct punt on the price of gold or other metals but on the profits that the mining companies can make.

Analysts compare the cost of mining an ounce of gold or a tonne of copper in any particular mine with the value of that commodity. A gold mine that has a fixed cost of \$1,200 an ounce will make \$10 profit when the price is \$1,210, but 10 times as much profit should it hit \$1,300, and 20 times as much should it go to \$1,400. Of course, it works the other way as well, although mines may shut rather than produce gold or other metals at a loss.

A big natural-resources company with many mines may have an average cost of bringing the metal to the surface. But the gearing effect still works through into the profit-and-loss account.

Unlike pure commodities, shares in mining companies and other similar organisations can pay regular cash dividends. If you hold shares through an investment or unit trust, you'll receive these dividends as well.

Exploring exchange-traded funds

Exchange-traded funds are creations from banks and asset managers. They enable investors to take a view – positive or negative – on anything from the health of the US stock market (via the S&P 500 Index ETF) to some very specialised areas such as obscure currencies or shares in hospitals. They're bought and sold in the same way as shares via stockbrokers and investors pay no UK stamp duty.

Scores of exchange-traded funds exist that cover soft commodities, oil and gas, metals and precious metals. And if you can't find the exact coverage you want in agriculture, for example, then buy into an exchange-traded fund that tracks firms that sell farm machinery, such as tractors. Cereal farmers tend to replace these more often when grain prices are high, so a farm machinery exchange-traded fund is a proxy for a number of commodities, such as corn and wheat.

Some exchange-traded funds are *leveraged* – they magnify both gains and losses according to the ratio to which they're set. Others are *inverse*. An inverse gold exchange-traded fund tracks the value backwards, making it the equivalent of going short (profiting from price falls), so if gold goes down, the holder gains.

Steering Clear of Commodity Scams

Sales of physical commodities – as opposed to unit trusts or exchange-traded funds or options investing in them – aren't regulated. If they were, these rules would impede a farmer selling wheat to a flour mill. And most people know nothing much about commodities. Add these two facts together, and you have a major attraction for phone and online fraudsters.

Here are three big scams:

- ✔ **The gold in the ground scam:** Fans of old black-and-white westerns will recall *salting* – shooting a small amount of gold into the ground to convince victims to buy the mine. The rest of the mine has nothing; they've paid top dollar for dirt. The updated version, which has been around for a few years, offers gold at $1,000 an ounce when it's trading at, perhaps, $1,500. That sounds like a bargain but there's a catch (natch!). The 'gold' is deep in a mine in Canada or South Africa and won't be available for at least two years. No gold exists and any mine has long since been worked to nothing, but the fraudsters run off with your $1,000 an ounce.

✔ **The 'you're making a fortune' scam:** Here, someone posing as an 'expert' advises you to invest £10,000 into commodities. He'll come up with all sorts of reasons why he knows where prices are heading and by how much. A week or two later, your £10,000 is now worth £15,000, but for so-called 'technical reasons' you have to leave it there for six months. In the meantime, the first success allows the fraudster to convince you to invest a further £20,000 because he's proved his expertise. The gains are doubly fictitious, because he never invested the money and the profits are imaginary. Meanwhile, the scam merchant disappears with all your money.

✔ **The rare earth mineral scam:** Few have heard of rare earth minerals (also called rare earth metals or rare earth elements) and even fewer can name them – there are 17 in all, including scandium, yttrium and lanthanum. Some aren't that rare; it's extracting them that's difficult. Tiny amounts are used in computers, phones and other devices. Scam callers try to convince you that their prices are going up fast (usually due to 'Chinese demand') and that you should invest £5,000 to £10,000 in an assortment of the metals to see your money treble in double-quick time. Whatever 'certificate' you may get, that's the last you see of your money. Rare earth minerals are rarely traded, and when they are, not in a way that's accessible for small investors. Electronic gadget makers know where to source these elements – and it's not from a private investor who's been conned.

This list is far from exhaustive, so make it a rule never to trust anyone who offers you investments out of the blue.

Part III
Collective Investments and Pension Funds

Defining Hedge Funds

Strictly speaking, the term *hedge fund* only refers to a specialised legal structure. A hedge fund is a private-partnership contract where the manager has a substantial personal interest in the fund and is free to operate in a variety of markets using a number of strategies. Think of a hedge fund as giving investors' money to a manager who has unfettered freedom to invest in areas other funds can't reach. These freedoms include the ability to

- ✔ Be flexible. Most hedge-fund managers can do what they like within wide parameters. They're not restricted by trust deeds to a narrow range of equities or bonds like traditional collectives, although some have stated strategies that limit their scope.

- ✔ Go short. Ordinary fund managers only select shares they think will do well and hence go up, a technique known as *going long*. Hedge-fund managers can also choose equities they think will sink, making money as the shares fall, a technique known as *going short* or *short selling.* If hedge-fund managers see a company in serious trouble, they can take a one-way bet on the shares going down to zero. When other investors see hedge funds attacking the company in this way, they sell as well, putting extra pressure on the share price.

- ✔ Employ derivatives, such as futures, options and some very exotic bets on interest rates, currencies and even *volatility*, which is the speed with which an investment moves up or down. Stacks of strategies exist here – enough to fill a whole shelf with *For Dummies* books on them.

- ✔ Move in and out of cash, currencies, commodities, gold and property as well as other investments at high speed.

- ✔ Use borrowings (known as *gearing* in the UK and *leverage* in the United States) in an aggressive fashion to improve returns. Of course, if they get it wrong then borrowing works against them.

Find out more about Investing at www.dummies.com/extras/investinguk.

In this part . . .

✔ Discover the wide variety of investment options on offer – there are thousands to choose from.

✔ Consider whether fund managers are good, bad or ugly – don't feel compelled to believe everything they say.

✔ Look for the reality behind the publicity hype – it's easy to go for the most advertised or the most novel fund on the market but it could be a disaster. . .

Chapter 12

Looking at Fund Management

*Y*ou can identify a fund-management advert from a mile away. It features a huge graph with the line heading to the stratosphere. It may even include a rocket heading for outer space, just in case you're too dim to understand the concept. (Some fund managers push the point home even further by naming themselves after planets or stars.) And the warnings, of course, are listed in tiny print.

As a potential investor, you're supposed to pay attention to the positive upward image and ignore or dismiss the negatives in small print as just regulatory noise that the Financial Conduct Authority (FCA) insists upon. And you won't even get the small print from the 'cheerleaders' – that's what I call the financial advisers who 'comment' on funds without declaring their interest in selling them – and the journalists who mindlessly reproduce their words without a wealth warning, especially if they find a good picture to go with the words.

Whatever the approach, fund promoters hope that you'll just send them your cheque as mindlessly as you'd buy a packet of crisps – perhaps less so.

Not if you're reading this book, you won't!

The history of investing is full of 'good ideas' that didn't work. At the turn of the century there was the tech fund bubble (cue pictures of scantily dressed women whose clothes were found on some online store at half the high-street price), and more recently, a fund that invested in Africa (cue beautiful wild animals) but forgot that buying and selling shares in Africa can be impossible.

Packaged, or *collective*, investments (the terms are interchangeable) – where a professional fund manager mingles your money with that of many others to run a portfolio of stocks and shares – have their place for most investors. In fact, some people don't want anything else but packaged schemes, such as unit and investment trusts. Nothing's wrong with that, provided you know why you're doing it and can deconstruct all the advertising and marketing tricks. That's where this chapter comes in. Read on.

Considering Packaged Funds

More years ago than I care to remember, I used to edit a publication with an amazingly high subscription price but ultra-low circulation – *Fund Management International*. Thanks to a keystroke mistake somewhere along the line, this publication became *Fun Management International*, which was enough for the magazine to be listed under *Leisure* in media guides. Dealing with leisure-industry publicists became a daily task until I managed to correct the spelling.

But fund management and fun management do have something in common, so here's one reason to put some of your money into collective investments: you want to have fun, and you want to have a life. If that's you then you probably don't want to spend your life poring over share-price graphs, annual reports and online dealing facilities. You'd probably rather pay someone else to take care of your investment money so you can read a good book or head down to the pub/gym/cinema/football ground/casino/other leisure venture.

Millions of folks are like this, and if you're one of them, don't think you've wasted your cash on this book. Choosing the right funds can be just as tricky as selecting the right individual shares. You find more managed funds of one sort or another listed in the back pages of the *Financial Times* than individual shares.

Buying a fund is like supporting a football team. A professional manager controls the individual players (or shares), but unless you know what's going on, you won't get the best out of your season ticket.

Wanting to have a life is just one reason for looking at packaged funds. Here are additional reasons:

- ✔ **You don't want all your investment eggs in one basket or even a few containers.** Diversifying so you get a good spread of stock-market sectors, foreign companies, and big and small companies is really important in risk reduction. You may own 5 to 10 individual stocks, but to get good diversification, you need a minimum of, depending who you ask, from 15 to 25. (Some say 50 to 80 is better, but I think anything more than that is just ridiculous.) Buying worthwhile amounts in another 10 to 15 investments may be more than you can afford. Buying a collective fund gives instant results for an affordable price. When you find further cash, you could either buy an individual share or top up on your packaged investment portfolio.

✔ **You can invest very small sums – perhaps on a monthly basis.** Many collective funds let you start with £500 or even less and you can also sign up to regular schemes with as little as £50 a month.

✔ **You want to fill in gaps in your investment spread.** You may fancy US or Japanese shares, but fancying is as far as it goes because you can't afford to, or can't be bothered to, buy individual US or Japanese shares in sufficient numbers to get diversification. Buying a well-selected and well-managed fund can plug that portfolio hole!

✔ **Seeing how the professionals operate can give pointers to which shares are in favour with the big buyers.** You can then either try to follow their lead or bet against them. Why bet against them and do the opposite? Perhaps because you believe the fund-management herd nearly always charges in the wrong direction. Later on in this chapter, I look at some top secret papers from investment firms that show how they think and what they do.

Understanding How Fund-Management Companies Operate

The packaged-funds industry in the UK controls a few trillion pounds in unit trusts, investment trusts, pension funds and insurance funds. (Note that unit trusts are also known as *open-ended investment companies*, which is a bit of a mouthful, so the term is often shortened to OEICs. And, okay, technically, a unit trust and an OEIC have different legal structures, but show me anyone other than a specialist lawyer who cares.)

All packaged funds work in the same basic fashion. You hand over your money to a fund-management company, which can be a stand-alone company, a life-insurance firm or a bank. The fund-management company adds your money to that of many others so the managers it employs can try to maximise your investment in a cost-effective way. The result is a fund that can be worth hundreds of millions, or sometimes billions, of pounds.

Because you and others have teamed up, you can now afford the professionals whose salaries would be prohibitive if you tried to hire them on your own – or a computer program if your fund just tracks an index by purchasing all the companies that are its constituents (such as the hundred shares in the FTSE 100 Index) in their correct ratios (so your biggest holding is the largest company by stock-market size in the index).

Flesh-and-blood fund managers look at the same factors as any potential investor. But because they control millions or billions, they get preferential treatment from brokers and research houses – they get to hear things before you can and ought to have the expertise to make better decisions than you can. But they also have to go further in their work than individual sharehold-ers because they must keep a number of juggling balls in the air if they want to keep their usually very well-paid jobs. And what's written on those juggling balls? The following words:

- ✔ **Performance:** The manager must beat the majority of direct rivals or come up with very plausible excuses. All investment managers know those soaring graphs sell funds, increase fund sizes and boost their bonuses.

- ✔ **Liabilities:** Many funds, especially those from insurance companies, have rules that insist they balance the desire to shine with a responsibil-ity to produce a basic return for investors and policyholders. These reg-ulations may prevent them from investing in some areas, acting either (you choose) like a brake on their creativity or a sensible limit on their gambling instinct.

- ✔ **Cost controls:** Some fund-management companies can spend money like it's going out of fashion. Most funds have constraints to prevent manag-ers from dealing all day long, eroding the collective's value in stockbro-ker fees. But these controls can be vague.

- ✔ **Publicity:** Managers want an eye-catching performance to attract more money and hence push up the value of their personal employment con-tract. Yes, it's the soaring graph again!

Your deal is with the fund-management company, not individual fund manag-ers, even when they're hailed as superstars. Managers may leave for a better job (if they're good) or get the sack (if they're bad), and even superstars have bad periods, retire or fall under buses. Over recent years, there's been a lively transfer market in good managers and a big cleanout of those who can be out-played by a five-year-old picking shares with a pin. Fewer than half of all funds have had the same manager for five or more years.

Funds can also be shut down or amalgamated, as I know to my cost. Many years ago I put money into a Latin American fund. Latin America was in the doldrums but I reckoned long term that it would turn out fine. It did – except that, on the way, the manager of my fund decided the fund couldn't make enough money out of Latin America, so he shut the investment down. I got some money back eventually but not nearly as much as if I'd been able to back my hunch all the way.

Calculating their crust

Most fund-management companies earn their money by taking an annual percentage fee from your holding. This fee can range from 0.3 or lower to 2 per cent or more of your money. They earn this percentage whether your fund is rising or falling. Obviously, the more it goes up, the more they get. They also receive a boost when new investors join, assuming that they outweigh those who want their money out.

Investors argue that it costs little more to manage a £200 million fund than a £20 million fund, so why does the management firm get ten times as much? It's a good point, and a small minority of fund-management companies, mostly in the investment-trust sector, offer lower fees as the amount grows – a feature called *economies of scale* and one worth looking out for.

The *total expenses ratio*, or TER, recognises economies of scale as well as the set annual fee. I consider this better way of looking at which fund offers the best value in Chapter 13. In brief, a fund with a publicised 1 per cent annual charge and 2 per cent in other expenses appears cheaper than a rival with a 1.5 per cent annual charge but only 0.5 per cent in other costs. It's not cheaper. Always look for the TER in unit trusts information.

A handful of managers also get success fees. These are extra payments based on a formula such as beating the averages or coming in the top ten funds. The idea is that managers deserve something more if they produce a better result. Success fees mostly operate in hedge funds, although some investment trusts feature them.

What's the big downside of success fees? Lousy performers still get to keep their basic contractual fee, which may be high anyway. The managers don't have to give you money back in non-success fees if they mess up. And many success fees are linked to a shares index. So if the stock market goes down 20 per cent and the fund only drops 15 per cent, they can claim to have outperformed their benchmark and grab extra cash. They get paid more for losing your money. Great job!

Swapping collective funds can be very expensive. Each time you change, you could pay as much as 5.5 per cent, so your investment must grow by that amount before you break even. Changing your mind twice a year over ten years would more than wipe out all your original stake money in costs, unless you were lucky enough to always pick the very top performer of the moment. Funds are for the long term, so budget to stay with a collective for at least five years or learn to use one of the online fund supermarkets where switching costs are far lower. Moving in and out of profitable funds may also land you with a capital gains tax bill – but paying tax on your gains is far better than nursing tax-free losses.

Examining the role of the marketing department

You won't see ABC plc advertising its own shares. Although the directors obviously want to see a healthy price, all sorts of rules prevent it from marketing its own equity. In any case, after it issues the shares, ABC's got its money – day-to-day price fluctuations don't affect its balance sheet.

Collective investments are different. Here, the promoters spend a fortune on advertising their wares. All this is regulated by a rule book the size of a telephone directory, but don't be fooled: you're out there on your own.

No guarantees exist, so if the investment turns out to be rubbish after three months, you can't take it back to the shop for a replacement or repair. Complaining that the advert appeared to promise you'd make money but the manager lost yours is pointless. The company will have that angle covered. The Advertising Standards Authority (motto: legal, decent and honest) barely makes a token attempt to control fund publicity.

So, don't be afraid to ask questions and query what you're told. It's your money after all, not the fund-management company's.

You should know about marketing tricks before you start. Here are some:

- ✔ Dividing all publicity between the big print designed to get effect and the small print, which absolves the fund-management company of any responsibility if things go wrong.

- ✔ Launching a flavour of the month. Fund-management companies love bandwagons. They see that a sector, a stock market or an asset has performed very well over the past 6 or 12 months, so they launch a fund to market that flavour. Sometimes they come up with ideas such as *focus funds*, which claim to concentrate on 'the top 20 ideas' or 'our favourite 40 stocks'. Now think ice cream and long term! All these concepts can be great if rum and praline are still going to wow them for the next five years. But they won't. They'll be replaced by ginger and honey, or coffee and chocolate chip. Avoid this problem by going for plain vanilla. Keep strawberry and chocolate chip for more daring moments – or, if you can take a five- to ten-year view, go for something that's out of fashion now in the hope it will return to the top.

- ✔ Claiming a fund is the top or best of something even if it's the fund-management equivalent of best marrow at the local gardeners' show. So you get publicity like 'the top quartile in its sector over three years'. Note that marketing people love quartiles, where you divide a list into four. If publicity misses out on a 'top quartile' showing then you can bet that the past performance was rubbish.

✔ Boasting about awards from investment trade publications. The thing is, so many categories exist that almost everyone gets a prize. There are even prizes for best administration or adviser service, which means these firms paying advisers with your cash. Anyway, these awards are dished out, so managers dress up and show up at £300-a-head award dinners where they can drink themselves stupid and be entertained for 20 minutes by a TV comic (who picks up £20,000 for the gig).

✔ Pushing optimism and relegating any thought the fund could lose to the statutory small print.

✔ Playing the percentages: fund managers may go for a high-risk strategy so if they get it right, they can boast about it, and if all goes wrong, they can hide the fund behind a cloak of zero publicity, or fold into another, more successful fund.

✔ Taking media-friendly independent financial advisers for a few golfing afternoons so they'll praise the products the next time a journalist calls for a quote or sound bite.

✔ Taking journalists on all-expenses-paid trips to exotic places, such as South Africa, Morocco and Hong Kong, with business-class travel and five-star hotels. That guarantees acres of favourable coverage.

Am I being excessively cynical? The investment industry would say I am. But always remember you can't take an investment back to the shop because you don't like it when you get home. So be a savvy investor by watching out for marketing tricks. After all, fund-management companies wouldn't bother with all this if they didn't think it paid them dividends.

Evaluating the Worth of Performance Tables

One of the most controversial issues in fund management is past performance and whether it has any relationship to the future. Academics have said that at roulette you have as much chance of picking a future winner by selecting the best from the past as you have of scooping the table based on the previous spin.

Regulators have tried to ban past performance figures but the fund-management industry has put up a spirited defence of the practice (without which it would have to rewrite most of its adverts), and its view has prevailed.

Tables used to be published once a month and then a month in arrears. Now you can easily find up-to-date figures on websites such as Trustnet (www.trustnet.com) or Morningstar (www.morningstar.co.uk). These allow you to sort funds according to your criteria, such as time periods, so you can see which ones have done well over ten years or over just one month.

Keep in mind, though, that comparisons don't always work that smoothly. Some funds are mobile. They move their asset mix over time and change sectors, usually to make the collective look better.

And sometimes the sector boundaries or even the name is altered, making it tough to follow a fund over the years. An even bigger problem occurs when funds merge. Usually, the fund with the better record continues, and the other is air-brushed out of history.

When examining performance tables, which are subdivided into sectors, keep in mind that coming in fifth in a sector of 200 is a real achievement, but coming in fifth in a sector of 10 is just average.

The ideal collective isn't one that's currently topping the table. Too many fund managers have succeeded in heading the league one day and propping it up by the time you've bought into it. Instead, look for consistency over the years. The fund that generally beats 60 or 70 per cent of its competitors on a regular basis is the one to aim for. If past performance shows anything, it's that managers who are consistently ahead of the majority provide better value for investors than those with flash-in-the-pan genius followed by down-the-pan disaster.

The same figures can tell different stories

All tables assume that you start off with a set amount (usually £1,000) and reinvest dividends after basic rate tax over a variety of time periods, usually six months, one year, three years, five and ten years. But after that, they can show two quite different scenarios. Most tables are cumulative so you see what you would've got after, say, three years. But others show 'discrete performance' and they can tell an altogether different story.

Cumulative tables give no idea of consistency. The good or bad performance may have been due to one great or one atrocious patch nearly ten years ago. Going down to shorter time periods may show the fund manager in a different light. A fund that has doubled over ten years sounds impressive. But scratch that a bit, and you'll see that it tripled over a few months nearly a decade ago and then lost money ever since! This could be due to changes in managers, fund emphasis or most likely a move from a lucky streak back to reality. So if you want to judge consistency and filter out one period of amazing good (or bad) decision-making, go for the discrete figures (see the following section for more info).

Tables that use discrete figures

Discrete-figure tables show every single time period taken individually. This would typically be every single year for the past five or ten years. If your table were dated June 2016, for example, you'd have the 12 months from 1 June 2015 to 31 May 2016, as well as the year from 1 June 2014 to 31 May 2015, and so on.

Discrete figures let you judge consistency and when any out- or under-performance occurred. A fund with a ten-year cumulative performance that was superb eight, nine and ten years ago and then reverted to a little below average would still look good over ten years. But the discrete figures would expose its less-than-inspiring performance since.

Here's an old bit of research (the basics haven't changed, so I still quote it). Out of the ten best US collective funds in 1990, only two funds were still in the best 10 per cent on a one-year discrete basis by 1995. Three were in the worst 10 per cent of all funds, and four others were below halfway. Fast-forward another ten years and the funds were scattered all over the table. Only one was still a real winner, a second had fared well, but many of the rest were average, below average or bottom of the heap. All this leads to the conclusion that funds that did well five or ten years ago are rarely the best deal from now onwards. Nothing's special about that US experience. The same exercise in the UK or elsewhere, and over different periods, would come up with the same findings.

Discrete-period tables are a powerful past-performance tool that most marketing departments would rather you didn't see. Trustnet (`www.trustnet.com`) is a good place to start your research.

What tables are strongest at showing

Although these tables are hit and miss in predicting future winners, they're better (okay, not infallible) at showing future losers. Funds that are down in the dumps seem to stay there. In fact, a number of UK adviser firms regularly publish lists of the losers. Some funds and fund managers seem to be permanent fixtures.

Past performance is most accurate in predicting really bad fund managers. Collectives that have spent most of their life in investment's equivalent of the fourth-division relegation zone tend to stay there. You can use this info to eliminate the no-hopers. Good funds may go down, and average funds may go up. But rarely does the total rubbish ever throw off that poor-performance mantle and shine.

Get savvy with fund performance-table talk

A *quartile* means that a table has been divided into four subsections. First-quartile performance is the top 25 per cent of the table, which may be anything from a few funds to more than 100. Anything from average upward appears in the top two quartiles. Third and fourth quartiles are for the also-rans.

A *decile* means that a table has been divided into ten subsections. The top decile of a table of 100 funds is the first 10. So top decile is better than top quartile, and bottom decile is worse than bottom quartile. Avoid funds in the bottom two deciles like the plague. Sad to say, but they rarely move up the lists.

Separating the Good Managers from the Bad

To divide the wheat from the chaff – the good fund managers from the bad – you need to ask lots of questions. If you don't get straight answers, move on to another fund. You've plenty to choose from.

Here are some pointers to test the fund-management company and its managers:

- ✔ What's the fund's purpose? Is it all-out growth irrespective of risk, total caution or something between the two?

- ✔ How will the company's fund managers work to fulfil the fund's purpose in practice? Look at the present holdings to see how they fit. Is the portfolio a ragbag, or does it have coherence?

- ✔ How frequently does the manager buy and sell? If the manager of a collective investment is forever buying and selling, costs will drag down performance. The practice may also show that the manager has no idea what to do, so the fund lurches here and there. But if there's very little activity, what are you paying for?

- ✔ What markets will the fund work best in, and what's the strategy for a change of market conditions? Fund-management companies are great at giving you a best-situation scenario. You want to know what'll happen if the worst occurs.

- ✔ Who's in charge? Is it a named individual, and, if so, who's the backup?

- ✔ What happens if the manager quits? How easy is it to get rid of a poorly performing manager? Or is there an anonymous team of managers?

✔ Does the fund-management company impose on individual managers a central philosophy or even central lists of shares to buy? Or does it let the managers think and act for themselves?

✔ If the fund is new (and most marketing tends to be around new funds) then what's the purpose? What new thinking does it bring to the party that previous funds don't?

✔ What's the history and track record of the lead fund manager? Experience is important. Don't get confused by statements such as 'Managers have 40 years of experience in markets'. Some funds may have ten managers; that's an average of just four years each! Or the average may hide that the team has one experienced fund manager with 20 or 30 years in the business and a group of college leavers.

Appreciating the Worth of Fund-Manager Fees

The collective-fund industry would rather not focus on costs. Instead, it would prefer to concentrate on benefits. But you can't separate the two. Whatever gains professional management may bring, you may lose them, and then some more, if you pay too much in fees.

The costs of buying into a fund aren't too much of a problem – and as you see in the next section, you can avoid them either completely or largely by signing up to a fund supermarket. But these fees aren't that different from those involved with purchasing individual shares. You generally aren't charged an exit fee from a unit trust (or an insurance fund, although few people now buy these because they only appeal to people with specialist tax needs), so think of the initial charge as a round-trip in-and-out fee. Many independent financial advisers, known as discount brokers, rebate part of the upfront fee.

Annual fees are where you're often hit hard. These fees are often shown at 1.5 per cent, but the counting doesn't stop there. Fund fees attract VAT (value added tax), making the real figure nearer to 1.75 per cent. Add on some compounding and, in rough terms, a fund held for ten years would give its managers around 20 per cent of your money, or about 9 per cent over five years. But some tracker funds can charge as little as 0.3 per cent each year.

To show value, a high-cost fund manager must add more than 20 per cent to a ten-year investment and around 10 per cent to a five-year holding for the holder to break even. Managers who can consistently deliver good results with the costs handicap can congratulate themselves. Frequent traders are harder hit by entry costs.

Filling Your Financial Trolley at Fund Supermarkets

Buying from a fund supermarket is little different from other online shopping experiences. You choose what you want, put the items in your trolley and pay at the checkout. And you'd expect to pay less than going to the old-fashioned store. Except, the sums involved here are going to be bigger than your usual grocery bill. In general, you pay nothing or very little upfront. If you buy directly from the investment company itself, you typically lose around 5 per cent of each investment in upfront charges.

Fund supermarkets typically offer around 1,500 to 2,000 unit trusts, which is enough for almost everyone. And after you've signed up to a supermarket – you could join more than one but the complications probably outweigh any greater choice – you can register all your existing holdings of similar funds as well. That gives a one-stop shop where you can see what you have and track your purchases, sales and dividends. Having everything in one place can be useful when it comes to filling in your self-assessment tax form. Look for 'consolidation' on the site. This tells you that you can list all your applicable investments.

What does the site get out of this? Unit trusts pay something called *trail commission*. This isn't a payment for going on a long-distance walk but an annual amount – usually 0.5 per cent of the value of the holding – that can be paid to the supermarket or to the independent financial adviser whose name might appear on it. It's one of the confusions of the supermarket that some are labelled either with their own name or with that of an adviser. Think of own-brand drinks at the real supermarket – they're all made by manufacturers with many brands, sometimes even supplying other supermarkets.

Fund supermarkets don't tell you what to buy. But they offer a whole range of tools such as tables and easy access to the investment firm's own website, where you'll find 'fact sheets'. These are really aimed at the professional broker but you'll find a whole range of useful information including statements from the managers and a list of the larger holdings in the portfolio.

The two totally dominant supermarkets are operated by Fidelity Funds (www.fidelity.co.uk) and Co-funds (www.cofunds.co.uk). Some discount brokers let you opt for one or the other – others tell you which one to have. Where you have a choice try both out, but it'll probably make no difference to your future wealth.

Don't go straight to a supermarket if you really want hand-holding advice. But don't be surprised if after a broker has created a portfolio for you, it ends up in a supermarket environment. It's just that it's much simpler to administer this way.

Understanding Tax and the Investment Package

Collectives such as unit trusts and investment trusts are taxable. Sorry.

Income tax

You pay income tax on dividends, although under present rules you don't pay tax if you're a basic-rate taxpayer (roughly earning less than £45,000 a year – check the HM Revenue & Customs website at www.hmrc.gov.uk for the current amount). The reason is because, under complicated tax legislation, companies pay dividends after a tax deduction.

If you pay at a higher rate than the basic 20 per cent, you must declare your dividends on your self-assessment tax return. You then must pay the difference between the basic rate and the top 40 per cent or 45 per cent level. The official self-assessment website run by HMRC does the calculations for you.

If you own shares in foreign companies, the dividends are really complicated. How much tax you pay depends on the country of origin – in a few cases, you could even get tax back. The self-assessment online website does the work for you. But if your total dividends from foreign companies are less than £300, you can treat them as UK payments, saving a load of time and trouble.

If you pay no tax at all, you can't reclaim the tax on collectives investing into shares. (Nor can you do so if you buy the shares directly for yourself.)

However, 0 per cent rate taxpayers can ask for a tax refund if they buy into bond funds or mixed bond and equity funds if the bond element accounts for at least 60 per cent of the total.

Capital gains tax

Capital gains tax, or CGT as the accountants call it, is normally payable on profits you make when you sell an asset. In most cases you can offset losses. The good news for unit and investment trust holders is that fund managers don't pay CGT on the ins and outs of their portfolios.

The bad news is that you may have to pay CGT when you exit the fund. The good news is that you have nothing to pay until your gains (what you get less what you paid) top your personal annual allowance. This allowance changes every year with rising prices but is £11,000 at the time of writing. It's use it or lose it, though; you can't carry it over from one year to another.

If you use the full allowance, you could collect a tax-free income worth £3,080 a year (before dealing costs). And you can use it, rather than losing it, with a few simple steps even if you don't want to change your portfolio to any great extent. After a little bit of tax history, I'll show you the legal workarounds.

Once upon a time, a very long time ago, taxpayers could 'bed and breakfast' shares – sell them and buy them back immediately to crystallise the gains. But that was banned and now you have to leave a month between the sale and repurchase. Here are two ways around this:

- Sell a share and buy into another very similar company or collective investment. For instance, you sell shares in ABC Brewery and buy those of XYZ Brewery, or you sell units in one UK index-tracker fund and buy the same thing from another fund manager.
- If you have a spouse or civil partner, one of you can sell, say, 1,000 shares in Toytown Bank while the other buys 1,000 shares in the same company.

Don't forget that married couples (and those in civil partnerships) each have an annual tax break. Nothing stops you transferring part of your holding before sale to your other half to make the maximum use of these allowances. This can double your household's tax-free allowance.

Investing tax free: The Individual Savings Account

An *Individual Savings Account* (ISA) gives tax-free investment into funds and bank accounts for the first £15,000 in each tax year (6 April to 5 April). You could put all of the investment into stocks and shares or all into cash accounts at a bank or building society, or mix and match the two, provided the total remains below the ceiling. And if you have old ISAs, you can move them from cash to shares or shares to cash as you like as many times as you want. You can invest your ISA – and every UK adult can have one – into a wide variety, including most shares, bonds, unit and investment trusts.

Virtually all unit trusts will put your money into an ISA at no extra cost. But many investment trusts make an annual charge that can more than outweigh tax advantages in some trusts. However, this fee is usually fixed, benefiting the investor with a big balance over the person with a few thousands because the charge is spread more thinly.

You don't have to reveal your holdings on an annual self-assessment tax form, and the ISA gives freedom from income tax on dividends and interest, and doesn't count for CGT. But the ISA tax freedom from CGT, no matter what the investment or the period held, comes with a warning. For what the tax-person giveth with one hand, the taxperson can taketh away with the other. The reverse side of the CGT freedom coin is that you can't count losses on ISAs against profits elsewhere in your holdings.

Although you pay no tax on dividend income from shares, basic-rate taxpayers don't gain because no one can reclaim the 'tax credit' that companies pay on their dividends. The news is better for higher rate taxpayers, though. Outside an ISA, they'd have to pay an additional charge – this is waived within the tax-free wrapper.

The deal is better for bond investors (or those in a mixed bond and equity fund where bonds make up at least 60 per cent of the total) because all the tax is refunded, giving benefits to the majority on basic rate.

Sadly, when an ISA investor dies, the tax freedom also dies. ISA holdings are subject to inheritance tax just like everything else left behind, and that could grab 40 per cent. So spend it while you have it!

Never let the tax tail wag the investment dog. Over the years billions have been poured into unsuitable and sometimes downright rubbishy investments by savers mesmerised by the words 'tax free'.

Chapter 13

Investing with a Trust

- -

In This Chapter

▶ Understanding how to own lots of shares for little cash

▶ Finding out about unit-trust charges

▶ Sorting out active from passive unit-trust fund managers

▶ Looking at ethical unit trusts

▶ Differentiating investment trusts

- -

*U*nit and investment trusts are the most important route for UK investors to buy a ready-made portfolio of shares or bonds backed by professional management. They're called *trusts* because most are based on a legal document called a trust deed. Of course, the fact that trust also means confidence does no harm in making these investments more marketable. Together these trusts are known as *collective investment*.

So what do unit and investment trusts give you that you can't do yourself? The best answer is that they offer a diversified selection of investments so you spread your risk. The only way that you could replicate this is if you were rich enough to invest meaningful amounts (and I'm talking £10,000 minimum here) into at least 30 to 40 shares. That adds up to about £300,000 to £400,000.

On top of that, you get someone – at a cost – to look after your investments for you. Effectively, you choose the area of investment – the UK, Japan or Russia, for instance – and someone to manage your money while the fund does all the legwork. And it can literally be legwork: fund managers often visit the companies they invest in, or may invest in, to check up on progress.

Both unit and investment trusts offer these ready-made managed portfolios. And although differences between the two exist – this chapter points them out – the similarities are more significant. Unless you really want to do it all yourself and have the £300,000 or so stuffed under your mattress, then you'll probably want to stick with trusts for the major part of your investment strategy.

The great thing about both forms of trust is that you can get started for as little as £50 (occasionally even £25) if you sign up for a monthly investment scheme, or £250 to £1,000 as a lump sum. Doing so gives you access to a professionally managed fund that diversifies your money into anything from some 30 shares to more than 200 holdings. You get an investment in a huge number of shares for not much money.

Don't get too impressed by funds with the longest list of holdings. No correlation exists between a large number of holdings and management success. In fact, some people think that having too many shares just spreads research and other fund-manager functions a bit too thinly. Others suggest that a really long list means the managers have no real ideas or convictions about where the market is heading so they go for the scatter-gun approach. And a third group says a strategy of holding many investments – perhaps more than 100 – is a form of *closet indexing*: that's buying all the shares in the index but charging for full management instead of very low index-tracking costs.

This chapter tells you what unit and investment trusts are and how they work, to help you decide whether investing in them is right for you, and points you towards sectors that meet your needs. Unit trusts outweigh investment trusts by a huge margin, so I start with them; then I look at investment trusts later on in the chapter.

Understanding What Unit Trusts Are

Unit trusts are so called because you hold a number of units in a fund that's legally set up as a trust. Simple. But don't get too hung up on the word *trust* because you can't always trust them to come up with the investment goods.

People sometimes refer to unit trusts with other names. *Mutual funds* is the title preferred in the United States, and it's becoming more common in the UK. *Open-ended funds* (because the number of units has no limit) is also a US term that's moving across the Atlantic. And in the UK most funds are, strictly speaking, defined as *open-ended investment companies (OEICs)*. But almost everyone still calls them unit trusts.

If you're really interested in all the fine print of a trust, you can get a copy of the trust deed. But don't bother (unless you're a committed fan of legalese). It won't help you in your quest for investment gains. Only specialist lawyers understand the differences – for the rest of us, the deed really doesn't matter.

Leaving aside the legal stuff that no one reads, unit trusts are a simple concept. A fund-management firm advertises a trust, and lots of investors send in money either directly or through brokers. After the firm subtracts around 5 per cent for costs, it invests the rest in whatever assets the managers are promoting. The assets can be anything from global equities to UK gilts to commercial property.

Examining why some trusts have more than one price

Unit trusts traditionally had two prices – one around 5 per cent higher than the other. The higher price, or *offer price*, was the one you paid on purchase, and the lower, or *bid price*, was yours when you sold.

–OEICs have only one price, whether you're buying or selling, a set-up called *single pricing*. Does that sound like you're free of the bid–offer spread? If only. Although OEICs have only one price, brokers can load the price by around 5 per cent when you buy, so you're back to where you were before single pricing came in.

Some OEICs can have far lower charges. They're available to anyone with a minimum of £250,000 to £500,000. And that's probably not you (or at least not yet). They're really intended for brokers who manage funds combining several trusts for their clients – unsurprisingly, these are called *funds of funds*. The adviser or broker doubtlessly adds on some 'management fees', so individuals end up paying the full amount anyway.

For example, suppose that a person invests £1,000 when the units are priced at £1 each. The investor now has 1,000 units, the value of which goes up and down in direct proportion to the underlying fund. The overall size of the fund obviously depends on the success or otherwise of the managers in picking the right investments. And that rests on whether money from the other investors is flowing in or out because they're buying or selling. The size of the fund, which is easy enough to find online, is based both on the success (or otherwise) of the managers in picking good investments and the flow of money in or out. Obviously, the two are connected.

No matter what happens to the size of the fund, however, you always have your 1,000 units, which can change in price. But unlike direct investment in shares, where your holding remains a fixed (if small) percentage of the company's capital, your units will vary as a proportion of the entire trust. Firms can create and destroy units as demand rises and falls. Unlike shares, you can have a decimal fraction of a unit as well as complete units.

Knowing How Much Unit Trusts Cost

You can't expect collective investment for nothing. Usually, you pay to get in and you pay an annual management fee. A few complex trusts also pay their managers a success fee, so if the fund beats a target, they get paid more. This is supposed to incentivise them.

Charges can be complicated, but here's a simple word of advice for starters. The worst deal you'll get is to buy your unit trust (or OEIC) directly from the fund-management company. Doing so is throwing money down the drain, as you can see in Chapter 16. Going straight to the company means you have all the costs but none of the benefits of dealing with a broker firm. Buying unit trusts direct is never better than the discount or investment supermarket routes. An *investment* or *fund supermarket* is an online facility where you can select funds to invest in yourself. However, you're legally the client of a financial adviser or stockbroker. Most advisers offer a choice of the two main supermarkets: Co-funds and FundsNetwork. Other advisers offer just one. There's really not a lot to choose between them (think Visa or Mastercard on your plastic).

The initial charge

The upfront, or initial, charge is levied when you buy the fund, whether through a broker or direct from the investment company. The charge can be either built in via the bid–offer spread or added on as a brokerage charge.

Alternatively, with a single-priced fund you may not pay the initial charge at all. Is this generosity? No. Because of a series of changes known as the Retail Distribution Review (RDR), some advisers charge an annual fee, usually based on a percentage of your holding, instead of an upfront charge. You may also pay trail commission – that's generally 0.5 per cent a year – to the broker company. The situation can get complicated, with some charging a fee but giving back the trail commission. But remember that all those small percentages add up over the years, and all the more so if your investment grows in value.

Brokers don't work for nothing. But they're supposed to give something back in terms of service and advice. Many (probably most) don't. So because the fund is the same whether you buy from Adviser A or Broker B, check out whether you'll get any extras such as regular market updates.

The annual charge

All unit trusts have a yearly charge. It can vary from 0.2 per cent to 0.3 per cent for the best-value UK tracker funds to 1.75 per cent or even more for some esoteric trusts. Most trust rules allow for higher charges, provided that you're given some notice. Over the years, annual charges have tended to rise. Managers have to pay the trail commission out of something. And you pay value-added tax (VAT) on top of that.

Hidden charges

With most funds, the annual charge is taken from the dividends received. So if the underlying fund earns 4 per cent and your charge is 1 per cent, you end up with 3 per cent. (This is a simplified example ignoring VAT.) Funds are generally managed to ensure that there's some income to meet the costs.

But with a minority of funds, mostly investing in bonds and other high-income assets, you're given all the income. This isn't generosity but sleight of hand. Instead of the fund taking the charge from the income, it's shaved away from your capital. The result? Fund-management companies can proudly proclaim a higher return on your cash than those going the conventional route of hitting your income. Looks good in adverts! Clever, huh?

Provided that you reinvest your income, the end result can be the same. Still, this route isn't a good idea. You get marginally more income to pay tax on. And if you spend the income cheque (and that's the main purpose of a high-income fund), your capital goes down year on year. Here's how (using very simplified maths):

You invest £10,000 after upfront charges in a fund yielding 10 per cent. Your first annual payment, ignoring tax, is £1,000. After ten years of 1 per cent annual deductions from capital (and assuming no gains or losses in the fund), your investment is now worth about £9,000. The 10 per cent yield now pays £900 a year.

Check on charges. Some funds are better value. No relationship whatsoever exists between high annual charges and better-than-average performance. High-charging funds argue differently, but then you'd expect that, wouldn't you!

Using TER to disentangle the real charges

The annual charge is just the start of what it costs to own a fund. But it's the only element that funds have to expressly disclose. Funds have other expenses, such as their own dealing costs and bills from their lawyers, custodians, auditors and other behind-the-scenes professionals, that aren't covered by the annual management fee because this goes straight to the managers.

Step forward, *Total Expenses Ratio* (or *TER*). This adds up all the various costs plus the annual management fee so you get one big number and know how much investors really get. An annual management fee of 1.5 per cent can easily turn into a TER of nearly twice that amount.

Some expenses, such as legal and audit fees, tend not to vary whatever the size of the trust. This means they can be spread more thinly over a large trust than a small one – that's an economy of scale that benefits the billion-pound collective over the 10-million one. And no one can do much about these essentials. But managers have control over a substantial slice of expenditure. If they decide to trade more often in and out of shares, rather than make fewer buy and sell decisions, then the costs rise. Managers are in a bind here. If they trade too much, they face criticism for running up big stockbroker bills. But if they trade too little, investors wonder what they're doing all the time.

Selecting the Best Unit Trust for You

To select the right unit trust for your needs, follow this step-by-step guide:

1. **Work out your asset-allocation strategy.**

   You need to calculate how much you can afford to put into the different investment types. Ultimately, the amount depends on how much you have, how much you're willing to risk and how long an investment period you have.

2. **Select your investment objective.**

   For example, is your objective income to boost your salary or pension, or long-term capital growth so you reap the rewards in maybe five to ten years' time, or a mix of the two?

3. **Decide on the proportion of your cash that you want in collective investments.**

   After you've worked out your long-term asset allocation moves, you don't have to carry them out all at once. This may be a good time to buy shares or bonds through a collective investment. But if it's not then nothing's wrong with holding your money back for a period. A good idea is to put this cash in a bank or building society account that you keep apart from your other savings.

4. **Ensure that the fund you choose will accept your level of savings.**

   Some trusts, for example, are aimed at really large investors with six-figure sums. But if that's beyond your cash league, you may find you can invest in them via specialist brokers.

5. **Refine your options by working through unit-trust sector listings, where you'll see all funds with similar investment patterns, such as corporate bonds, North America or Europe excluding the UK.**

All trusts are classified in sectors so that you can see funds pursuing roughly similar investment objectives when you need to compare performance. The sectors change from time to time, but currently around 30 exist. An unwieldy number, yes. And with more and more trusts following all sorts of clever and complex strategies, the old, easy division between income and growth just doesn't work anymore across the board. Income sectors and growth sectors still exist, but a lot of sectors are neither one nor the other. So the Investment Management Association, which creates and controls the sector breakdown, uses a number of other broad classifications as well. The following sections provide details of the main ones.

Watch out for sector switching – a fund that looks a dud in a tough sector can, with a tweak of its investments, appear in a less-demanding category where it looks good. Also, many advisers tout the newest fund as the next 'best thing'. Yes, new is exciting, but after a few months the varnish often becomes tarnish. Little correlation exists between a new fund and long-term success.

Unit-trust sectors

The unit-trust world is divided into sectors that cover the broad range of all that's on offer, from the safe to the scary. Each main sector is then subdivided – so, for example, capital growth includes Japan and Europe as separate lists. You can't really compare Japan's shares with those of Europe (think of apples and oranges), but both these sectors may appeal to investors looking for growth and higher risk from overseas equities rather than income and lower risk from government bonds, for instance.

You can sort out the super-smooth sectors from the rollercoasters with _volatility_. This measures monthly ups and downs, usually averaged out over three years. The short-term money market category is the 'safest' with a volatility factor of just a few basis points (a _basis point_ is 0.01 per cent). At the other end of the scale, you have China with a recent volatility factor of 5.2. To put this into context, the UK gilt fund category would weigh in at around 1.6, property at 2.5 and the UK all companies category at 3.9.

The low-risk sectors

In this section, I look at unit-trust sectors that appeal to the safety-first investor. Here are the funds principally targeting capital protection:

✔ **Money market:** These invest at least 95 per cent of their assets in money-market instruments (cash and near cash, such as bank deposits, certificates of deposit, very short-term fixed-interest securities or floating-rate notes). But never forget that these assets can go down – near cash isn't really cash! So this isn't the home for money you need in the near term – it should be fine for a year or so, though.

✔ **Protected:** These are funds, other than money-market funds, that principally aim to provide a return of a set amount of capital to the investor (either explicitly protected or via an investment strategy highly likely to achieve this objective) plus the potential for some investment return. Remember that protected isn't the same as guaranteed. And going for one of these funds is pointless if you really believe your chosen investment will soar – you pay for the protection in lots of ways including ceilings, which mean your gains can be limited to a set figure.

Income funds

Moving up the risk/reward ladder, the next sector consists of unit trusts that aim to produce a mix of dividend income and some capital growth as well. These trusts can be useful if you need a regular boost to your earnings or pension. Here are the funds principally targeting income (by asset category):

✔ **UK gilts:** These invest at least 95 per cent of their assets in sterling-denominated (or hedged back to sterling), triple-A-rated, government-backed securities, with at least 80 per cent invested in UK government securities (gilts). The UK is no longer triple-A with some ratings agencies, but that downgrade doesn't matter too much because many other bonds from governments, including the US Treasury, were also cut down a notch or two.

✔ **UK index-linked gilts:** These invest at least 95 per cent of their assets in sterling-denominated, triple-A-rated, government-backed, index-linked securities, with at least 80 per cent invested in UK index-linked gilts. They should protect your savings against rising prices with a little bit over. Super-safe. But super-safe involves the risk of being left behind when other assets rise. Super-safe is always super-low returns.

✔ **Sterling corporate bond:** These invest at least 80 per cent of their assets in sterling-denominated (or hedged back to sterling), triple-B-minus or above, corporate-bond securities (as measured by Standard & Poor's or an equivalent external-rating agency). This excludes convertibles, preference shares and permanent-interest-bearing shares (PIBs). Some risk of loss exists.

✔ **Sterling strategic bond:** These invest at least 80 per cent of their assets in sterling-denominated, fixed-interest securities such as convertibles, preference shares and PIBs. Investors face some risk of loss but also the chance of low-level rewards.

✔ **Sterling high yield:** These invest at least 80 per cent of their assets in sterling-denominated bonds with at least 50 per cent of their assets in below BBB-minus, fixed-interest securities including convertibles, preference shares and PIBs. High yield is the polite term for junk bonds.

- ✔ **Global bonds:** These invest at least 80 per cent of their assets in fixed-interest securities in any country of the world except the UK.

- ✔ **UK equity and bond income:** These invest at least 80 per cent of their assets in the UK, between 20 per cent and 80 per cent in UK fixed-interest securities and between 20 per cent and 80 per cent in UK equities. These funds aim to have a yield in excess of 120 per cent of the FTSE All Share Index. Here you should get some growth with six-monthly payments, which you can spend or reinvest into the trust.

Equity sectors

Equity funds present a higher risk of loss than those I've mentioned so far but also offer the potential of greater long-term reward. These two sectors aim to mix and match growth prospects with growing dividends. Some investors use a facility to plough back their dividends into new units until the day when they need the income.

- ✔ **UK equity income:** These invest at least 80 per cent in UK equities and aim to achieve a historic yield on the distributable income in excess of 110 per cent of the FTSE All Share yield at the fund's year end.

- ✔ **UK equity income and growth:** These invest at least 80 per cent of their assets in UK equities; aim to have a historic yield on the distributable income in excess of 90 per cent of the yield of the FTSE All Share Index at the fund's year end; and aim to produce a combination of both income and growth.

Funds targeting growth

These sectors aim for outright growth with little or no consideration for dividends or any other form of regular income. In some cases, the dividends are so low that they don't even pay for annual fund-management charges.

- ✔ **UK all companies:** These invest at least 80 per cent of their assets in UK equities, which have a primary objective of achieving capital growth. Tracker funds are usually in this sector. This is the biggest sector of all in terms of the number of funds available with more than 400 on offer. It's a different story with the total value of the funds. All companies' funds are worth £170 billion, and that's easily outweighed by Global Bonds, a fund sector which is worth £380 billion in total. Global Bonds are investments in government and corporate loans from all over the world.

- ✔ **UK smaller companies:** These invest at least 80 per cent of their assets in UK equities of companies that form the bottom 10 per cent by market capitalisation. Here you're taking a chance on the market's Tiddlers – they often go up before larger companies but can crash farther and faster than the big firms.

Overseas equities

Going overseas increases risks because investors have to concern themselves with currencies and exchange rates as well. Here's a list of the main equity sectors from outside the UK.

- ✔ **China/Greater China (Hong Kong and Taiwan):** Funds must invest at least 80 per cent of their assets in companies quoted in these markets. This is a new sector, reflecting the growth of China in the world economy.

- ✔ **Japan:** These invest at least 80 per cent of their assets in Japanese equities.

- ✔ **Japanese smaller companies:** These invest at least 80 per cent of their assets in Japanese equities of companies that form the bottom 30 per cent of the Japanese stock market by capitalisation.

- ✔ **Asia Pacific including Japan:** These invest at least 80 per cent of their assets in Asia Pacific equities, including Japanese content. The Japanese content must make up less than 80 per cent of assets.

- ✔ **Asia Pacific excluding Japan:** These invest at least 80 per cent of their assets in Asia Pacific equities and exclude Japanese securities.

- ✔ **North America:** These invest at least 80 per cent of their assets in North American equities. This is really Wall Street but can include Canadian companies.

- ✔ **North American smaller companies:** These invest at least 80 per cent of their assets in North American equities of companies that form the bottom 20 per cent by market capitalisation.

- ✔ **Europe including UK:** These invest at least 80 per cent of their assets in European equities. They may include UK equities, but these mustn't exceed 80 per cent of the fund's assets. This sector is small – it's really better to go for Europe and the UK separately rather than invest in a fund that's neither one nor the other.

- ✔ **Europe excluding UK:** These invest at least 80 per cent of their assets in European equities and exclude UK securities.

- ✔ **European smaller companies:** These invest at least 80 per cent of their assets in European equities of companies that form the bottom 20 per cent by market capitalisation in the European market. You could get some UK shares in these funds.

- ✔ **Global growth:** These invest at least 80 per cent of their assets in equities and have the prime objective of achieving growth of capital. You buy this sector when you just want foreign investment. You need to look closely at each fund's fact sheet to see what you really get. You can easily find fact sheets online.

✔ **Global emerging markets:** These invest 80 per cent or more of their assets directly or indirectly in emerging markets as defined by the World Bank, without geographical restriction. Effectively, most of the money goes into Brazil, Russia, India and China (probably via Hong Kong), Nigeria and South Africa, but it could go into many countries, some of whose economies and stock markets you may know little about, which can be very risky.

Mixed-asset sectors

Investors who aren't sure where they want to place their money can opt for someone else to make those big decisions for them. With the mixed-asset sectors, the main choice concerns level of risk. Some advisers create their own with funds of funds (see the later section 'Going with a Fund of Funds'). Many of these sectors have been renamed to give a better idea of what they really do rather than vague terms such as *cautious* or *managed*.

✔ **Mixed investment zero to 35 per cent shares:** Funds in this sector are required to have a range of different investments. Up to 35 per cent of the fund can be invested in company shares (equities). At least 45 per cent of the fund must be in fixed income investments (for example, corporate and government bonds) and/or cash investments. *Cash* can include investments such as current-account cash, short-term fixed-income investments and certificates of deposit.

✔ **Mixed investment 20 to 60 per cent shares:** These invest in a range of assets with the maximum equity exposure restricted to 60 per cent of the fund and with at least 30 per cent invested in fixed interest and cash. The fund should do what it says on the tin and produce some gains, but gains that are generally of a moderate nature and not those that will collapse overnight should markets turn suddenly. This used to be called *cautious managed*.

✔ **Mixed investment 40 to 85 per cent shares:** Here funds offer investment in a range of assets, with the maximum equity exposure restricted to 85 per cent of the fund. At least 10 per cent of the total fund must be held in non-UK equities. This sector was once known as *balanced managed*.

✔ **Flexible investment:** These funds ratchet up the risk/reward ratio another few notches and offer investment in a range of assets, with up to 100 per cent in equities and at least 10 per cent of the total fund in non-UK equities. The funds in this sector are expected to have a range of different investments. However, the fund manager has significant flexibility over what to invest in. No minimum or maximum requirement exists for investment in equities, so funds can have a high proportion of shares. This sector used to be labelled *active managed*.

Specialist sectors

These narrow funds invest in one specialised area or use techniques that go beyond the usual buy-and-hope-it-goes-up method that most fund managers adopt.

- **Absolute return:** These are managed with the aim of delivering absolute (more than zero) returns in any market conditions. Typically, funds in this sector expect to deliver absolute returns on a 12-month basis. This sector, with techniques derived from hedge-fund managers, has become very popular with investors who can't decide whether markets are rising or falling. The returns won't be spectacular but neither – if the managers are competent – will you suffer from big falls. But no guarantees exist.

- **Property:** These predominantly invest in real estate and some shares in property companies. Many of these funds have small-print clauses that allow the managers to close the fund for a period (often six months) if too many investors want their money out. This is because selling properties, such as the office blocks or shopping centres in which these trusts typically invest, takes time.

    In order to invest predominantly in property, funds should do either of the following:

    - Invest at least 60 per cent of their assets directly in property.

    - Invest at least 80 per cent of their assets in shares or bonds from property companies.

- **Specialist:** This is the heading given to funds that don't fit into a mainstream sector, such as South Korea, India, Switzerland, Germany, Thailand and Australia. This is a ragbag because you can't compare a Swiss shares fund with an Australian natural resources trust. All aim at growth and many are rated a 'scary risk'.

    When several stocks cover the same area, they sometimes qualify for their own sector. So healthcare, financial companies and mining shares have their own breakout listings. Mining funds can often be a good way of getting into a commodity boom because they invest in gold, copper, zinc and other raw materials.

- **Technology and telecommunications:** These invest at least 80 per cent of their assets in technology and telecommunications sectors as defined by major index providers. Some are survivors from the dotcom boom way back in 1999, when fund managers launched into what was then the latest craze. But their managers say an interest in backing technology will always exist, whether for communications or to help deal with global warming, so some funds now specialise in alternative energy sources. Risky to very risky.

- **Unclassified:** This is a total ragbag and largely meaningless. It contains funds that don't want to be classified into other sectors, such as private funds and funds that have been removed from other Investment

Management Association sectors due to non-compliance. More than 450 unclassified funds exist but many are the same funds with different charging structures, and a large number are very small. These are unlikely to appeal to any but the most devout unit-trust watcher.

Comparing Active and Passive Fund Managers

Active fund managers buy and sell shares and other assets hoping that they'll perform at least better than average and preferably hit the big time. Most funds that are designated as unit trusts (or technically OEICs) are actively managed. They are the product of research.

Passive fund managers in the unit trust world don't care about doing their research homework. In fact, they don't even need to know the names of the companies in their portfolios. The reason is that they're usually computers, not people, without too much in the way of sentimental feeling. They buy all the constituents of an index in the right proportions (or occasionally come up with sampling methods to ensure that a fund doesn't have to cope with hundreds of tiny company shares). Because they follow an index, they're usually called *tracker funds*.

The result of passive fund management is that what you see is what you get. If the fund tracks the Footsie (the FTSE 100 share index of the UK's biggest stock-market-quoted firms) then your fund will go up and down along with the index. You'll get an income calculated as the average yield on the basket of shares your fund follows, less the annual management charge. You'll also know what level of risk you're taking.

Most passive funds in the UK track either the Footsie or the wider All Share Index. But you can buy passive funds that follow markets in other countries; that buy into sectors worldwide, such as technology or pharmaceuticals; or that only invest in an index of ethically and environmentally approved companies. A growing area of passive investment is to buy the replication of an index through exchange-traded funds. *Exchange-traded funds* are traded via stockbrokers just as if they were real shares. They're big in America and getting much bigger in the UK.

Active versus passive has always been the big fund-management debate. Both sides can come up with good (and sometimes bad) arguments:

- ✔ Active managers say that they can add value because they can sift out the wheat from the chaff.
- ✔ Passive managers say that they don't have to second-guess the future.

✔ Active managers say that they have a wider range of investments, including smaller companies with a great future.

✔ Passive managers say that most of these small-company bets fail. And even when they do well, they have little effect on the overall fund because holdings are minuscule.

✔ Active managers say that they offer strategies that vary with market conditions.

✔ Passive managers say that the market as a whole automatically adjusts to different conditions.

✔ Active managers say that passive funds end up with too many shares that have peaked. The trick is to look for shares that are growing fast enough to knock on an index's door.

✔ Passive managers say that a lot of active managers just buy big-index stocks but charge up to five times extra for the privilege – a practice called *closet indexing* in the investment trade. You can sometimes spot a closet indexer because all their big holdings (see the fact sheet that usually lists at least the ten most significant investments) are virtually the same as the biggest stocks in the index.

✔ Active managers say that passive funds often fail to track their chosen index properly. No real defence to that exists other than to claim the opposite!

✔ Passive managers say that they win on costs. They reckon that active managers have to do about 1.5 per cent better a year than the index – a tough call year on year. That's because passive-management costs in a unit trust are typically less than 0.5 per cent annually.

✔ Active managers say that they can spread their investments more efficiently. They don't have to buy and sell whenever firms go in and out of an index. They can talk to companies and sometimes influence the stock market. But, they say, passive fund managers must buy stocks they have no control over and at whatever price the market dictates.

✔ Passive managers say that although they'll never top a table, they'll never be below halfway for long either. They say that active funds that beat them one year probably won't do so the next. Owing to costs and other factors, a good index fund should always end up around 38th to 42nd place in a group of 100 funds over a typical year. Performing this way consistently is better than rocket performance one year and rubbish performance the next – unless you're quick enough to spot the gains and then move to avoid the falls, but actually no one's really that clever.

Active and passive fans will continue to swap insults and statistics to prove their cases. Don't get caught up in their ego trips. Instead, you could go for a core and satellite strategy. Put the bulk of your money in low-cost index funds and leave it there. This is your core. Invest the rest in selected managed funds (avoid the closet indexers), such as smaller-company trusts, or go for specialist areas overseas.

Taking Ethics into Consideration

'Ethics? That's a county to the east of London!'

That's an old City joke and probably not one of the brightest, especially if you live in Essex. But all jokes have some element of truth, and this one says that the mainstream neither invests nor even cares about selecting investments with a green or ethical tinge.

But many private investors and members of a growing number of pension funds want to feel that their money is backing firms they approve of. The ethical investment market has gone from zero to about £50 billion over the past 30 or so years. Some £6 billion of this sum is in unit trusts representing 5 per cent or so of all equity investment in mutual funds. The UK has a long way to go to catch up with the US, however, where 12 per cent or more of equity funds are managed ethically.

Ethical investors want to avoid investing in companies involved in tobacco, armaments, hardwood logging, animal experimentation, nuclear power, gambling and pornography, or in organisations that support repressive regimes or that manufacture goods using sweatshops in less-developed countries. Equally, ethical investment (often called *socially responsible investment*, or *SRI*) buys into firms involved in positives, including alternative renewable energy such as wind farms, and recycling and waste management. SRI also includes buying into firms at the forefront of good employment practice and those providing high-quality services or goods that clearly benefit the wider community.

Shades of green: Ethical unit trusts

SRI enthusiasts with a large investment pot can go to a specialist stockbroker for a bespoke portfolio. For the rest of us, a specialist ethical or environmental unit trust is the only serious route. These funds come in two shades of green.

Dark-green funds work on an exclusion basis. Stocks of companies involved in any of the forbidden activities are dubbed *sin stocks*. They won't appear in the SRI trust portfolio, which cuts out about half the stock market. If a company moves into a sin-stock zone then the fund sells the shares.

Even dark-green funds have a threshold. If a sin activity accounts for a very small proportion of a company's sales – say sales of tobacco in a big high-street supermarket group – then the fund managers or their ethical advisers look for positives to balance out the banned activity. Some dark-green funds invite unit holders to take part in meetings that debate where the fund is going. Also note that negatives change over time. Thirty years ago, alcohol sales were a definite no-no. Now, more tolerance exists for the demon drink. Meanwhile, attitudes to global warming and deforestation have toughened.

Light-green funds take a different line. Their fund managers say that dark-green funds exclude too much and too many sectors of the business world. So although they cut out the worst of the sin stocks, they're willing to look at the least reprehensible company in each sector. Searching for firms trying to upgrade their SRI credentials is known as investing in the *best in class.*

Fund managers of both shades engage with companies by telling directors how they could improve. For example, fund managers of light-green funds don't sell if a company strays into sin. Instead, these managers try to use their voting power as shareholders (they, and not the actual investors who put up the cash, hold the voting rights in a collective) to change matters for the better.

Balancing act: The pros and cons of ethical investing

Some investors are passionate about SRI. They should skip this section. Others believe that a sin-stock portfolio of tobacco, armaments and pornography publishers works best. They should skip this section as well. You can read what you like into past performance statistics, depending on the period you select and the funds you look at. What you really need to do is balance the pros and cons of ethical investing:

- ✔ **Pro:** Stocks screened out come from dinosaur old-economy industries, such as mining, tobacco, chemicals and armaments, where growth is more limited and government controls are stricter.

- ✔ **Con:** Fund managers can't perform their job if they're limited by non-investment criteria imposed by non-investment people. And sometimes sectors such as tobacco or mining do very well – they were some of the better investments in the first decade or so of this century.

- ✔ **Pro:** SRI-approved stocks tend to be young, dynamic firms that benefit from the general move away from dirty industries towards a cleaner future.

- ✔ **Con:** SRI companies may be less profit-conscious because they're too concerned with their employees or the neighbourhood they work in. And too many go bust because they have a good idea but either can't carry it through or find their markets were either never there or have moved on.

> ✔ **Pro:** Companies that show the management abilities to move to a more sustainable way of doing business are probably brighter and less stuck in the mud elsewhere.
>
> ✔ **Con:** SRI funds concentrate too much on volatile smaller companies.

Going with a Fund of Funds

Most unit-trust investors start off with a UK fund, often a tracker. Then they add to it with more UK-based trusts, and then they venture overseas. But as they build up their portfolio, they have to make decisions. They have to choose the best in each sector that they select and then monitor their holdings.

The do-it-yourself approach has two big failings: massive costs are involved every time an investor switches from one fund to another, and investors may have to pay capital gains tax on profits. The alternative is to hand over money to a fund of funds manager, who invests in a number of other funds but in such a way that minimises switching costs and has no capital gains tax worries within the fund.

Do funds of funds beat a buy-and-hold strategy? The jury's out. But the fund managers must be specially gifted to overcome the drag of two sets of charges. You pay annual fees to the fund of funds manager and yearly charges on the underlying funds. If you pick a manager badly, you end up paying more for less investment performance.

So far, no one's come up with a fund of funds of funds!

Don't confuse fund of funds, where one manager buys and sells units in different trusts to come up with an overall package that matches the amount of risk you want or the area you're interested in, with manager of managers. With *manager of managers*, a fund, usually a poor performer, sacks its own managers and hires in others to do their job. The stated plus points include the fact that you can hire and fire managers very quickly in this way, maybe with as little as a month's notice, and that you can find specialist managers for each part of your fund. So if you had a European fund, you could take on a specialist for France, another for Spain, a third for Germany and so on. This all sounds great in theory, but in practice it's been a bit of a flop. By the time the manager gets around to hiring the best managers on their past performance, they may well have passed their peak! Investment managers should come with a use-by date, just the same as groceries.

Delving into Investment Trusts

Investment trusts offer ready-made portfolios of shares from professional fund managers but, unlike unit trusts, they rarely advertise themselves. They don't pay financial advisers either, which is another reason they're low on the horizon. In this section, I introduce you to investment trusts, and look at both their advantages and their drawbacks.

Seeing how investment trusts differ from unit trusts

Investment trusts are the UK's minority route to collective investment. In total, investment trusts are only worth a small percentage of the value of unit trusts. In some ways, they're similar to unit trusts. For instance, managers operate a portfolio of shares and other investments on behalf of individuals. But, at a more technical level, they're different. *Investment trusts* are companies whose sole business is investing in other companies. And that means the value of an investment-trust share is whatever the stock market decides. It can be more, but more often it's less than the underlying value of its portfolio.

Here are some more features of investment trusts:

- ✔ They offer investors a ready-made portfolio managed by professionals intended for medium- to long-term holding.

- ✔ You can invest anything from as little as £50 via a monthly savings scheme.

- ✔ Managers take an annual fee but it's often low – especially for very big investment trusts.

- ✔ You get a wide range of choices – everything from shares in China to shares in pub companies! Most of the biggest trusts, and the ones most popular with private investors, buy into a wide range of shares across the globe.

In terms of both numbers of products on offer and the total amount invested, investment trusts are very much the little sister of unit trusts. Oddly, they're also the older sister – the first investment trust dates back to 1873 but unit trusts started in the late 1920s.

So why did investment trusts, with their 50-plus-years head start, turn into a minority route? The answer comes down to marketing. And although it sounds technical, the most important difference between unit and investment trusts is what happens to them from their launch.

Unit trusts are what's known in the investment trade as *open ended* – the amount of money in the fund depends on the amounts investors purchase and withdraw. When investors are pouring their money in, the amount under management grows. And vice-versa: as investors lose confidence, the fund shrinks and managers have to sell their holdings to pay them back. Hence, unit-trust firms have to continually market their wares to investors to ensure the funds under management grow rather than shrink. When unit trusts launch, it's really important to make them as big as possible – and then ensure they keep growing.

Investment trusts are quite different. They're launched with a set target – perhaps £100 million. And after the trust achieves the target, it doesn't notice whether investors are buying or selling. It has its money and can continue to invest irrespective of the short-term actions of investors. The trust doesn't have to market the shares after the launch period; one reason that the investment-trust world is so much smaller than the open-ended-fund universe.

Think of an investment trust as a company like BT or Sainsbury's. BT took the money from its initial share launch and invested it in telecoms; Sainsbury's likewise took the money from its share offers many years ago and invested it in food stores. Investment trusts don't buy telephone exchanges or supermarkets but shares in other companies instead.

When investors buy shares in BT, the money they pay doesn't go to BT but to the seller of the shares. BT's managers can continue to invest from their balance sheet (borrowings and past profitability) whatever the day-to-day fluctuations in the value of the firm's equity. Likewise, investors selling shares in Sainsbury's receive their money from investors buying, not from the Sainsbury's group itself. The underlying strategy continues. Of course, if too many investors sell and no one's keen to buy, companies have to take notice of market sentiment and perhaps change direction or their directors. But that doesn't happen on a daily basis.

Companies like BT and Sainsbury's, as well as the thousands of other quoted companies, have two values:

- ✔ **The worth of each share.** Multiply it by the number in issue and you get the *market capitalisation*. So 10 million shares each worth 50p in the stock market gives £5 million. This is the value shareholders look at.

- ✔ **The underlying worth of the company's *assets* –its property, machinery, value of patents, cash at the bank and so on.** The underlying worth could be more or less than the market capitalisation (or *market cap*, to use the jargon).

Investment trusts are no different. One calculation looks at the value of the assets they hold less any liabilities such as borrowings. This is called the *net asset value* or *NAV*. The NAV is similar to a unit trust's value.

Now for what really divides investment trusts from unit trusts. Because investors have to make a decision about the future course of the NAV, you get buyers and sellers. If buyers outweigh sellers, the market value of each share goes up – or vice versa when sellers outweigh buyers. The difference between the net asset value (NAV for short) and the actual price of each share is called the discount when the NAV is higher than the share price and the premium when the share price is higher than the NAV. This discount or premium is unique to investment trusts so the following section gives more information.

Discovering the discount

The value of each share isn't linked to its NAV or the underlying worth of the portfolio but to whatever investors are prepared to pay. The share price could be greater or less (occasionally the same!) than the NAV. When it's greater, it's said to be 'trading at a premium to NAV' and when it's lower, investors talk of 'trading at a discount to NAV'.

Although they go up and down, most investment-trust shares generally trade at a discount.

The discount tends to magnify market movements compared with the same portfolio in an open-ended fund. When the underlying assets go up in value, demand increases and the discount narrows, so investors get a double benefit. For instance, an investment-trust share has a 100p NAV and trades at a 15 per cent discount so the price in the stock market is 85p. Its managers are seen to be bright and they get the NAV to 120p – a gain of one-fifth or 20 per cent. But clever managers increase the demand for the shares so the discount falls from 15 to 10 per cent. Now the shares are worth 108p – a gain of 27 per cent. Investors have won twice over.

Of course, when the opposite happens, the underlying value or NAV falls and the discount usually widens so investors lose twice over.

More occasionally, investment-trust shares trade at a premium. When the premium increases, investors gain more than the underlying increase in the portfolio. But when it falls, they can lose more than the decrease in the portfolio value.

Should you worry about discounts and premiums? Well, they can increase volatility (that's the speed at which prices can go up or down) because both discounts and premiums can magnify movements in the underlying value of the portfolio. But many unit-trust advocates, financial advisers and some people in the media exaggerate the problem. Over time (and I'm talking long-term products) the discounts tend to even out and stabilise. Investment trusts can sometimes control their discounts. If they're seen to widen too far for a time, some buy in their own shares and cancel them. These tactics are called *share buy-backs*. By reducing the number of shares against the underlying portfolio, the value of each share should rise.

Discounts can be good. If you pay 85p for a share with a NAV of 100p, you receive the dividend income on 100p, not 85p. This gives more bangs for your bucks.

Gearing: Not just for bicycles

Because they're stock-market-quoted companies, just like BT and Sainsbury's, investment trusts can borrow money from banks and other sources to increase the size of their investment fund. This process is called *gearing*. Borrowing more is called *gearing up* or *higher gearing*.

Now, get on your bike. When the wind's behind you and the slope is in your favour, high gears mean you go much faster. Similarly, when an investment trust's managers are making the right decisions, higher gearing works in their favour. They now have more money than before – and the gains are greater than the interest they have to pay for the loan.

When cyclists get to a hill, they move down into a lower gear. High gears are painful on steep upward slopes. It's the same with investment trusts. When they hit difficult conditions, the high gearing turns against them. They still have to pay for the borrowings but now they cost more than they're worth. Managers need to 'de-gear'.

But although cyclists can change down through their gears with a simple flick of a lever, getting rid of borrowings isn't so easy. During downturns, gearing works against fund managers, magnifying the discount.

Look at the average gearing for investment trusts similar to the one in which you're interested. You can find this on the Association of Investment Companies website (www.theaic.co.uk). If your trust is higher then it's taking extra risks to gain potential higher rewards.

Examining Monthly Investment Plans

Most investment and unit trust funds have investment plans for regular savers. Some start as low as £25 a month, although most have a minimum £50 or £100. These take your money from your bank account through a direct debit on a monthly basis and buy units in the plan (or shares in an investment trust) at whatever the price is on the day of purchase.

They're sometimes called *savings plans*, although, unlike bank or building society savings, you aren't guaranteed to ever get your money back. These are risky investments.

Savings plans have no minimum savings periods, so you can stop when you like and either cash in or leave your money to grow (hopefully!).

Besides the ability to fund a scheme with small sums, you also benefit from not having to worry so much about timing. Your regular sum buys more units when prices are low and fewer when they're high, so you iron out the ups and downs of investment prices. To stop or sell you need to make a positive decision, however: you have to know what time's best for your needs.

Regular investment plans are very flexible because you can change your amount each month (as long as it stays above the minimum for your plan). You could, in theory, stay in for just one month. In practice, people invest affordable sums for many years. It's often money they don't really miss each month. But when they do cash in, they're often amazed at how well they've done.

Note that savings plans are rarely available through discount brokers or supermarkets. So you must expect to pay the full upfront and annual fees for your investment.

Chapter 14

Saving Up for Your Retirement

· ·

· ·

Your pension is almost certainly the most important investment you'll ever make. It may not be worth as much as your home, if you own it, but the decision making could last all your working life and beyond – and is more complex than buying a roof over your head. Pensions never used to be like that. Once, you could count on the state, and often an employer, to shoulder the burden of providing an income when you stop working. These days, you're effectively left on your own with plans where the buck stops with individual holders and their decisions.

In this chapter, I look at strategies that enable you, as a pension buyer, to achieve the best possible retirement income – without taking undue risks. The focus is accumulation – building up as big a fund as you can while you're earning. The next chapter looks at *decumulation* – jargon for taking a pension fund and turning it into an income for the rest of your life. You can, of course, only decumulate after you've accumulated.

Seeing How the Pension Situation Has Changed

When I was researching the first edition of *Investing For Dummies* some dozen years ago, I wondered whether I should include a chapter on how to employ the best investment strategies to maximise your retirement income. At that time, I concluded that there was little point.

I assumed – rightly at the time – that most readers would retire on a mixture of state benefits and workplace pensions. This combination probably wouldn't add up to a champagne and caviar lifestyle, although it would ensure a reasonably comfortable time when work was finally over and they could look forward to a well-earned life of leisure.

More to the point, talking about investing for a pension gave no significant advantage. But a lot has changed in the past 12 years, and to start off, you need to know about how the two kinds of pension have shifted.

The state pension

Everyone is entitled to a state pension. What pensioners get from the state depends on how many years' worth of national insurance they have contributed. This governs whether they will get a full basic pension. For many, the government also provides a state second pension, which is calculated according to a complex (and sometimes changing) formula based on some or all earnings over a working life. This second pension will be phased out over time starting in April 2016.

No amount of investment skills can boost your state pension, nor can investment stupidity diminish the sum you will receive. State pensions are paid out of tax revenue, and require no investment.

These days, the state pension isn't fashionable. Tens of thousands of warnings from pension providers and financial advisers focus on how little you'll get from the state. They're true. The UK state pension is one of the least generous in Europe and few people will find it sufficient to maintain more than the most basic lifestyle.

But for all its imperfections the state pension exists, and almost everyone has paid into it and therefore qualifies for it. And unlike most money-purchase pensions (see the following section), it will, based on its past history, increase each year in line with inflation.

Assuming you're going to retire sometime after 6 April 2016, and that you have national insurance contributions covering 35 or more years, you'll get at least £148.40 a week – probably £150 because politicians like to start a scheme with a nice, round headline number. That's £150 a week, or £7,800 a year, that you don't have to worry about. All your other retirement income will go on top of that. And, providing they also qualify, any spouse or partner will also have that amount.

But your state pension could be more than £150 a week if you qualify for the *additional state pension*. Qualification depends on your earnings up to April 2016 and is applied to men born on or after 6 April 1951 and to women born on or after 6 April 1953. The additional state pension was formerly known as the state second pension and before that the state earnings-related pension scheme. Whatever name you know it as, the pension also increases each year in line with inflation.

If you delay taking your state pension, your eventual payments will increase to compensate. This is known as *deferring* and it affects your eventual payments. However, the percentage rate of increase will decline from 6 April 2016. Until then, it's the equivalent of an additional 10.4 per cent a year. From that date, the annual rate will almost halve to 5.8 per cent, making putting off your pension far less attractive.

Keep in mind that the state pension, both before and after April 2016, has something in common with all other retirement income. What the state gives with one hand, it can take away with the other. Your state pension counts as income and is liable for income tax.

The state pension forms the base of pensions planning because it's an amount you receive regardless of investment conditions, which allows you to perhaps plan a different strategy for your other pensions. For example, when you want to de-risk your pension pot (see the later section on lifestyle pensions), you may decide that you don't need the very lowest risk category – cash in the bank – because that very slice of your future retirement income is there already, covered by the state pension. This could mean that you follow a more adventurous strategy in the decade or so before your expected retirement date.

The workplace pension

In the past, many people received *final-salary pensions* (also known in the pensions trade as defined benefit, or DB, because you get what the maths dictates). Whether individuals had to pay into it from each salary cheque or not, the end result was based on just three factors: how many years a person had been in the scheme multiplied by their salary in their final year at work and then divided by a figure known as the *accrual rate*. With the years and salary, the higher the number, the better. With an accrual rate, the lower the number (it's often 60 or 80), the better.

Workplace pension fund managers invested contributions from you and your employer, but because the benefit was defined by salary, length of service and accrual rate, how well the managers did was of no real concern to scheme members. Whatever happened, you'd get your pension at the agreed rate. If the investments did well, your boss wouldn't have to put so much in next year. And if they sank then the firm would have to top up the plan. The employer took the risk.

True, there was always a small minority, mainly the self-employed, who had to fend for themselves pensions-wise. Generally, they handed over their cash to life insurance companies, which invested on their behalf in special funds known as *with-profits*. These were supposed to iron out the ups and downs of stock markets with a process called *smoothing*. All the investment decisions came from the managers, leaving the pension buyer with nothing to decide except how much to put in each year.

The workplace pension picture now looks like this:

- **Final salary schemes are closed to new members.** Outside the state sector – teachers, army, local government workers, National Health Service employees and civil servants – it's now rare to be able to join a final-salary scheme when starting a job. Schemes are closed to new members and many have been shut down altogether. However, a few employers now offer *career average* schemes instead, where the pension calculation depends on progress over your total career rather than just the last year. This is less costly.

- **Money-purchase schemes are growing.** An increasing number of employers are pulling the plug on their final-salary scheme plans full stop. Although they won't take away benefits already built up, employees are left to organise their own pension by investing a mix of their own money and, usually, a contribution from the employer. These are known as *money purchase* – investment professionals prefer the term *defined contribution* (or DC) because you only know the amount going in. You have to invest your money to produce a pension pot – under current rules you can take 25 per cent of this as a tax-free lump sum once you reach 55 or older and you have a wider-than-ever variety of options for the balance (see Chapter 15). Defined contribution schemes can range from having no choice other than to be in or out of the plan, to a complete do-it-yourself approach.

The pensions risk has been transferred from employer to employee in the money-purchase plan. If investment markets misbehave or the pension owner makes a bad call then retirement could be little better than bread and water. That's why you can't afford to ignore pensions – even if you're still in your twenties or thirties with retirement way beyond the furthest horizon. You won't know what your pension will be until you finally stop investing into it and decide what to do with your pension pot. But the chances are the pot will be bigger the earlier you start and the more you contribute.

By the way, if you're lucky enough to be in a final-salary scheme, you still can't afford to skip this chapter. Your next job may be in a money-purchase plan. And even if it's not, you could well have to make investment decisions on top-up plans known as additional voluntary contributions (AVCs), which are almost universally (except for a few government-employee plans) based on the money-purchase concept.

Knowing When You'll Retire

Older readers may remember all that 'How to have a great retirement at 50' advice from pensions firms and the media two or three decades ago. It was a load of rubbish – very few ever retired that early (unless forced to) and pensions at that age are poor. After all, a 50-year-old has contributed for far fewer years than a 65-year-old, and the fund would have to support that person for a greater number of years. Besides, few would find retirement at 50 to be anything other than boring.

You can no longer retire at 50 – the minimum age is 55 under present legislation. That's the age you can take a personal or company pension. The state pension age is different. It has increased for women past the traditional 60, and will be going up for men as well. Depending on your age, think 68 to 70 for the state pension.

But a bright side exists. The longer you stay at work, the more you'll collect into your plan and the greater it will be. As I explain throughout this book, time is the greatest ally of the investor. Investment is for the long term, and if you have 20 or 30 or 40 or more years before retiring, you can afford to ignore all the short-term news in the media and concentrate on the message that, over time, taking measured risks works out better than the safety of cash in the bank.

Retiring later also means any *annuity* (that's an income for the rest of your life from an insurance company) you may receive will pay more each month because the money is spread over fewer years – obviously, the average person lives for fewer years when starting from 70 than from 60. Oh, and working more years is also good for your physical and mental fitness. The next chapter has more info on annuities.

Beware of so-called *pension liberation schemes* that promise to unlock your pension pot before you even reach 55. These are scams, although some just about manage to get around the law thanks to some clever small print. Many divert your pension into a self-invested personal pension (SIPP) that then invests into non-existent, highly risky or overpriced schemes such as Amazonian forestry or bonds based on US lawsuits. These assets then 'disappear' – besides being worthless, they're also controlled by the folk who sold you the liberation scheme. But even if you lose all your money in a liberation scheme in this way, you could still have to pay a 55 per cent penalty to the tax authority for taking the benefits early.

Expecting Something from Your Employer

Bosses are mostly now obliged to contribute towards your pension, and by early 2017, every single one will have to pay in something for all those earning £10,000 a year or more (that's the 2014–15 level but it can change). It's called *auto-enrolment* – this means that providing your earnings top the minimum level, your employer has to provide a scheme and a payment.

The employer contribution can be based either on your entire salary before tax or on the amount from the minimum national insurance level up to the maximum national insurance level, if you earn that much. These minimum and maximum amounts are £5,772 to £41,865 a year in 2014–15 (these will vary in subsequent years).

When you're in the scheme, your boss has to pay in 1 per cent of your applicable or *qualifying* earnings, rising to 3 per cent in 2018. Of course, nothing stops your employer being more generous.

You have to pay in as well – currently, you pay in 0.8 per cent of qualifying earnings (4 per cent by 2018). You can choose to pay more. If you don't want to pay then that counts as an opt-out and you don't get the employer contribution.

All the payments go into a plan chosen by the employer, thereby reducing the costs. This could be an existing pension plan or – and this is aimed primarily at smaller companies – the default option, an investment plan called Nest.

Nest, which stands for National Employment Savings Trust, features low charges. It puts your retirement money into a fund of mixed assets, similar to many other large pension schemes. This will change a little over time but the percentages into the four main assets are roughly shares 42 per cent, bonds 30 per cent, property 17 per cent with the balance – 11 per cent – going into cash. There are plans to introduce a more adventurous portfolio, with a higher ratio of equities. This is intended to appeal to younger savers who have longer before their retirement age.

In common with other pension plans, you get income tax relief on your contributions – an upper limit of £40,000 a year exists for this relief but that's unlikely to concern many.

Outside of auto-enrolment, many employers put around 6 to 8 per cent into schemes, with some increasing that amount for older employees. Some may also add to any extra amounts you choose to put in – the most generous match that sum and others boost your payments by 25 to 50 per cent.

Don't expect even the most generous boss to just hand you the firm's contribution to invest as you like. It's not that your employer thinks you'll spend the money on partying; you're expected to be a member of the employer's pension plan. At most places, you have a choice of joining the official scheme or doing without your boss's contribution. This is a no-brainer. Take the money for your future.

A second great advantage of a workplace scheme is that your employer bears the costs. The gap between the 1.5 per cent per year you could pay and the zero in the firm's plan doesn't sound a lot. Over the years, however, it adds up to a fortune. Here's an (admittedly simplified) example:

James pays £100 a month for 20 years into his own scheme with costs of 1.5 per cent annually. Janet pays the same into her workplace plan for the same 20 years, and her employer carries all the costs. Both funds grow at 7 per cent per year, and after 20 years both have put in the same £24,000. James, with his costs, ends up with £43,560. But Janet, in her company scheme, has £52,088. She has over £8,500 more in her pension pot – money that she's kept away from advisers and pension firms that she can now use for a better retirement.

Examining the Investment Deal

The one investment advantage of being outside the company plan is choice. The vast majority of employer schemes either offer no options at all or a limited range, and most have a default where contributions are spread over a number of assets – shares (in the UK and elsewhere), bonds, property and cash. A typical default fund has 35 per cent UK equities, 30 per cent overseas equities, 25 per cent bonds, 5 per cent property and 5 per cent in cash deposits.

Assets in a pension plan are free from capital gains tax, income tax on bond or cash holdings and any additional tax on share dividends.

Many also allow you to select how much you want to put into each of these admittedly basic funds and let you switch. So you could have 100 per cent in overseas equities or your money split equally between bonds and UK equities. The vast majority also give a lifestyle option (see the later section 'Dealing with the Lifestyle Option') for those approaching retirement.

This restricted choice keeps costs down but, more importantly, ensures employees keep to the middle of the road and don't risk all their retirement future on one huge bet. The default option will never shoot the lights out, but neither should it go down to zero. Think of the tortoise and the hare. The fund that sets out with a fast pace will often fail to keep up later when its higher-risk investment strategy is no longer in fashion. In investment, slow but sure can often be better.

How youth and investment hope go hand in hand

Take a look at the history of financial markets over the past four decades. Ups and downs have occurred – some severe in both directions – and very few were foreseen by market professionals. Nevertheless, for those who have the luxury of time on their side, the longer-term trend remains that equity investment beats bond or property strategies, which, in turn, do better than cash at the bank. Little point exists in being cautious when you're 30 because the safety-first option for the next 35 or 40 years will almost certainly leave you with a poverty-stricken retirement. The return on cash may not keep up with rising prices, let alone produce real gains.

Does a lack of choice matter? Those selling expensive schemes with links to 999 different funds claim it does because it restricts your potential, you miss out on some great opportunities and you get middle-of-the-road managers who are only interested in their own bonus cheques. Yes, these critics are right – if you're confident and clued-up enough and have sufficient energy and time, you can try to do better. But you have to beat the competition by a margin that's enough to overcome the extra charges.

Another reason to favour the employer plan over the investment deal is that you won't have to worry about the short-term noise that surrounds investment markets. The media – and commentators from the investment world – have to fill up space. So they talk up small swings one way or the other as major crises or monster gains.

 Being outside an employer plan is the only option open to the self-employed or for those with some spare-time earnings. They don't have the luxury of someone else picking up the plan's tab. My advice? Go for the cheapest cost option you can find and then concentrate on basic tracker funds. High costs or clever investment strategies rarely equal high performance.

Putting Your Marker on the Risk Spectrum

Assign a rating ranging from super-cautious to super-adventurous to each fund into which you can put your pension contributions. Here's my risk spectrum for pension-fund investors. The higher the number, the greater the risk over the short term, but also the greater the potential of long-term reward.

1. Cash

2. UK inflation-linked government bonds

3. UK government bonds

4. AAA-rated corporate bonds

5. International bonds

6. Commercial property – UK

7. International property

8. UK equities

9. Junk bonds

10. European equities

11. US equities

12. Japanese equities

13. Far Eastern equities (not Japan)

14. Emerging markets

15. Frontier markets (parts of Africa and Latin America)

Benefiting from pound–cost averaging

Pound–cost averaging is the posh name for drip-feeding a fixed sum of cash into investments every month. Because this sum automatically goes into the pension fund each month after you set up your plan, it saves you from having to make decisions about the best time to invest.

Most pension buyers invest on a regular monthly basis. The investment comes out of their salary payment. Even if you're self-employed with a less certain monthly income, you should still attempt to put money into the plan every three months on a set date.

Regular investing helps avoid concerns about the price paid for assets, because when markets are falling, purchasers get more units in their chosen fund, which should then subsequently rise. Rising prices mean people purchase fewer units but those already owned go up in value.

In the majority of cases, using pound–cost averaging produces an eventual bigger lump sum than investing the same amount in a large lump sum (assuming you had it!), but like everything else in *Investing For Dummies*, no guarantee exists.

The only time you make a real loss is when you sell your investment. Because a pension is a long-term plan and you can't get your money back anyway, sticking with a more adventurous strategy as long as you have time on your side should work better than a premature switch into safety. Remember that no upper age limits exist for pensions, and you may not need all your pension savings if you have earnings from work or payments from other retirement plans.

Never put all your eggs into one investment basket, but aim for the part of the risk spectrum that's best suited to your needs (assuming you have a choice of funds). Someone with 30 or 40 years to go before retirement should settle among the high numbers at the lower end of my list. By the time these pension buyers reach retirement, many emerging markets will have become mainstream. Don't fret about day-to-day fluctuations – all the worrying in the world does nothing to stop them. You may be taking greater risks with your future retirement income by going for the safer options.

As an example, an adventurous investor may put 50 per cent into emerging markets, 20 per cent in the Far East and spread the other 30 per cent among the US, UK and Europe, with a small slice in property. A younger person with a more moderate attitude to risk may invest 80 per cent in UK equities with the balance in property or international bonds.

When you have a strategy, stick to it. Nothing's worse than going for an adventurous mix and then moving to something safer after a shock. This is the classic error of switching out at the bottom, especially because you may well have moved in when prices were much higher. Let time come to your aid.

Dealing with the Lifestyle Option

The *lifestyle option* has nothing to do with tastes in music, art, food or clothing. Instead, it's the term the pensions industry applies to schemes that automatically move holders from risky to less risky assets over a period of time.

This movement is gradual and normally starts some years before your chosen retirement date. Although no final age exists for taking your pension, many schemes still assume either 65 years or the state retirement age (which has already increased from 60 for women and will soon go up from 65 for men) as the selected date. The age when women can get their state pension goes up each month and will reach 65 for those born in December 1953. After that, the age for both men and women will rise to 66 by October 2020 – affecting those born from December 1954 onwards. Later on, the government plans to increase the state pension age still further towards 68, and perhaps 70, although there are no firm dates for this that I can tell you about. Many schemes use the state retirement age for their own retirement age. They don't have to but it is convenient for them.

Lifestyle is an option, not an obligation. You can opt out of it if the scheme automatically signs you up at a certain age – or you need never opt in. Alternatively, most schemes allow you to spread the lifestyle option over a different time-scale.

Lifestyle swaps the opportunity for higher rewards for more certainty of outcome. Take a look at the risk spectrum for pension-fund investors (see

'Putting Your Marker on the Risk Spectrum', earlier in this chapter). As you get older and approach retirement, time's no long so much on your side and able to heal and overcome the volatility of difficult to predict markets. So then it's time to move towards the lower numbers on the list.

Exactly when you should start to de-risk the portfolio is a matter of debate. Some say ten years, others five. Starting earlier makes sense if you may want to take your pension before your state retirement age, but you can put it off if you intend working as long as you can. And, of course, you can avoid de-risking altogether if you have other assets that would see you through a sudden downturn in share prices.

You always pay a price for safety. Equities, with their higher-risk profile, nearly always return more than other assets over time.

Lifestyle starts with a medium attitude to risk. It assumes that most of your pension portfolio is concentrated around assets in the middle of my risk spectrum – international property, UK equities, junk bonds, European equities and US equities. It then dampens down volatility by moving eventually and gradually to assets at the start of my risk-spectrum list.

A five-year lifestyle plan would move 20 per cent of your pension fund each year from the higher numbered assets to those in the first five assets of the spectrum. A ten-year lifestyle would switch 10 per cent a year. Some plans would even move relatively safe bonds into cash over the last one or two years.

Pension companies often lifestyle by moving the fund each year into a new and less risky one. So if you were in the default fund, with its emphasis on equities, you may find yourself in a new fund that has lower equity exposure, and then the following year you may move into yet another fund that has a far greater bond orientation. The effect is largely the same, although less visible.

Always check on how lifestyling works in your pension plans to ensure that it doesn't override your own preferred strategy. Remember, it's your choice.

Swallowing the Whole Pensions Glass with a SIPP

SIPPs – or *self-invested personal pensions*, to give them their real title – are a variety of personal pensions where the holder is in charge of what goes in and out of the portfolio. The ultimate responsibility for what's in the fund lies with the pension buyer, rather than with an investment manager. Advisers and many people in the media tout SIPPs as the latest and the very best thing on the retirement planning block. But are they?

They've certainly been sold like crazy, with advisers and pensions firms raking in huge sums in commission and profits. And I've been involved in many a dinner party discussion where anyone without a SIPP 'wasn't quite all there' – people see the SIPP as the grown-up route to retirement income.

SIPPs are certainly a great idea for some pensions purchasers, but not for everyone – even active investors.

Dispelling some common myths

First, I'll deal with a few SIPPs myths:

- ✓ **They're new and shiny.** SIPPs have actually been around for 20 years and more. It was only the great pensions simplification in 2006 that made them more accessible with easier-to-understand rules.

- ✓ **They're only for big pension pots.** Although they're generally aimed at those with large sums who are close to retirement, some start with as little as £5,000. These are aimed at younger people who hope to build up their fund over time or those who have other pension investments that they can put into their SIPP later on.

- ✓ **They offer a whole new range of pension possibilities.** SIPPs are a money-purchase pension plan that replaces an external fund manager with the individual, or a chosen adviser or stockbroker, making the selections. Other than having a greater investment choice, you can't do any more with a SIPP than you can do with any other personal pension plan. But because, as the holder, you have a greater say in what goes on within the plan, you have increased flexibility.

- ✓ **You have to be an investment expert to own one.** You can get involved in the investment process as much or as little as you like. You can make daily investment decisions (probably best avoided!), or you can leave the investments untouched for months or even years. If you want, you could hand all the choices over to a third party such as a stockbroker or investment adviser.

- ✓ **Valuation.** SIPP providers want to be able to value your holdings on a day-to-day basis. This rules in conventional financial assets such as bonds and shares but can rule out shares in family-run firms.

Almost any asset (other than residential property; banned because it would make tax avoidance too easy) can go into a SIPP. This can include assets that are effectively scams. So-called 'financial advisers' have sold high-priced, although virtually worthless, shares for SIPP inclusion. Some pension savers have been conned into buying carbon credits, rare earth minerals and even percentages in US divorce settlements. None of these assets are formally banned, even if they're certain to end in investment disaster. Most SIPP providers draw the line somewhere and prohibit these kinds of assets. However, fringe SIPP firms exist with lower standards; sometimes they're connected to scam firms. Remember, responsibility comes with freedom – and that includes the responsibility to slam down the phone very hard on those trying to turn your pension savings into their fortune.

The SIPP shopping list

Here are the main asset classes that SIPPs can accept (although not all SIPPs accept those I list – some plans are restrictive, limiting themselves to a narrow range in return for lower fees). It's a long list but most have one thing in common – the assets are quoted on main stock exchanges or, like contracts for difference, are derived from quoted assets.

- ✔ Bonds traded on recognised exchanges
- ✔ Cash funds
- ✔ Commercial property (held directly or via a unit trust) – see the later section, 'Moving your place of work into a SIPP'
- ✔ Contracts for difference (a form of betting on shares – see Chapter 20 for more details)
- ✔ Deposit accounts at banks or building societies
- ✔ Hedge funds
- ✔ Insurance company-based pension funds
- ✔ Investment trusts
- ✔ National Savings & Investment products
- ✔ Shares traded on recognised stock exchanges in the UK and overseas
- ✔ Traded endowment policies
- ✔ Unit trusts, open-ended investment companies (OEICs)
- ✔ Venture capital trusts (these invest in start-up companies)

Some assets on the list aren't practical for pension purposes. For example, you wouldn't include venture capital trusts because they have tax advantages outside of a pension, but within a SIPP these tax plus points are no better than any other asset, and contracts for difference are essentially short-term assets.

Some SIPPs restrict you to OEICs, others to OEICs, pension funds and UK shares. But all allow for cash deposits. Restrictive SIPPs are often called *supermarket SIPPs* and you can buy these online. Other SIPPs take in the whole (or almost the whole) list and are known as *full SIPPs*. The more you pay, the greater the flexibility. But do you want that?

SIPP suitability – is it for me?

A SIPP could be a good move if

- ✔ You believe you can handle the investment strategy better than the professionals. Or you have an adviser or stockbroker that you trust to do better than pension-fund managers.

- ✔ You have a ragbag of poorly performing or high-cost funds with other pension firms that you can consolidate into one, easy-to-manage fund. Transferring is simple – your new SIPP provider does all the work after you give the go-ahead.

- ✔ You want to delay taking your retirement income and need to manage your money using *income drawdown* (that's a way of having some pension income but putting off turning the pot into an annuity; see Chapter 15).

Never transfer a final-salary scheme into a SIPP. If you do, you give up the guaranteed pension for a risky unknown. The SIPP remains a personal money-purchase pension with all its risks. And it rarely makes sense to transfer one of the very old-style personal pensions that come with guaranteed payouts on retirement. These can be very large at current levels.

Deciding what to put into a SIPP

Although the range of investment possibilities is many times greater than a conventional pension fund, exactly the same basics apply. If you're young and years (perhaps decades) away from retirement, you can take the risks and rewards inherent in equities. As you age and approach pension age, you should de-risk via bonds, property funds and eventually cash. Holding a SIPP still means taking 25 per cent of the pension pot as a tax-free lump sum.

Costing a SIPP

As I say many times in this book, costs count.

On a full SIPP, expect to pay setup costs of around £500 plus annual management charges of about £600 and charges for every transaction you undertake. These can range up to £1,000 if you decide to include commercial property in your fund. On top of that, you also pay management charges for any unit trusts or pension funds included in your SIPP.

Joining the SSAS

Directors and senior employees of small companies have a further option – the SSAS. This bit of alphabet spaghetti stands for Small Self-Administered Scheme. It's rather like a SIPP but where the contributions come out of the company rather than individual pockets. SSASs are complex and may have knock-on effects on other investments. They require specialist advice tailored for the specific company situation.

Supermarket SIPPs can be free to set up. They earn from a share of the management fee in any existing investments that you transfer. Additionally, they can charge for each transaction plus a quarterly or annual fee. These regular fees are often based on a percentage with a cap so the annual total isn't often more than £250 or so.

All plans charge when you want to turn all or part of your pension pot into an income either via drawdown or an annuity. These charges can vary immensely.

Moving your place of work into a SIPP

Small business bosses and those in partnerships can hold their office or other workplace premises in a SIPP (assuming they're not renting). In many cases, such as a professional partnership, the property may be the one tangible asset the firm has. It can absorb a substantial slice of capital.

Additionally, SIPP holders can borrow from a bank a sum of up to 50 per cent of their SIPP fund to buy commercial property. This property doesn't, however, have to be the SIPP holder's workplace. It can be any commercial property. But residential property is banned. After the property is in the fund, the SIPP has to take in a commercial rent from the occupiers.

Relying on one property for all or the bulk of your pension means you've taken the risk of putting all your eggs in one basket. If its value falls – maybe the area becomes unattractive – or worse, if your firm goes bust and you can't find another tenant, then the pension pot suffers.

Chapter 15

Disinvesting During Your Retirement

In This Chapter

▶ Discovering the biggest pension changes for a century

▶ Understanding tax rules

▶ Calculating your needs

▶ Creating investment strategies

▶ Returning to basics with traditional annuities

*T*he tearing up of practically all the rules about what you can do with your personal pension pot when you retire has been dubbed the biggest pension change for 100 years. That's only a slight exaggeration: it's really only the most important rule change in the past 95 years. But it's so mega that you'll have to excuse the hyperbole of an extra five years or so.

I wrote every other edition of *Investing For Dummies* with old, restrictive pensions rules in mind. But the new setup announced in March 2014 radically altered the pensions picture in the UK, so out with the old and in with the new: this entirely new chapter that helps you plan for your retirement.

Other than those who are already drawing a pension (and a large number have put this off to see how the new setup works) the changes to pensions affect the majority of the adult population. That includes everyone who expects to retire, or at least reduce work levels at some future stage, and who's building up or has built up a personal pension pot.

In this chapter, I outline the main options. These include leaving your pension untouched to grow, taking the whole pension as cash and spending it, or opting for a traditional annuity – that's where you hand over a lump sum to an insurance company which promises an income for life – whether you live a month or many decades. Whatever course you take, remember that 25 per cent of your pension pot is tax-free.

Pensions choices can be complex – many permutations exist. And everyone is different. Sorting your pension involves the biggest and possibly the most irreversible earnings decisions of your life that may have to last you for 30 or even 40 years. So always take advice from a qualified and regulated professional financial adviser.

Deciding What to Do with the Freedom

From April 2015, virtually no rules exist about what you can do when you reach 55 and want to turn the pension sum that you've created over your working lifetime into an income intended to last you for the rest of your life. That could be a very long time. It's estimated that at least 700 people currently alive will see their 105th birthday. Getting to 90 is already no big deal – witness the number of 'Happy Ninetieth' birthday cards in shops – and 100 is increasingly common.

After you reach the stage of wanting to use your pension pot to provide an income – known in the pensions world as *decumulation* (the opposite of the accumulation in Chapter 14) – you can do anything you like with your pension savings. Some ideas are good, some absolutely terrible. This is the price of freedom: you're free to make big mistakes that will leave you in pernicious pensions penury as well as take sensible strategies that will enhance your life and that of your family.

You're free to use your entire pension pot to purchase a Ferrari. But given that the typical retirement lump sum is around £35,000, many wouldn't get much further than the wheels. You're equally free to spend an amount each year on riotous living. It's a version of *SKI-ing* (spending the kids' inheritance). You can buy a new kitchen or put the latest massive-screen 3D television in every room in the house. Or you can pay off all your credit card debts.

Nothing stops you doing any of that. And for many, having a bit of blow-out on retirement is a reward for a life of work. That's fine, provided you keep within bounds. For after you stop working, your ability to contribute further to a pension is also likely to cease as well. You've left accumulation and are in the decumulation phase.

I assume in this chapter that you won't blow all your pension on a Bentley. I also assume you'll sit back, either during the years just before your planned retirement date or afterwards if you have some other income, to plan a strategy. This is the biggest financial decision of your life. Moving home or changing a mortgage if you make a mistake isn't hard. However, reversing some retirement income decisions can be tough, or even impossible.

Driving the change

Pensions freedom was driven by the unpopularity of *annuities* – products from insurance companies that guaranteed an income for the rest of your life, and sometimes that of your spouse as well. Annuities, which remain an option (see later in this chapter), fell out of favour because they locked in your money until you died so you only had one opportunity to make the right decision – one that some insurance company-based pensions providers tried to hijack so you made the wrong decision. It didn't help that

rates paid fell sharply. You may have to live for 20 to 25 years before even getting back the money you invested.

On top of all that, annuities are *opaque* – that's finance industry jargon for something that advisers can't or won't explain to the customer. Everything about annuities, from the way rates are calculated to the commission advisers receive, is covered in multiple layers of impossible-to-penetrate maths and jargon.

The new freedoms allow you to plan what you want, when you want. You're not forced to do anything, so you can arrange your affairs around other earnings – perhaps from renting a property or part-time work or the state pension or pensions from employers. You have choices. One course of action may be to plan for a rising income for the rest of your life. A second could involve a few years of expensive living – those dream holidays, perhaps – followed by a decade of standing still with more to spend in your later years when illness may intervene.

Along with pensions freedom is the government's 'guidance guarantee'. At the time of writing, it wasn't clear what this would entail. The best-off probably already have financial advisers and can afford to pay their hourly rates. The rest of us may end up with a mix of online generic advice with face-to-face backup. Because it's free, ignoring the guidance would be daft – even if you later decide that the advice isn't for you.

Pensions freedom doesn't apply to those in *defined-benefits schemes* (also known as *final-salary schemes*) where your employer promises to pay a pension based on a percentage of your earnings in your last year (sometimes averaged over three or five years), multiplied by the time you've been in the scheme. These pensions are very valuable because they generally include annual increases plus generous provision for your dependants. You can transfer a defined-benefits pension into a personal pension (known as defined contribution) but this is rarely a good course of action. However, unscrupulous advisers try to persuade you to the contrary.

Considering the Tax on Your Pension Pot

Pensions freedom is not freedom from income tax. The next section shows how you could end up losing nearly half your pension pot if you decide on the option which allows you to take the lot and spend it. Remember that the first 25 per cent of any withdrawal does escape the tax net.

Paying income tax on withdrawals

Firstly, the good news. You can still take 25 per cent of your pensions pot as a tax-free lump sum. Whether you've saved up £10,000 or £1 million, the first quarter is yours to take and invest or spend as you like. Nothing has changed here. Most see taking the tax free sum as a no-brainer decision unless they have very old pension plans that guaranteed an income for life at levels that can't be replicated under present conditions. But with pensions freedom, no harm exists in leaving the lump sum until you need it.

After that 25 per cent, whatever you take as cash from your fund is taxed as if you earned it that year. It's added to all your other income.

Be warned: taking lots of money out of your pension plan to spend can lose you up to 45 per cent in tax! The tax measure prevents you taking all the pension and spending it. Tax can build up to such a massive amount that you need to consider it before working out an investment strategy.

Here's how the tax on pension withdrawals works. (The following examples are calculated using 2014–15 tax rates; although the numbers are subject to change, the basics won't alter.)

- ✔ Richard has a state pension of £7,500 a year and no other income. He doesn't currently pay income tax. He's built up a pension of £40,000. He takes £10,000 as his 25 per cent tax-free lump sum. He decides to cash in the £30,000 balance. This is now added to his £7,500-a-year income to produce a total of £37,500. He has to pay income tax on the £27,500 amount above his personal allowance of £10,000. He'll be taxed at 20 per cent, meaning he'll lose £5,500.

- ✔ Jean has a state pension plus part-time earnings adding up to £20,000 a year. She has a £100,000 pension pot. She takes a quarter (£25,000) tax free and decides she wants the balance of £75,000 to spend. She adds this to her income to give £95,000 and subtracts her £10,000 personal allowance. Her taxable income is £85,000. The first £31,865 is taxable at 20 per cent; the remaining £53,135 attracts a 40 per cent rate. Her bill is £27,627.

And the situation would be worse for someone with a very large pension pot because he'd end up in the top 45 per cent tax band. A person retiring with £500,000 would find at least £350,000 of it taxed at the 45 per cent rate – effectively losing nearly half his savings.

You only become liable for any income tax due when you withdraw money from your plan. Pensions freedom means most people leave the balance after their tax-free lump sum in a scheme, so they withdraw income as they want and don't get into high-rate tax bands. They can either keep the money with their present pensions provider or move it into a self-invested personal pension (SIPP). See the later section 'Leaving money in the pot'.

Factoring in your pension after you die

Until very recently, if you died with money still in a pension plan, it was taxed at a very high 55 per cent. Now this 'death tax' has been abolished. The new rules state that if someone is under 75 when they die, the dependants pay no tax if they continue to draw an income from the fund. And if the person is over 75, those who benefit from the fund pay tax at their own top rate of tax – the income is added to their other earnings.

This could be a vital factor in how you choose to manage your decumulation because dependants can use any pension fund remaining to help carry on with their lives. Many other pension schemes only offer reduced benefits to partners or non-adult offspring after the main scheme holder dies.

The freedom could have a major impact on your retirement investment strategy, especially if you have a substantial pension pot. If you thought more than half of what was left in your fund on death would go to the state, you may have decided on high-income investments that you then spent. Now – assuming you have enough for day-to-day living – you can look further ahead, selecting assets for longer-term capital growth.

The ability to plan for the future instead of trying to spend as much as you can for the present means you can adopt an investment strategy offering potential protection against rising prices and those additional needs that can affect extreme old age. It reduces the fear that you may run out of money.

Leaving money in the pension fund, instead of spending it or moving it, makes sense. Suppose you withdrew the money to purchase a buy-to-let property investment. You'd pay tax at your top rate on that cash – almost certainly at 40 per cent – and then, on your death, the flat or house would go into your estate and be taxed at a further 40 per cent through inheritance tax. The same maths would apply if you withdrew your pension money to buy an Individual Savings Account. The ISA has no income or capital gains tax – just like your pension fund – but it counts as part of what you leave on death for inheritance tax.

If you can leave some of the money in your pension fund after your death, your family will be better off. Of course, you don't have to leave the money to your dependants or family if you don't want to.

Leaving money in the pot

The preceding sections largely read like a tax manual with very few mentions of how to invest your money. But elsewhere in this book I say you should never let the tax tail wag the investment dog. A very good reason exists for this apparent contradiction. Outside the ISA, most investments that come with tax benefits carry a high risk or a very high risk of failure, such as Venture Capital Trusts (VCTs) and companies in the Enterprise Investment Scheme (EIS). You can too easily see the magic words 'tax free' or 'tax saving' and throw caution and common sense to the wind. Never invest in anything that carries one of these labels if you wouldn't be prepared to put your money into that asset without any tax benefits.

Your pension in retirement is different. You have to make decisions about your dependants and about tax – to take the pot and spend it, or to keep it in the plan – irrespective of any investment strategy. Whether what you do with your money is ultra-cautious, middle of the road or verging on the adventurous, you'll have more of your own money if you keep your pension pot in its fund, or transfer it into another specially designed *drawdown fund* – that's one where you can easily switch investments and withdraw money when you need it. Most drawdown funds are varieties of SIPPs. At this stage of life, aiming for the lowest-cost plain-vanilla version makes sense.

Pensions freedom ends all complications around drawdown pensions such as the need to have a minimum pension from other sources or working out whether capped or flexible drawdown is better. Now you can do what you like and withdraw your money as you want. If you have income from earnings, you may also be able to increase your pension pot with further contributions.

Think of your pension fund as a box (the pensions industry prefers the term *wrapper*). As long as your money remains in the box, it's safe from the tax authority. After you take it out, you have to expect to pay some tax. The trick is to only take out what you need, when you need it. The Treasury, which makes the rules, argues that as you (and your employer) have had tax relief on the money you put into the pension when you were accumulating it, so it's only right that you should pay tax on the proceeds when you come to spend it in retirement.

Working Out Your Personal Accounts

When I wrote the first edition of *Investing For Dummies* in that dim, distant world of over a decade ago, annuities were the only option. You had to buy one when you reached 75, although most people purchased this income for the rest of their lives when they were far younger – typically, their early 60s.

The annuity buyer didn't get much choice. Options were limited to taking the maximum on offer (knowing that if you died the next day, the insurance company providing the annuity kept it all), or having a dependant's benefit, or taking a plan that promised annual upgrades in line with inflation. The second two choices – and variations and permutations on these themes – paid less.

That's all past tense these days. Now the annuity is just one of several choices. Those approaching retirement need to assess, perhaps with their families, just what they want out of their pension savings. That means working out a projected income and expenditure account to last the remainder of their lives. It's personal budget time!

Determining income

The personal pension pot is a source of income. But for some it won't be all they receive.

On one side of your household balance sheet is the amount you (and any partner) will get each year from any, some or all of these four potential sources of income:

- **State pension:** Almost everyone qualifies.

- **Occupational pension:** Many can count on something from former employers.

- **Guaranteed pensions:** The 'too good to be true' guaranteed pensions from old-style personal pension funds (mainly those taken out before 1986) – these offer rates so high to the holder that they're almost impossible to replicate in current financial conditions.

- **Earnings:** The idea of every male retiring at 65 and every female at 60 years of age (and their collecting an inscribed carriage clock from grateful colleagues) has long since gone. Retirement is now flexible, and although the average age for quitting work is around 62, many continue well past that. Retirement depends on your occupation – carrying on with a manual job is more difficult than one that demands less physical energy – and it may depend on whether you enjoy what you do. Many elect, of course, to work fewer than the standard five days a week.

On the other side of your budget, you need to produce a realistic estimate of your running costs – that's everything from food to holidays, from insurance to transport, and from entertainment to repairs and replacements.

Remembering all you spend in a year isn't easy (and you have to do a full year because some payments, such as home insurance or the television licence, can be annual), so fish out your old bank and credit-card statements. Adjust for any changing spending patterns on retirement such as not needing to travel to work and not needing such smart clothes, to requiring more heating at home because you're no longer out so much. Then add 10 per cent to cover the unexpected.

Setting a strategy

The income and expenditure on your personal account (see the preceding section) end up in one of the following configurations:

- ✔ Income is larger than expenditure.
- ✔ The two sides of the equation are roughly equal.
- ✔ Spending is greater than income.

Which category your personal budget falls into determines your investment strategy.

Because you have the freedom to be flexible, you can adjust strategy as you go along. So, for instance, someone who works part-time may consider he'll stop entirely in five years' time. Many people also come up with an 'ill health' strategy that reflects higher costs as well as – sorry to be blunt here – a potentially shorter lifespan. However, people are, on average, living longer. If you reach 65, you'll typically make your early eighties if you're male and your mid-eighties if you're female.

Most of the pension ideas that I list in the following sections are also suitable if you're already in a drawdown pension plan. But if you turned your pot into an annuity, you're stuck with it, for better or for worse. This is, of course, one of the biggest disadvantages with an annuity – what you take out at 65 may not be the best idea when you reach 85 or 95. (For more on annuities, see the later section 'Taking the Route of Least Resistance with an Annuity'.)

Giving up a guaranteed pension from an employer or an old-style personal pension is almost never a good idea. And the state pension comes as standard. But not all personal pension plans are geared up for flexible withdrawal. You may also have a number of smaller plans that you want to consolidate. In these instances, you need to transfer your pots into a SIPP drawdown scheme.

Bringing in more than you spend

Lucky you. You don't need your pension at the moment and may not want to dip into it for some years. On the other hand, betting the whole pot on forestry in France or gold in Gambia would be more than stupid.

Take a look at your existing investment strategy. You may well have avoided the 'lifestyle' investment option that I describe in Chapter 14, where over time your portfolio moved from equities into less-volatile assets such as cash and bonds.

You can afford to take a moderately adventurous route, keeping the fund invested in stock-market funds, or (and this needs more work but entails lower costs) directly in shares. Over most time periods, even those as low as five to ten years, equities have outperformed other assets. Your retirement could last 25, 30 or more years, so you really could do well over that time with shares – even if no guarantee exists.

TIP

Look at middle-of-the-road, 'generalist' investment trusts, tracker funds and unit trusts in mainstream equities in the UK, with some global reach in addition. Choose equity-income funds so you take a mix of capital growth and dividends rather than aim at all-out capital appreciation.

But what if this happy scenario were to end? What if the work dried up or your costs increased? This shouldn't happen overnight, so you have time to 'de-risk' the portfolio, moving more into bonds and cash. If change does happen suddenly, however, this strategy allows for a quick exit. Provided you don't put all your eggs in one basket (or put them all in baskets with holes in them), you should be able to move some of your assets into cash without too much pain.

Balancing present income with current spending

This isn't a bad place to be. But although life's good for the moment, the glow may not last. Aging often brings fewer earning opportunities, if you're reliant on wages from work, and additional costs such as employing people for tasks like decorating or gardening that you once did for yourself.

Here are two strategy ideas:

- ✔ Use the portfolio ideas in the previous section, but reduce your holdings in equities by the amount your household needs to live on for one year. Keep that cash in your pension drawdown account. It's a buffer. If you need it in the future then it'll give you time to sort out other assets. If you don't need the buffer, it'll carry on being there for you. Think of it as a sort of insurance policy against the unexpected whose premium is the gap between what you can expect as interest from cash (not much!) and the likely return from equities.

✔ Aim your pension pot at more aggressive dividend payers in shares via higher-yielding equity-income funds coupled with property investment and corporate bonds. Access all these via unit trusts for simplicity. An alternative would be a portfolio of absolute and real-return funds – the two labels are much the same – but this area is unproven over any real long-term time period, so it's not a sector for more than perhaps a quarter or at most a third of your pot.

Needing more than is coming in

This is the most frequent of my three scenarios; hardly surprising because retirement for most is running down what they built up during their working lives. Depending on how big your pension pot is, you may bridge the gap between income and spending with dividends from unit trusts at the high yield end. This is taking the 'natural yield', leaving your capital intact and available to grow.

Dividend yields tend to be more stable than capital values. This strategy should mean income is constant, and maybe rising a little, even if the underlying value of your investments has dropped or is proving volatile.

But the time may come, sooner or later, when that's not enough. You'll have to dip into your capital, even though doing so will erode future possibilities in both income and growth. This gives the option of taking gains on winning investments before any downturn.

Ignore advisers who suggest maximising income. Going for the highest dividend payers and dipping into capital isn't difficult, but unless you need the money, taking it out of your personal pension portfolio is pointless. You'll have less investment power for the future and hand over more in taxes.

Consider bond funds for consistency of long-term payouts, but don't expect too much out of any capital growth. Bond prices have been chased up to some of the highest levels ever seen, so the potential to go further ahead is limited. Meanwhile the chance of prices falling is great because interest rates are more likely to go up (bad for bond values) than come down further.

Look out for innovation as pensions freedom grows in importance. Low-cost, no-frills drawdown vehicles are designed to appeal to those with smaller pension pots. And some product providers are working on drawdown plans with specified monthly or annual income. This is 'annuity-very-lite' – someone with a £30,000 pot may be offered £100-a-month income, much like a classic annuity but with no guarantees. The product managers work out how this payment is funded. The plan holder is free to take his money elsewhere or buy an annuity or change the amount each month as he likes.

Taking the Route of Least Resistance with an Annuity

Annuity sales started to tumble the moment pensions freedom was announced, even though that was a year before the idea turned into reality. Many of those who could afford to do so delayed taking their retirement benefits. The number taken out halved overnight – and the share prices of specialist providers followed the same steep downward curve.

Surprise? No. The real shock is why anyone at all should want an annuity if he doesn't have to buy one, given all the well-publicised disadvantages (see the earlier sidebar 'Driving the change').

Here are some reasons for choosing an annuity:

- ✓ **Not small enough, not big enough:** Those with up to three funds worth no more than £10,000 each can take their entire pension pot in cash under 'trivial commutation rules'. Those with six-figure personal pensions can afford to look at drawdown strategies, including those I set out in the section 'Bringing in more than you spend'. This leaves those in the middle, typically with £25,000 to £50,000, whose pots aren't small enough to take in cash but not big enough to be seen as worthwhile candidates for drawdown.

- ✓ **Inertia:** It's the easiest route to a retirement income. You don't have to do anything – you can even accept the deal from your pension provider, even though regulators say that this rarely offers the best value.

- ✓ **Longevity insurance:** An annuity is a life insurance policy in reverse. With life cover, you pay each month and the beneficiary collects a large lump sum should you die. The annuity provider, usually an insurance company, pays you each month and collects your lump sum when you die. Annuity firms are now pushing their products on the grounds that they offer insurance against living a very long time and exhausting the pension pot. It's their top sales line when faced with pensions freedom.

Here are three key points to keep in mind about annuities:

- ✓ After you buy an annuity, you can't change your mind.

- ✓ Nothing stops you buying a series of smaller annuities over time should you like.

✔ All annuities look at your age but they're no longer allowed to differentiate between women and men (women came out of that change better).

✔ Annuity income is taxable like all retirement income, including the state pension.

Annuities come in all sizes, from as little as £5,000 to the sky's the limit. More importantly, they come in several shapes, with more to come because many of the rules governing annuities are also set for the scrapyard. Here are some of the 57 varieties which I have listed in value order – those that pay the most immediately get pride of place.

✔ **Level annuity:** Pays a set sum each month or year until you die.

✔ **Guaranteed annuity:** Promises to pay for five or ten (and perhaps more) years even if you die earlier.

✔ **Escalating annuity:** Payments rise each year in line with inflation or another measure.

✔ **Joint life annuity:** Pays out until both die but the second to die may have a lower payment.

✔ **Impaired life annuity:** This is for people in bad health or who smoke or who are substantially overweight. It recognises that they may die earlier than average, so the payment is greater. Some specialist annuity providers offer rates for those diagnosed with terminal diseases.

✔ **Postcode annuities:** Those living where life expectancy is lowest die on average eight to ten years before those inhabiting the highest-life-expectancy neighbourhoods. So these annuities recognize that those from deprived areas, where life expectancy is low, won't generally be able to claim for so long. As with the impaired life annuity, insurers compensate for the greater likelihood of dying earlier with higher payments each month. But even though, the rates for those likely to die earlier are better, they are never good enough to compensate for the fact they will probably be paid for fewer years. Here's the maths (and the figures also apply to many impaired life annuities). Someone in a deprived postcode receives 10 per cent more at £770 a year in return for each £10,000. They live for ten years so they get £7,700. The person is the high health area gets £700 a year but lives for twenty years making a return of £14,000.

Chapter 16

Selecting a Stockbroker or Financial Adviser

In This Chapter

▶ Knowing the level of service you want

▶ Sorting out advice from non-advice

▶ Discovering the costs

▶ Considering what questions to ask

▶ Understanding the sign-up process

Stockbrokers used to have an image – deserved or not. They supposedly wore pin-striped suits and bowler hats, arrived at work in the City from their large country homes around 10:15 a.m., went out for a long lunch at their club around 12:45 p.m. (where they started with several large gin and tonics and ended with several large brandies), returned to work at 15:30 p.m. and went home again around 16:30 p.m., travelling first class, of course. These days most stockbrokers work very long hours and take a sandwich lunch – but they can still earn enormous salaries and bonuses.

Financial advisers also used to have an image. Theirs was probably more deserved. They were people who found double-glazing sales too ethical and knew every trick in the book to fool customers into signing up for whatever product paid them the highest commission. That's no longer true either; although that change is just a few years old. Commission chasers are largely out of business, leaving what should be better-trained advisers who focus on your needs rather than their personal bank balances.

These days most investors never find out about either the lunching habits of stockbrokers or the new skills of financial advisers. Because the reality is that only a small minority need the services of a stockbroker and many do without financial advice – but not without financial advisers.

Selecting a stockbroker and financial adviser is a big decision, and one you want to get right. So this chapter explains what you need to know in order to choose an adviser or stockbroker to best meet your individual needs.

Understanding the Difference between Stockbrokers and Financial Advisers

Stockbrokers concentrate on buying and selling stocks and shares. Investors need the services of a stockbroker for most buying and selling transactions in shares and bonds, even when they don't want or require any help or advice in coming to decisions.

Unless you're determined to invest only in individual shares and bonds, you'll probably end up with a financial adviser as well. *Financial advisers* focus on collective investments such as unit trusts, but may also advise on pensions, mortgages, life insurance and other forms of protection insurance such as critical illness and income protection cover, as well as planning for other aspects of the future such as inheritance tax and university fees.

Two types of financial adviser exist:

- ✔ **Independent**: Financial advisers like to be called independent financial advisers or IFAs. But only some advisers can call themselves independent. They have to be able and willing to discuss the full range of investment options, from National Savings Premium Bonds to investment trusts, although that does not mean they must do so in every instance. These independent advisers are able to consider and recommend all types of retail investment products that could meet your needs (though they rarely venture past a select number of firms and funds). That doesn't mean, of course, that everyone needs everything.

- ✔ **Restricted**: These advisers can't use the independent label because they focus on a more limited selection of investment products and/or product providers. In some cases, they sell products from a substantial number of companies; in others they only sell products from one company. But whatever the number, they offer less than the 'whole of market' that the independents have to provide.

Both independent and restricted advisers must pass the same qualifications and meet the same requirements to ensure they're providing suitable advice. Firms should only employ qualified individuals who've had to pass a series of exams before they can be let loose on investors. These exams have become progressively more difficult to pass.

An adviser or firm has to tell you in writing whether they offer independent or restricted advice, but if you're not sure which they offer, you should ask for more information.

Many of the distinctions between stockbrokers and financial advisers are now blurred. Stockbrokers dealing with retail investors (as opposed to pension funds and other large institutions) often have either a financial advice arm in their organisation or close links to a financial advice firm. And some financial advisers can also arrange the purchase or disposal of stock market assets. You may, of course, have more than one adviser or stockbroker.

The few times when you don't need a stockbroker

Investors generally need a stockbroker when purchasing and disposing of shares and bonds. Brokers are there to take care of the mechanics involved in buying and selling rather than as sources of investment wisdom.

But you don't always need a stockbroker yourself (although sometimes one is working behind the scenes for the organisation you're dealing with). Here are some instances:

- ✔ Shares purchased during a flotation (also known as an initial public offering, or IPO).

- ✔ UK government stocks bought at the time of issue or the return of your investment if you hold the bonds until maturity.

- ✔ Investment trusts purchased through savings plans. You can sell these back to the scheme.

- ✔ Shares bought through a dividend reinvestment scheme, but not any subsequent sale, although a few companies with large registers offer share special dealing facilities from time to time.

- ✔ Special deals offered by some companies to investors who want to buy or sell. They may have a number of days in a year when you can buy without costs, for example, or promote special deals where you can dispose of very small amounts of shares that would otherwise be uneconomical to sell. Often they suggest giving very small amounts of shares to a charity.

- ✔ Unit trusts bought directly from a fund manager, including those bought via regular savings schemes.

And regarding that last item, here's a little tip for you: never buy unit trusts from fund managers directly unless they offer a big discount. Otherwise you end up paying more but receiving a lower level of service than buying directly from a financial advice firm gives you. And that's plain stupid. Most financial advisers offer a big upfront discount on the initial charge of around 5 per cent. How can they do that? They get a 0.5 per cent payment each year from the fund company. This is known as *trail commission*. Commission is now a tricky subject and only applies if you buy without advice, technically known as *execution-only*.

Deciding whether you'd like that service with or without advice

Any firm involved in dealing with the public on investments in the UK must be authorised by the Financial Conduct Authority (FCA). The FCA website (www.fca.org.uk) enables you to check on this matter.

Never deal with any firm that's not authorised. This warning includes financial concerns whose marketing material is 'authorised' by an FCA-approved adviser when the firm itself isn't on the list. Scam companies operating from tax havens sometimes hire UK lawyers to put their name to their adverts as 'approving the marketing material'. This marketing material usually consists of nothing more than the name of the firm and a phone number (often a UK number, but that's just to fool you). So all they're approving is the firm's name and phone. Not much, is it? Other scam firms clone the details of approved firms, including the names of their staff. Watch out for too-good-to-be-true offers that come to you out of the blue via telephone cold calling.

Click on to a number of IFA websites and you'll find details of recommended investments and, sometimes, a second list of those to shun. Click again, or apply for the same material by post, and you could be buying or selling the assets mentioned if you already have an agreement with this firm and it has details of your bank account. Remember that there is no easy or cost-free way of going back so make sure of what you want before you agree to buy or sell.

You may find a great deal of information, but if you think this is 'advice', think again. UK financial regulators have a different view of what constitutes 'advice' to most other people.

Your relationship with an adviser or stockbroker comes under two distinct headings, which also determine the nature of her remuneration (she has to earn her crust, after all).

- ✔ **With advice:** *Advice* here means you get individualised buy and sell recommendations that are designed to take in a whole range of your personal needs, including your attitude to risk, family circumstances, overall wealth, investment aims and any other investments you may already have. So here, you have contact with the adviser or broker, either face to face at your home or her office, on the phone or, more rarely, in writing. Financial advisers generally justify their advice in writing.

- ✔ **Without advice, or execution-only:** Here, you fill in a form in a newspaper or magazine, or reply to a mailshot the adviser or broker has sent, or click on a website. Unless you then opt for the individual advice service (see the preceding bullet), your relationship counts as 'without advice'. It doesn't matter that what you see has your personal details on it or includes terms such as *strongly recommend*, for example – it's still without advice according to the FCA. Execution-only can be a controversial area when it appears as though you're getting individual advice.

Many stockbrokers and financial advisers offer filtered lists of good-performing unit trusts and other investments. Some refine this further; for example, by offering lists specifically for people wanting income, for people approaching retirement or for people who are prepared to take above-average risks. Legally, these are recommendations and not advice. But such lists are a basis for your research.

Some IFAs send out leaflets that advertise funds. The funds themselves have paid to be included on these leaflets, so don't count these as a real recommendation from the IFA.

Pinpointing the Levels of Service Available

Stockbrokers dealing with private investors offer up to three levels of service. Two of the levels, advisory and discretionary, have been around for decades. The third, execution-only, is more recent and is the level most frequently sought by small investors.

Advisory service

The *advisory* level of service is where the broker contacts you personally and recommends a course of action. You're free to accept or reject this recommendation.

Discretionary service

With the *discretionary* level of service, you discuss your needs with a broker, such as a need for longer-term capital growth or a need for income now. Your stockbroker takes your money and then puts it into shares on your behalf.

The advantage is that someone's doing the work for you and is able to reduce the costs of individual share dealing by dealing for a number of clients requiring the same sort of portfolio at one go. The downside is that the stockbroker won't tell you about every transaction, although you receive regular updates.

With this level of service, you usually pay an annual fee rather than pay commission on each trade. The advantage of a fee over commission is that it removes any temptation for the broker to *churn* your portfolio – to make money from unnecessarily frequent trading.

Discretionary services are often a good idea for those with around £100,000 or more to invest and who want to hand either the whole amount to a professional or perhaps a large proportion so they can concentrate on managing the balance themselves. Some brokers offer discretionary services for those with smaller sums, but they're often based on investment and unit trusts rather than individual shares.

Execution-only service

This service has nothing to do with capital punishment! Instead, *execution-only* means you decide exactly what you want to do based on your own research and your own understanding of your needs. When you've come up with a buy or sell decision, you contact the broker, who'll then execute the deal for you via the stock market. This is the service level most frequently used by small stock-market investors.

Most execution-only services are online, but many brokers still offer phone dealing (likely to be more expensive) and a few deal by post. Postal buying and selling is usually confined to infrequent traders – perhaps those dealing once or twice a year. Many high-street banks also offer execution-only share-dealing services.

If you deal by post, the share price is determined when the broker carries out your order, not when you sent the instructions. The price can move either in your favour or against it in the meantime. This movement can be substantial. Dealing online or by phone minimises this risk. But because share values can be in constant flux, even a ten-second delay could mean prices move.

Knowing What You Can Expect to Pay

Financial advice and stockbroking services aren't free. Advisers and brokers generally expect a good lifestyle, irrespective of whether their input into your investment planning is successful. Only a tiny minority work on a success basis, and even then, you're still likely to pay some costs.

Commission

Until recently, IFAs worked for *commission*, a percentage of the amount you invested. A typical unit-trust deal paid the adviser 3 per cent of your money when you invested and a further 0.5 per cent per year of the value of your holding in *trail commission* thereafter. Lump-sum insurance investments, including with-profits bonds, paid the adviser up to 8 per cent. This gave scope for *product bias* – telling investors to buy one product rather than another because it was more profitable for the adviser (and often less profitable for the individual).

Commission is now banned – but only for advice (rather than execution-only recommendations). Besides product bias, the regulators stopped it because too many investors thought they were getting something for nothing because they didn't directly pay for the advice.

Advisers have to eat, of course, so they must be remunerated in other ways. These can include:

- ✔ An annual or monthly set fee.
- ✔ A fee based on a percentage of the funds the adviser advises you on, paid via a cheque from the client or a deduction from a client's investment.
- ✔ A rate per hour for the work carried out – in much the same way as lawyers and accountants often charge. If the adviser charges per hour, ask for an estimate of how many hours the work should take. Expect to pay between £100 and £200 per hour.
- ✔ A mix-and-match menu of the preceding options.

Your adviser should put all this in writing and also make it clear what happens to any commission that comes from investments you already have. Your adviser would normally rebate this against your costs.

Platform payments

Commission still applies when the adviser gives no advice: the investor has opted for execution-only. And because you buy most unit trusts via platforms – notably Co-funds or Fidelity Funds, although some big IFA firms, such as Hargreaves Lansdown, operate their own – understanding the cost structure is worthwhile. The platform can levy fees on the investor which end up with the adviser. Remember, whether it is called commission or not, there are fees to pay.

Payments for platforms have changed to bring greater clarity to the process, so you can see exactly where your money goes:

- ✔ **The old system** of paying commission applies to funds bought before 6 April 2014 unless they've been topped up with a lump sum. Investment companies adjusted unit prices to pay the various parties with an involvement in the annual management charge (AMC) – the adviser, the platform and the fund manager. Usually, you paid an AMC of 1.5 per cent. This would be divided up so the fund manager typically got 0.75 per cent, the intermediary (or adviser) 0.5 per cent and the platform itself collected 0.25 per cent.

- ✔ **The new system** applies to investments made on or after 6 April 2014. It allows for 'commission-free share class funds' that have a lower AMC; generally, 0.75 per cent. This sum all goes to the fund manager. The platform makes a separate charge – generally around 0.2 to 0.25 per cent. And the adviser may get nothing because you're already paying the firm in some other way, such as an annual fee or a percentage-of-funds fee. Most new investments now end up in the commission-free class. This new way of paying also applies to Individual Savings Accounts (ISAs).

Advisers can still charge commission on non-investment products such as life insurance. Arranging a £500,000 insurance-bond deal involves no more work than arranging one for £100,000. But the adviser could earn five times as much on the larger sum. So if commission still applies, you've scope for haggling.

Based on the level of service

Stockbroking costs vary based on the level of service you choose:

- ✔ **Advisory service:** Expect to pay around 2 per cent on each purchase or sale deal. After that, you could pay up to £250 an hour for the broker's time. Unless you're a very rich client, you're likely to have a junior broker as your personal adviser.

- ✔ **Discretionary service:** A wide range exists, but typical charges are around 1.5 per cent on each transaction, plus a 2 to 3 per cent annual management charge.

- ✔ **Execution-only service:** If you're reading this book, this is the most likely service level you'll aim for. You'll almost certainly deal on the Internet, although less choice exists than there once was. At the height of the dotcom boom in 1999–2000, some 40 firms were chasing business. Most have now amalgamated one with the other out of necessity or just gone out of business. So the result is the end of some of the cut-throat competition where many brokers offered free (other than stamp duty) dealing for a fixed period. Those that are left usually charge the same amount no matter how big your buy or sell order is. Expect to pay a minimum £35 for a basic sale and £40 plus stamp duty for a purchase – more if you deal by phone. Post can be cheaper, but both buying and selling take time. Some services amalgamate all their orders over a period such as a week or a month.

Getting carried away by online dealing is all too easy. At its simplest, you click a button and have either bought or sold. But you're dealing with real money (and your own money), not Monopoly money. Execution-only stockbroking means no one's around to say, 'Stop! Think before you act because you could be making a big mistake!'

Knowing What to Look at When Selecting a Stockbroker

If you come from a fabulously wealthy background, you probably already have a family stockbroker. If not, read on.

Considerations with discretionary and advisory services

Discretionary and advisory services rely on at least some face-to-face contact between you and a stockbroker and the broker's need to find out exactly what you want out of your investment strategy. So you may need to do some shopping around to find a stockbroker who's right for you. Areas to look at include:

✔ **Size of portfolio:** Make sure that your personal wealth is well within the broker's parameters. If the broker wants a minimum £25,000 then having £25,001 isn't much help because you could easily fall below the line if markets turn against you. Ask what happens if your fortune shrinks either through bad decisions or because you choose to spend some of your money. In reality, the broker who sets the minimum at £25,000 really means £50,000.

✔ **Level of service:** Consider the experience of your contact or account executive, as well as whether she'll send out email alerts and regular newsletters or other forms of stock recommendation. Find out whether the broker offers a portfolio based on unit trusts, investment trusts or exchange-traded funds.

✔ **Costs:** This shouldn't be your first consideration, but it's essential all the same. Excessive costs can wipe out gains from a clever investment strategy. Very excessive costs can turn good decisions into instant losses.

✔ **Protection from churning:** Unscrupulous brokers try to earn more from your investments by over-frequent buying and selling. You can agree to a limit on their trading activity.

For a listing of potentially suitable brokers, contact APCIMS, the Association of Private Client Investment Managers and Stockbrokers, at `www.thewma.co.uk/`

Considerations with execution-only services

Investors who want to make up their own minds don't need advice, but they do need a broker to carry out the transaction. Most dealing is on the Internet.

The advantages of online dealing are obvious: being able to buy and sell anytime, from anywhere; seeing how your portfolio is performing in real time; and getting up-to-date prices, charts and news. But drawbacks exist too. The obvious one is backup if your computer or Internet connection fails. Some online brokers have a telephone alternative.

Most Internet broker security breaches occur because investors – while at their workplace – leave their computers connected to the broker site or leave password details lying around for anyone to find. Don't.

Sticking to one broker

Try to use one broker for all your transactions. This isn't a legal necessity, but the way online brokers operate and charge makes having more than one broker difficult. Many online brokers offer terms that make sticking with one organisation cheaper. You have to set up a bank account if you do anything more than occasional dealing. And setting up portfolios that reflect your trading at another broker is very difficult.

Online charges are low because very little paperwork is involved. You won't normally receive certificates because your portfolio is in a nominee account with Crest (the London Stock Exchange centralised settlement system) so the broker can instantly buy or sell on your behalf. Most online brokers insist on a nominee account and an associated bank account so that cash for purchases can move out without fuss and you have a receptacle for money you generate on a sale.

Most online brokers hold your money in an account in their name, so the company you're investing in doesn't know that you're a shareholder. You may lose your rights to shareholder material, such as annual reports (but you can usually find these online at the company's website), as well as voting privileges and any other shareholder perks. Most investors live without voting, and worthwhile shareholder perks are few and far between. If these points are important to you, your broker may offer you an individual nominee account, but that could cost more. Some companies now offer arrangements for individuals to use the votes that come with their shares held in broker nominee accounts.

Small print points to ponder

If you're considering an execution-only service, here are some additional points to consider:

- ✔ **Computer compatibility:** Not all stockbroker sites support Mac- or Linux-based machines. A few financial sites struggle if you don't use Microsoft Internet Explorer as your Internet browser.

- ✔ **Trading range:** All brokers cover mainstream UK shares. But if you fancy tiny UK companies on the ICAP Securities and Derivatives Exchange (ISDX), traded options or overseas shares then your choice may be more limited.

- ✔ **How many extras you get:** Look for easy-to-use EPIC code finders (these are the letters that professionals use – for example, Marks & Spencer is MKS), a good stock-history facility, easy access to company statements and stock-exchange filings, research reports and analyst ratings. Are these things free?

- ✔ **How much money you need to open a trading account:** Some brokers are only interested in the very wealthy and demand that you deposit big sums. But all want something to cover your trades, otherwise they can't deal for you. The days when a 'gentleman' would be allowed to run up large bills are over, except maybe for the most blue-blooded brokers and their wealthiest clients.

- ✔ **Extra charges:** These charges may be for statements of dividends and capital gains (or losses) so you can file your annual tax return more easily. You may also pay a fee for sending proceeds of sales to another account.

- ✔ **Whether the broker is set up to offer another service channel:** Does the broker offer a phone or postal service if the Internet breaks down or if you want to deal occasionally on an obscure overseas market?

- ✔ **Whether the service is in real time:** Does the broker act on your decision at once, or does it depend on email? That matters if you're a frequent trader.

- ✔ **What interest, if any, the broker pays on your cash balances:** You'll have cash balances with your broker either because you've deposited cash ahead of purchases or because you have cash from a sale of shares or bonds. Either way, many brokers offer you interest while the money is under their roof. But don't expect much. Interest can be as little as 0.1 per cent.

> ✔ **Whether a fill or kill facility exists:** With this kind of arrangement, you set a maximum price for a purchase and a minimum acceptable price for a sale. If the broker can't fulfil your instructions, the deal is automatically terminated.

Many brokers have a sampler service, meaning you can try out the site on a dry-run basis. You may find that you're willing to sacrifice some services and pay more for a broker that offers a site that's easy to navigate. Once you click Go, you've dealt, so don't make mistakes.

Signing Up with a Stockbroker

You can't just use a stockbroker, online or in any other form, in the same way as a grocery store. You have forms to fill in and bureaucracy to satisfy.

After you choose an online stockbroker for execution-only services (where you make all the decisions, leaving the technical bits of buying and selling to the broker), you need to open an account.

Brokers have to follow rules designed to combat money laundering, so they need to check that you are who you say you are. This process involves sending in your national insurance number online and may be followed by a request for hard-copy documentation, such as your passport and proof of address from a utility bill (gas, water, electric, fixed-line phone). If you've moved recently, you may have to provide details of past addresses for the previous three years. In addition, the broker needs details of your main bank account and needs to know whether you're a UK citizen.

After you complete these formalities, which can take two weeks or more, you need to send cash to open your trading account. The minimum varies from £100 to £50,000. Most brokers arrange for you to move the cash electronically from your bank account. Some want a cheque, primarily as a further security check. The cheque may take up to two weeks to clear if it comes from a building society. Allow a week otherwise.

You may also want to transfer investments into your new account. If you're moving all your stocks and shares from another broker then the broker you're ditching and the new broker whose services you're signing up to should be able to sort everything out after you've given permission.

Getting a new broker is a good time to dematerialise all those old share certificates and put them on an electronic basis so the broker records all your purchases and sales on a computer. You end up with a statement that you can print. It's just the same as dealing with your bank where you get an electronically generated statement and not the actual bits of paper. Share certificates are nothing but a nuisance, especially if you lose them.

A few old share certificates have collector-item value. You can arrange to have them cancelled and returned to you.

Dealing with IFAs

Most investors deal with stockbrokers for just a small part of their overall wealth. Only a handful of investors concentrate on individual stocks and shares to such an extent that they can do without financial advisers.

For the rest, areas such as collective funds, insurances, pensions and tax advice on investment matters probably involve financial advisers. But this isn't to say that you need an IFA for advice. If you've read this book and other *For Dummies* titles on personal finance, you're probably as clued up as an adviser. However, you need a financial advice firm to carry out the mechanics of investment and pension purchase and disposal. And although you can do almost anything that advisers do yourself, doing so rarely saves you any money. In fact, in many instances going it alone could cost you money.

It's impossible to repeat too often that dealing directly with a unit-trust company or an insurance company or a pensions provider is no cheaper than going via an adviser. That sounds counter-intuitive – in most other purchasing decisions, the nearer you are to the source, the cheaper it gets. But financial companies aren't interested in dealing with individuals. Their whole sales focus is on the financial adviser, and they don't want to annoy these people by allowing you to undercut them.

Finding a discount IFA

The secret to finding the best place for your non-advised dealings is to find a *discount IFA*. These should rebate all or most of the upfront commission they'd otherwise earn. This rebate can be substantial. It's normally 3 per cent on unit trusts, but can be up to 8 per cent on some lump-sum insurance bonds. It can be money for old rope – it comes out of your savings, whatever the firm says, so you have less for the future. Most financial advice firms now offer rebates to execution-only customers.

So how do discount IFAs earn their living? Via one of the best-kept secrets in the broking world – *trail commission*.

Every year, the company behind your unit trust or most other investments (but generally not investment trusts) calculates how much your holding is worth. Then it sends 0.5 per cent of that amount to the person who sold you the product. This adds up to a huge amount if you hold a trust for 10 or 20 years.

Financial companies such as unit trusts and pensions providers claim that they pay the trail commission out of their own pockets, leaving the customer unaffected. Now although this may be strictly true, ponder it for a while. Before trail commission was thought up around 20 years ago, the average unit-trust annual charge was 1 per cent. Now it's typically 1.5 per cent. So although no specific deduction exists, the customer pays for it one way or another.

Always ask the adviser what you'll get in return for trail commission. It's supposed to pay for continuing advice and help. All too often, the commission is just a way of making money out of you. Ask whether you get (the best is first and the worst is last):

- ✔ A named individual who'll be available to discuss your investments and other financial affairs with you. This could count as real advice, in which case commission is banned although some advisers continue to collect trail commission on older investments for a year or two yet.

- ✔ A regular personalised update showing your investments, their value and whether the firm recommends you should carry on holding them or switch to another investment.

- ✔ A regular general update on financial markets, giving views but leaving you to make up your own mind. This may be an email.

- ✔ Sales material on new launches and other products that may be of use to you.

- ✔ Nothing.

A number of discount brokers share trail commission with you. If you feel you're getting no service or one that's inadequate for your needs from your present IFA, you can switch these investments to another adviser who'll rebate trail commission. In some cases, the broker will return all the money except for an annual fee of around £35 to £75. If the fee is £50, you'll make a profit if your holdings top the £10,000 mark.

Don't expect great service from advisers who do nothing other than share this commission with you, but it's a lot better than giving cash to another firm each year and getting little or nothing back. The track record of many IFAs who don't share commission can be little better.

Signing up with a financial adviser

This should be very simple. All you have to do is to buy a product and produce identification documents. The documents required vary from adviser to adviser but generally consist of national insurance number, a copy of a recent bank statement to show your address and a copy of a passport or driving licence.

Determining whether the adviser's adding real value

Is your adviser really adding value, or just reading to you what's available on the Internet for free from packaged product makers – or copying that info word for word and sending it out as the advice firm's view? Obviously, advisers need a reference because no one can learn and remember all the facets of a portfolio. But the interpretation is what makes the difference.

A good test is to see how critical the broker or adviser is of heavily advertised products. An adviser who says 'I don't know' is at least being honest and not trying to sell something doubtful. Some advisers bombard their client list with 'flavour of the month' funds or those that are just about to be launched.

Never send a financial adviser additional fees unless the service is limited to recovering all or some of the trail commission.

Chapter 17

Hedging Your Fund Bets

. . . .

. . . .

*T*he reputation of hedge funds is appalling. I can't put it a nicer way. It's bad, terrible, dreadful. People blame hedge funds for almost everything, from the collapse of banks to the collapse of currencies to the collapse of jobs. And I've probably left out a few collapses. Additionally, many are unregulated and offshore, or if they're subject to a rulebook, it's a very slim one.

But although many make huge sums for their managers and investors, many also fail. You hear a lot less about the duds than the stellar performers. Hedge funds are very risky and about as far as you can get from a one-way bet to riches. Thousands fail every year, mostly in total obscurity, even secrecy. The majority make nothing for their investors, although promoters probably turn a pretty penny.

So why look at hedge funds then? The simple fact is that you can't ignore them. They wield enormous market power. They're part of many pension investment plans; although, controversially, Calpers – the California State Pension, which is worth around $300 billion – is halving its hedge fund investments. Others may follow – or perhaps not; no rulebook exists.

As importantly, hedge funds (or funds run on a similar basis) are increasingly available to investors outside the millionaire bracket. One increasingly popular mainstream form of collective is the absolute-return fund that I describe in this chapter. Additionally, many investment trusts, including those aimed at savers investing perhaps £100 a month, now feature hedge funds in their portfolios. So your future fortune may be riding on one of these funds without your knowledge. They're the genie that you can't force back into the bottle.

For all these reasons, you need to know about hedge funds and how they work, even if you can't or don't want to invest in them. Most people won't take their money to these funds, but knowing how they operate helps you better understand what's going on – and perhaps gives you some tactics that you can use. That's where this chapter comes in.

Defining Hedge Funds

Hedge funds – sometimes (and confusingly) called alternative investments even though they have nothing in common with old-style investment alternatives such as classic cars or stamp collections – have been around since the late 1940s. Literally tens of thousands of them exist around the globe. Strictly speaking, the term *hedge fund* only refers to a specialised legal structure. A hedge fund is a private-partnership contract where the manager has a substantial personal interest in the fund and is free to operate in a variety of markets using a number of strategies. Think of a hedge fund as giving investors' money to a manager who has unfettered freedom to invest in areas other funds can't reach. These freedoms include the ability to

- Be flexible. Most hedge-fund managers can do what they like within wide parameters. They're not restricted by trust deeds to a narrow range of equities or bonds like traditional collectives, although some have stated strategies that limit their scope.

- Go short. Ordinary fund managers only select shares they think will do well and hence go up, a technique known as *going long*. Hedge-fund managers can also choose equities they think will sink, making money as the shares fall, a technique known as *going short* or *short selling*. If hedge-fund managers see a company in serious trouble, they can take a one-way bet on the shares going down to zero. When other investors see hedge funds attacking the company in this way, they sell as well, putting extra pressure on the share price.

- Employ derivatives, such as futures, options and some very exotic bets on interest rates, currencies and even *volatility*, which is the speed with which an investment moves up or down. Stacks of strategies exist here – enough to fill a whole shelf with *For Dummies* books on them.

- Move in and out of cash, currencies, commodities, gold and property as well as other investments at high speed.

- Use borrowings (known as *gearing* in the UK and *leverage* in the United States) in an aggressive fashion to improve returns. Of course, if they get it wrong then borrowing works against them.

Note that *hedging* is a term that's been used in commodity trading for over a century. It denotes a technique where producers and users of a commodity, such as silver or sugar, protect themselves against sudden price shocks. It has to do with risk reduction. Likewise, some hedge funds set out to cut back on risks, but many were established to take higher-than-average risks in the hope of really big rewards. A few are huge, with billions of dollars in assets. (The whole hedge-fund world works in US dollars wherever they're based.) But many hedge funds are small so that managers can operate freely and without the trading constraints that moving a billion or two in financial markets invariably brings.

Hedge funds came to prominence first in the 1990s as top fund managers quit unit and investment trust firms to make more money for themselves by setting up their own hedge funds. Hedge-fund managers take performance fees. If they do well, their contract gives them a hefty slice of the gains. If they flop, they earn comparatively very little, even if it's still a lot compared with your salary slip. Of course, they rarely give investors a refund of their earnings from the good times if they make a mess.

You can only access hedge funds via a stockbroker or other regulated professional adviser. Getting information on funds can be difficult because most are secretive, and many of them operate out of tax havens where corporate governance rules are lax. Whatever you're advised to do, always check that you're happy with the management firm and where it's based before considering moving a penny in its direction.

Choosing Strategies

Broadly speaking, hedge funds fall into categories. Firstly, every hedge fund exists either to maximise returns or to offer a safe haven while trying to return more than an investor would get from leaving his money in cash deposits at the bank. Around half of all funds are run on a long–short strategy (see the section 'Opportunistic strategies' for the details). Beyond that, eight other well-defined strategies are available for managers to pursue. These strategies come under three main headings: relative value, event driven and opportunistic.

Relative-value strategies

This tactic is at the lower-risk end of the hedge-fund spectrum because it doesn't depend on whether or not the market is enthusiastic for oil companies or banks or food producers or automotive engineers, just on the relative values of two closely connected stock-market investments such as two banks or two oil companies. This is because the factors affecting one company in a sector are similar to those affecting a competitor company, especially over the short term. But the factors aren't so similar as to be the same.

With relative-value strategies, the hedge fund tries to profit from price gaps between the same or similar investments in different markets. For instance, some shares are quoted and traded on more than one stock market. Minor differences between the two may exist, often only available for a minute or so, as local prices react to something happening in another country, or because the local stock market is more enthusiastic (or less keen) on shares themselves that day. You can also exploit currency differences. These differences are often minute, but multiply them by the millions of pounds, euros or dollars a hedge fund can throw at the difference and then do this several times and you can make a little bit more.

Keep in mind that in investment, the gap between the best and the worst often comes down to either a few lucky trades that make big bucks, or being able to score a tiny extra percentage over competitors most of the time. Scoring a few hundredths of a percentage point over the opposition each day is really where a fund wants to be.

Three main types of relative-value fund are available:

- ✔ **Convertible arbitrage:** Some shares have convertible bonds as well as conventional shares. Exploiting price differences can be profitable.

- ✔ **Fixed-income arbitrage:** This one is for the rocket scientists who try to make money by buying and selling bonds with the same credit risk (so they stick to UK gilts or US treasuries) but with different maturity dates or different headline interest rates.

- ✔ **Equity market neutral:** Traditional collective-fund managers try to find shares that will go up, but equity-neutral managers aren't concerned with the direction of markets or shares. Instead, they look for differences between shares and derivatives, so they may sell a bank share but buy a bank-based derivative. Another route is to sell overvalued shares and buy undervalued shares. It's up to the managers to decide which are overvalued and which undervalued – no flags fly here.

Event-driven strategies

This tactic focuses on shares in companies that are involved in takeovers, acquisitions and other forms of corporate restructuring. Big rewards await those who get this strategy right, and huge losses occur if all goes wrong.

Here are the main types of event-driven strategies:

- **Merger arbitrage:** This type concentrates on companies that are either acquiring or being acquired through takeovers. The shares often have a life of their own, independent of general market forces. Hedge-fund managers using this tactic hope to make money out of the fears of other investors that the deal will be scuppered by other shareholders or government regulators.

- **Distressed securities:** Here, managers try to make money from equities and bonds on the verge of collapse. Some hedge-fund managers end up with significant stakes in the company concerned, so they can influence any rescue attempt. Sometimes, the hedge fund wants the company to collapse to maximise its strategy. Because the hedge fund looks to the short term, it's probably not interested in long-term reconstruction attempts.

Opportunistic strategies

These are the riskiest hedge-fund strategies, promising high returns or threatening big losses. The hedge-fund managers bet on stock-market directions – up, down or sideways. But they can also invest in other areas, such as commodities, bonds and currencies.

Here are the main types of opportunistic strategies:

- **Long–short:** This is the big one, accounting for about half of all hedge-fund activity. The idea is that expert managers (often with a track record in equities or bonds elsewhere) aim for positive returns from a small portfolio of shares in companies they know well by either selling them (going short) if they think the price will fall or buying them (going long) as they see fit. Some go for more complicated tactics such as buying what they consider to be the best share in a sector and selling the weakest. So they sell the worst (in their opinion) oil company, for example, and buy the best. Or vice versa.

  Short selling usually involves shares that the fund never owned. Techniques to exploit price falls are more complicated than those used to gain from rising prices.

- **Macro:** With this tactic, the managers take bets on big worldwide movements in all sorts of markets but especially those where their activities are hidden by huge amounts of trading by others. They hope to second-guess market moves.

✔ **Short selling:** This type specialises in techniques to make money out of falling equity and bond values. It's a very high-risk tactic. If the investment moves the other way, the losses can be massive. Purchasers of shares who hope the price will rise can only lose their stake if the asset falls to zero. Now suppose that you sell a share with a £1 price, hoping to buy it back later at 50p and take out 50p a share profit, but you get it wrong. That share could soar to £2, £5 or who knows how high. So short sellers face limitless losses. And when markets are rising steeply, short-selling funds have to stay on the sidelines.

✔ **Emerging markets:** This type is really for the ultra-courageous. These are the riskiest hedge funds because they invest in less well-developed markets where information is sketchy, legal and administrative systems are often unstable, local politics are volatile, and the companies themselves are often run by managers who either lack experience or are corrupt. Most investors run a mile from this type. But hedge-fund managers see it as an opportunity to try to profit from the very problems that scare off others.

Finding an Easy Way In: A Fund of Hedge Funds

The easiest (and for many investors the only) way into hedge funds is via a Financial Conduct Authority-recognised fund of hedge funds. Managers of these funds buy into anything from 5 to 40 other funds, trying to spread the risk by diversifying managers and management styles. Some of these funds have the Individual Savings Account (ISA) annual limit, meaning that you can invest with £15,000, compared with the £100,000 minimum that most hedge funds want from individual investors. A number of these funds won't even send an application form to someone with less than £250,000 to invest.

The advantages for investors in funds of hedge funds are:

✔ Access to areas that are normally restricted to the ultra-wealthy

✔ Professional management, including constant monitoring

✔ A greater information flow than from often secretive funds

✔ Access to a variety of fund types

Many funds of funds come from major UK management groups, so investors have a good idea whom they're dealing with. Managers from these companies tend to sidestep hedge funds that don't comply with high disclosure standards. Your bet here is to hope the managers of your fund know what the managers of the other funds are doing. Some funds come surrounded by investor wealth warnings.

No strategy and no manager will always beat the odds. A manager who's successful in one market situation may fail in another. And a manager who's a big hit when heading a large team run by a major investment house may fail dismally as a hedge manager without the props of a team and a huge fund-management house employer. You have little comeback against a manager who fails to deliver. You have zero comeback if you buy into an offshore hedge fund that then goes bust.

Private investors with up to £15,000 can invest in a fund of hedge funds through an ISA. That's not quite the same as going directly to a hedge-fund manager, but your money will be in a variety of hedge funds.

Taking Hedging Some Stages Further

The big advantage of hedge funds is that they can make money when share prices fall as well as when they rise. But if the truth be told, many investors are scared of hedge funds or think they're only for those with hundreds of thousands, if not millions, to spare. So mainstream investment companies, such as unit-trust management firms, have come up with some new ideas based on hedge-fund thinking, but not carrying that label, that are accessible to investors with relatively small sums. Many start at £5,000 and some take as little as £1,000.

Only look at these fund ideas if you're experienced and able to withstand periods of losses. They're not intended for the first-time investor. Always check on how the managers intend to reward themselves. Some have been known to prioritise their own remuneration before that of their investors, so be careful.

Absolute-return funds: Hedge funds-lite from the mainstream

Absolute-return funds are aimed at the private investor, using many of the hedge-fund techniques I list in the previous sections, but in a UK-regulated fund. Their numbers have grown substantially, with many investors attracted by their aim of gaining in both rising and falling markets. You have around 60 UK funds to choose from, worth around £40 billion.

Don't be fooled by the name – there's nothing absolute about these funds and the returns can range from very positive to highly negative. Many managers now prefer the label *targeted return* to show they aim at slow but steady gains in all sorts of investment weathers.

Absolute-return funds are hedge funds in all but name. Their managers operate a flexible strategy: they can borrow, *sell short* (sell stocks they don't have) and go into futures, options and almost anything else they can think of to enhance their returns. Some adopt a strategy known as *market neutral*, where most of the fund aims to match the stock market, leaving a small proportion over for a handful of investments that the managers expect to rise substantially in price.

Their aim is to give a better return than cash in the bank but minimise the risks involved in big one-way bets on equities or bonds, where managers hope to make relative returns (that's relative to each other and not to any other investor requirement). But absolute return tries to give you gains over and above a set benchmark, such as what you'd get from a bank account.

Why have the funds become so widespread? They're approved by the Financial Conduct Authority, but more importantly, they appear to offer a new route to gradual gains, away from the big ups and downs of traditional funds. Making gains is far harder in a low-inflation, low-interest-rate environment. So absolute-return funds set their sights lower – and they're not afraid to put all or a large part of the portfolio in cash if other assets are uncertain.

So do these funds deliver what they say on the tin? Most absolute-return funds are still wet behind the ears, so the jury is still out on whether they work or not. Early indications show that most have neither made nor lost much money. Managers stress that investors shouldn't expect the funds to gain every single month. Instead, judge them over a five- to ten-year period during which almost anything can happen.

Absolute-return funds tend to charge higher fees than relative-return funds, so managers have to justify their high earnings. You pay annual fees plus a performance-related fee, which is usually high. The performance part should be charged on the amount a fund produces over and above a minimum level. Check that any fund you invest in has a high-water mark. This means that if a fund falls, it has to make up the losses and get back to where it was before it can charge again. Always check this high-water mark to see where it is. Some funds use cheeky tricks to move it down so that the managers earn more. Most absolute-return funds aim for cautious management, so if a fund screams 'exceptional returns' then it's likely the managers have taken big risks.

Don't expect absolute-return funds to shine if equities are soaring ahead. The higher that percentage, the greater the potential rewards but also the larger the possible risks. A fund advertising itself as cash plus 5 to 7 per cent would be higher up the risk ladder than a fund offering 2 to 3 per cent over the cash return. The first would appeal to adventurous investors; the second to more cautious savers.

Making money from yo-yo asset prices

How do you make money if interest rates stay stubbornly low and share prices end each year roughly at the same level they started? The answer to that problem could be to play *volatility*. This is a bet on whether short-term movements will be sharply up or down, or whether they'll show little difference day in, day out.

Volatility ignores whether markets are rising or falling. It's the speed and intensity of each move that counts. Investors usually concentrate on market indexes rather than individual equities, so if the Standard & Poor's index of US shares moves up 10 per cent one day and down 10 per cent the next, that's greater volatility than if it moved up 0.1 per cent and then down 0.1 per cent. Of course, in both instances the market is almost unchanged over two days. (The *almost* is because a percentage up and then the same down doesn't bring you back to zero.)

Think of a yo-yo. When it's working well, the ups and downs are substantial even though you end up in much the same place.

The most used measure of volatility is the VIX index, which is quoted by the minute and traded on stock markets. Investors can go for greater or lesser volatility with a number of strategies. In case you're wondering, VIX is short-hand for the Volatility Standard & Poor's 500 Index, and it measures movements in mainstream US stocks.

Some Do's and Don'ts: A Hedge-Fund Checklist

Because very few investors other than the ultra-rich have ever bought into a hedge fund, and because hedge funds are rarely mentioned in the press, precious little help and advice is immediately on hand for the average investor. So you have to tread very carefully. Here are the basic do's and don'ts:

✔ Do ensure that a hedge funds management company reveals just how it selects and monitors the hedge funds it includes in the portfolio you invest in.

✔ Don't let hedge funds hold more than a limited place in your portfolio. Most advisers say to limit them to 10 per cent of the portfolio's total value. So add up all hedge holdings and never put more than 10 per cent of your investment money into them.

✔ Do check that the adviser or broker understands hedge funds and is up to date with information on them. Some brokers offer free education packages to private investors.

✔ Do always be sure that you know about fees and charges. They can be significant and erode stated gains. Look for the high-water marks I explain in the section on absolute-return funds earlier in this chapter. But also look at what the fund compares itself against. Some increase fees when the fund beats a benchmark. Check to see whether this benchmark is easy or hard to better.

✔ Do take individual advice from an expert adviser to confirm that the investment is suitable.

✔ Don't invest if you're in doubt about a hedge fund or a fund of hedge funds. Hedge funds and your cash make a highly volatile mix, so if you're in doubt, just don't do it.

Following the trend to success

Were you ever accused of being a copycat at school? Are you worried about being a tracker rather than a trendsetter? One bunch of hedge funds is proud to be a copycat in investment fashion. They're called trend followers and they use computers to look for trading patterns across the globe. When they identify a trend, milliseconds later they go in on their coattails.

Trend followers are the fashion victims of the hedge funds world: funds that make money by copying exactly what everyone else has been doing. As with many investment ideas, trend-following trading strategies have gone in and out of fashion. For most of the past decade, computer-driven hedge funds have profited from identifying patterns across hundreds of different markets, and have managed to make

money consistently. The investors who place money with these so called *black box funds* rarely understand fully how they work, but are confident that they'll generate returns for their portfolios. Some complex algorithms are at work – so difficult that promoters can't exactly explain why they work, only that they believe in them. They do say, however, that they work best when markets are sharply differentiated – and that when they're correlated (different assets all singing from the same hymn sheet), they do less well.

The trend followers had a bad run in the wake of the financial crisis, but – proving that all fashions can come back (well, maybe not some '70s hairstyles!) – they subsequently recovered.

Chapter 18

Investing at Random and with the Intellectuals

Don't worry about the title of this chapter. You don't have to have worked through Aristotle or Einstein or Freud, or worried about the point of life with the French writers of the 1950s (although *Existentialism For Dummies* is a really good read). Instead, this chapter looks at how some of the leading investment brains in the world view the subject and what you can do with their knowledge.

You don't have to follow these intellectuals' thoughts. But you do need to know what they think so you can better understand the investment process and how it affects your savings. It doesn't matter whether these theories are right or wrong now. They'll have been right at some stage and they have a huge influence on the way professional money managers move their billions. And what these money managers do sets the scene for what you can achieve.

This chapter starts on a subject most investors have been conditioned to believe is pure fiction. It's not. It's about how you can perform as well as the average fund manager or stockbroker using no technology more complicated than a pin. I used my own children as guinea pigs in this. (Don't worry: my kids were old enough to handle a pin, and no animals were harmed in the videoing.)

Pinning Your Hopes on Chance

One of my all-time favourite investment books is *A Random Walk Down Wall Street* (WW Norton, 1973) by US writer Burton Malkiel. The book was first published in the early '70s, and since then it's been updated at least eight times and has been constantly in print. Much of the book is high-flown investment theory, but Malkiel also describes the most devastating puncturing of the postures of highly paid experts.

You can do as well as most professionals with nothing more complex than a pin and a list of shares. Way, way back in June 1967, bored journalists on US investment magazine *Forbes* were sitting around in their New York office, discussing the way top fund managers produced results that ranged from marvellous to miserable each year and the way that a manager who did well one or two years in a row rarely made that three or four. In fact, over five years, only a tiny handful managed to perform consistently well. (This remains true to this day.) A Wall Street contact had joked that a blindfolded monkey stabbing a share price page with a pin could do as well as some of the chumps working for big fund groups. So they decided to test the theory, which is now known as the Random Walk. The rest is history. Tested and tested again in subsequent years, the pin beat most of the professionals – even more so because the pin, unlike the experts, cost nothing!

In the 1990s I regularly featured a New Year portfolio chosen with a pin (selected by my then young children, Zoe and Oliver, from the share price pages in the *Financial Times*). It started as an antidote to those New Year share prediction articles, which promised to foretell the future but probably only wrote up shares already held by the writers' sources.

Most years, the portfolio selected by my offspring outperformed the average UK fund manager; one year it was in the top 5 per cent and did better than all the professional newspaper tipster columns. Okay, on two occasions out of the ten times we did this it fell below the average, but not disastrously. The results were third quartile rather than bottom of the fourth division.

Why did I stop? The newspaper I used to write for shut down its business pages. (Nothing to do with my contribution; well, unless it was my scepticism that led to a dearth of fund-manager adverts.)

Looking at the Worth of Fund Managers

So why should anyone bother with fund managers? They sound like redundant, overpaid throwbacks to investment's Stone Age. So let me put the record straight: the Random Walk or 'picking shares with a pin' approach isn't for everyone. For starters, you have to make the effort to buy the shares yourself.

I can honestly say that some of my favourite people are fund managers – or at least those who make an effort and don't try to pass off just tracking the market as their own work! No one really needs to pay active management fees, which can be five times as expensive as a passive tracker, to someone who just tracks the market – a technique known as *closet indexing*.

The fund-management companies that employ fund managers do perform a number of useful tasks, which many individuals don't want to or can't do. Fund managers:

- ✔ Carry out all the purchase and sales dealing with stockbrokers, taking advantage of economies of scale
- ✔ Deal with all the paperwork associated with dividends
- ✔ Take care of taxation within the portfolio
- ✔ Offer access to a diversified portfolio for a small sum of money
- ✔ In some cases, make asset-allocation choices, such as moving from shares to bonds
- ✔ Provide you with the comfort factor of being able to blame someone else if your investments head nowhere

Knowing the Limits of a Random-Choice Portfolio

The pin is a pretty good investment-choice tool, but it's not all-powerful. It's not a guarantee against losses. No collective manager can insulate against a falling stock market, and neither can the random-choice-method investor.

You need a long time span

You need time and patience for a random-choice approach to work. Remember that doing nothing for ten years is worth a lot. In rough terms, investing £10,000 into a market that doubles would give you about £19,700 after a decade of doing nothing. The £300 loss is down to purchase costs and stamp duty. In comparison, with an active fund manager taking 1.5 per cent (plus VAT in many instances) annual fees plus the internal costs of dealing in and out of shares, you'd be lucky to have £17,000.

Paid-for managers would have to be really on the ball to overcome that cost handicap. A minority of them manage to do so. A few do even better. The problem is that you don't know which funds will succeed and which will fail, but the failures always outnumber the winners over time. And the failures get worse as the years progress.

Note that if a market stood still for ten years, your buy-and-hold portfolio would be worth about £9,700 after costs. The same investment with a high-cost collective manager would go down to just over £8,500. (All these figures ignore dividends, by the way. Dividends really boost your fortune if you reinvest them. Remember that active fund managers grab about half or more of your dividend to pay for their champagne lifestyle.)

A compromise route for equities is to diversify and split your share cash – investing half via whatever the pin lands on and half into a low-cost global growth investment trust. Some very low-cost lump-sum investment and regular savings schemes are on offer. Look at the Association of Investment Companies website (www.theaic.co.uk) for further details.

Diversification is the posh way of saying that you don't put all your investment eggs in one basket. It's been a mainstay of investing thinking for decades. Everyone – including me – has stressed that you need to spread out your savings across a wide variety of asset classes before you even start dividing your money up between individual shares, bonds or funds. The idea has always been that each asset class is 'uncorrelated' with any other. So what happens in the property market doesn't have any relationship with what's going on in shares or bonds or currencies.

But since the big bank collapse in 2007 to 2008, this assumption seemed questionable because you suffered no matter which basket you used. But it should still work better over a period than sticking all your eggs together. Investment tends to return to some sort of normality after once-in-a-generation shocks. And although everyone has to learn from these events, they can't be paralysed forever by fear of a recurrence.

Traditionally, you need to select assets

The toughest take in any investment decision has always been to select your asset classes. You have to decide what proportion of your money you want to go where. (And if you've read the stuff about Random Walks in the earlier section 'Pinning Your Hopes on Chance', prepare to put your pin away. You can't select asset classes in this way.)

The black swan swims into view

Before people from Europe went to Australia, they assumed all swans were white. Then they discovered the black version and had to rethink the whole colour thing. If swans can be recognised, philosophers say, by the shape of their body and neck then, theoretically, a red swan or a blue one may exist. A *black swan event* is a happening that's so impossible to predict from what we knew before that it creates an entirely new world. Impossible to predict, and yet when the black swan appears, some investment gurus claim they knew about it all the time!

With the big crash over 2008 and 2009, the black swan was a ripple effect from the sub-prime mortgage crash, which everyone had said would never happen. But it did. It didn't matter what assets you held: everything was a disaster. And diversification didn't insulate you from a problem in one area – difficulties in any one allocation area spread to the others like a nasty disease. That black swan knocked a tidy US$20 trillion or so off our combined wealth.

Ninety-nine per cent of the clever people – bankers, economists, fund managers, media commentators – had not only failed to see this black swan, but their minds weren't even open to the possibility that something unforeseen could happen. The other 1 per cent were ignored, drowned out by the noise of the overwhelming majority.

The vast majority had failed to understand that banks holding bonds based on these sub-prime mortgages (loans made to those with a bad credit record) were vulnerable to the slightest shock because these investors hadn't spread their risk as they thought – they believed they were insulated against failure because they'd diversified across many hundreds of thousands of mortgages. They'd invested in a house of cards rather than solid property. When one mortgage started to go wrong, it brought down the structure, because the value of the properties that backed the loans collapsed. Investors saw that what they had bought was so complex and so clever and they forgot that no investment is never, never, ever so clever as to be foolproof.

The word 'never' is the most dangerous word in investing. The whole purpose of money markets is to deal with the unexpected – if everything in the financial future was known, trading assets would be pointless because they would have a fixed value.

The next most dangerous words are 'new paradigm' – the idea that investors can forget the past completely because they're entering a fresh era of investment peace and light. Sadly, a black swan is always swimming around the next corner to spoil this vision. The 'new paradigm' phrase first came into prominence during the 1999–2000 technology stock boom (and subsequent bust). The belief was that the Internet would change everything so much that companies with no track record, no earnings and sometimes just a short-term rented office as an address were worth billions and that all the traditional companies would fade, if not collapse. This theory brushed aside what should have been obvious – that the world doesn't always follow the paradigm or pattern that investors convince themselves that it should.

The moral of the story: a red, green or a rainbow swan may be coming next. Never say never in investing.

The basic advice has always been that you need to allocate your savings between these big-picture items:

- ✔ Equities
- ✔ Bonds
- ✔ Property
- ✔ Cash

These days, you may add commodities to the list – I look at this asset class in Chapter 11.

Only after you've made the allocation decision can you get down to fine-tuning your holdings. You have to decide first of all that, perhaps, 35 per cent of your money should be held in bonds before working out which bonds or bond funds to buy. And although you can choose to ignore foreign holdings, bond and equity purchasers, whether in the UK or overseas markets, can't escape them altogether. Many of the biggest companies have large businesses in other countries so they are partly, sometimes largely, overseas based and a number of companies in the FTSE 100 listing are primarily or completely overseas organisations, all of which may involve foreign investment.

Understanding Modern Portfolio Theory

Diversification is based on something called *Modern Portfolio Theory* (MPT for short). Volumes upon volumes are devoted to the theory. Some of it's really, really difficult to understand, but you don't need a doctorate in investment science or even a spreadsheet to get the basics.

First, know that MPT isn't actually modern any more. It was first invented by Harry Markowitz in an economics dissertation for his doctorate degree at Chicago University in 1952. Markowitz, incidentally, went on to win a Nobel Prize in 1990, so his thinking wasn't a one-day wonder.

MPT starts off with the assumption that investors aren't wild speculators or saloon bar gamblers. They want returns, but want to avoid risk as far as they can, although they know all life has some risks. (After all, leaving cash under the mattress risks fire, vermin and theft, and it earns nothing.) And regarding their return, most investors are content to aim somewhere near the average.

Traditional investors focus on analysing each component share or bond in a portfolio. They prefer Bank A to Bank B because they like the former's chief executive, or they prefer Oil Company C to Oil Company D because the latter is involved in exploration in an expensive (and unlikely to produce) area.

Now for the really clever bit, according to MPT followers. Instead of looking at the risks in individual stocks, you measure how they all react with each other and calculate the overall risks inherent in your portfolio. MPT says that you can then get a higher return from the whole thing compared with the risk of each component stock. Using something called the *efficient frontier*, you can build a portfolio that maximises the return while minimising the risk.

So instead of looking at companies like a traditional fund manager from a business point of view, including factors such as management, profits and prospects, you look at how a share moves up and down in relation to the market as a whole and to the other holdings in the portfolio.

MPT goes beyond the individual risk and looks at the overall risks in the portfolio. The idea is to see how portfolio components react or correlate with each other. For example, a hot weather spell is good for breweries. People drink more beer when it's warm. A hot weather spell is bad for gas sales because people turn off their central heating. So brewery shares rise and gas producer stocks fall. And in a cold spell, the sums work in the opposite direction. So it's like a see-saw with the weather playing a big part in deciding what's up and what's down. But by owning both beer producers and gas companies, you've reduced the risk of being hit by unexpected weather.

Now suppose your portfolio consists of a warm outdoors coat company and a heating-oil firm. If the winter weather is unexpectedly cold, both companies do well because they're correlated. But if December, January and February are unexpectedly mild, both do badly. You've spread your holdings but in a way that the risk – the weather here – impacts either very positively or very badly.

High oil prices are good for fuel companies but bad for airlines, which need to stock up with their products. Here again, a low correlation exists. So a portfolio is better diversified against the unexpected by having one brewery, one gas company, one fuel firm and one airline than by having four banks or four of anything else.

MPT needs time to work. It's like an insurance company. In a bad weather spell that may only last a day, an insurance company loses money to flood and tornado claims. The company also knows that wooden homes are a greater fire hazard than those built of brick. So it has lots of risks. But although each policy may represent a huge loss, the insurance company knows that if it gets its maths and customer mix right, it will make some money for its owners over time.

It's all to do with making your portfolio a safer place to be – anyone can take wild gambles (and if you follow through to Chapter 20 you can see how to take your investment market ideas to a bookmaker and place a bet) but do you really want to do this with your life's savings or your pension money?

Monkeying around with just two investments

A firm of London investment advisers was once known as No Monkey Business. These days it goes by the more prosaic name of Fowler Drew, but it continues to have a different way of looking at the world.

The Fowler Drew people reckon that most ideas about how to construct portfolios have led to increased risk taking, and more wild cards instead of making someone's money do what the investor wants. Investment theories have their fans and their detractors – mostly economics professors rather than practical investors. If you want to know more, prepare yourself for some very complex mathematics.

The Fowler Drew folk say that most portfolio theories fail to offer investors what they target and increase their risk of misery. Each new idea is rather like an improvement to a car engine to make it go faster. But in the automobile business, every power upgrade is matched by better brakes, tyres and steering. Investment theories don't tend to come with any corresponding safety enhancements.

So this firm, and others like it, go right back to investment basics. Put in a nutshell, the firm tells its very well-heeled clients that only two components should exist for their investments. The great bulk of their money goes into *index-linked gilts*, UK government bonds that guarantee to keep up with inflation and then offer a little more to ensure holders always keep a little ahead of rising prices. And the balance goes into riskier elements such as shares in emerging markets.

This approach swims against the tide that says you should diversify your assets as far as you can because here everything is in one of two baskets. Why? Because Fowler Drew believes that so many assets depend on one another –

even when people think they shouldn't. It suggests that assets in various classes are more correlated – they act more in concert – than most people believe. So bonds knock into currencies and shares and property and just about everything else. You can rewrite that sentence starting with other asset classes, so currencies knock into bonds, or shares affect currencies. In the 2008–2009 crisis, for instance, assets that were supposed to be differentiated, such as residential property and bonds, were so sliced and diced that they ended up back where they started! The snake was swallowing its own tail.

Fowler Drew reckons it can now look back with the benefit of hindsight and see that most of the evolution of techniques, structures and strategies for transferring, transforming and managing financial risks are doomed not to survive. Ouch!

What it all comes down to is that those who thought they understood what was going on were the same people who created all those complex structures that I have mentioned in this chapter. The hard fact is, they really didn't understand their creations and no one else did either, but – touch of the emperor's new clothes – everyone had to pretend they did. So all those risks transferred elsewhere weren't really moved at all. And no one understood that.

But who could blame them? Only the authors of all those millions of pages of computer models of advanced mathematics ever read, let alone comprehended, what it was all about.

No free lunch exists in the investment world. If the Fowler Drew theory teaches anything – and plenty around say it doesn't work – it's to keep matters simple and have no faith in anything complex enough to need more than half a sheet of paper for the explanation.

MPT assumes that investors want to minimise risks and not take wild punts. It doesn't work well among the penny dreadfuls or tipsheet favourites, where small-investor hope and greed overcome reason and moderation. But if you can get the mix right then you've reached MPT's nirvana – the efficient market frontier.

MPT has remained in the investment theory room for more than 60 years. It has gone in and out of fashion over the period, and will probably continue to do so. At the time of writing it's 'out', but some clever person will probably rediscover it and do well out of it until the fashion wagon rolls on. And those six decades are substantially longer than the six months or so that Hybrid Portfolio Theory lasted. This was even more difficult to understand than MPT, and for a very brief period it was everywhere in the investment world; but then it disappeared. If you're interested, search for articles online, but check the dates of these. They're all clustered around 2009, so perhaps Hybrid Portfolio Theory was just some theoretical investment expert reacting to the 2008 crash.

Trading in the Blink of an Eye

Most investment decisions are considered; they take time. But now a new breed of investor, whose main aim is always to be faster than anyone else, is moving to the centre-stage. But you won't find this investor celebrating after a profitable day's work, because it's a computer (and a very big one!).

The idea is called *high-frequency trading* or HFT, and it uses sophisticated technological tools and computer algorithms to trade bonds, equities and currencies with strategies employing enough processing power to move in and out of positions in fractions of a second. Some now manage 100 or more transactions a second.

The amount of assets traded in this way is enormous; well over half of all trading in some instances. The idea is to make a percentage of a percentage of a penny on each asset traded – so you need huge volumes – and hope that all these mount up into something worthwhile.

High-frequency trading activities go largely unnoticed in the wider world because firms involved don't accumulate positions or hold their portfolios overnight. It's the low margins, with incredibly high volumes of shares or bonds, frequently numbering in the millions, that should make it worthwhile.

High-frequency trading strategies are controversial. Because the computer can trade in a fraction of a millisecond, and that sets off other computers, sudden large and unexpected movements can ensue, known as a *flash crash*.

Some suggest that high speed trading techniques manage to *scrape*; that's a trader word for taking a percentage when index-tracking funds have to change their balance or their constituents, because their computers can be in and out in microseconds before the human traders have even had time to push a button. However, you can also argue that machine-driven deals make markets more effective, and reduce trading costs for all major participants.

High-frequency trading is an investment theory that you can't try out at home. But you need to know about it all the same, because of its huge influence on other big players.

Part IV
Property and Alternatives

What's good about commercial property?

Commercial property, such as offices, factories, warehouses and retail premises, is a lower-risk investment with a good return if the price is right and it's the right property in the right place.

Commercial-property ownership is generally structured so that you need a minimum £50 million to £100 million to be considered a player – and even more to get a really diversified portfolio. However, some commercial-property investment opportunities exist for those whose fortunes lack most of those zeroes, usually via a specialist collective vehicle.

In a nutshell, here are the long-term benefits of commercial property:

✔ Rental yields arc up with higher-risk corporate bonds but with less likelihood of financial problems.

✔ Rents tend to increase; some properties have automatic increases every five years.

✔ Demand for top-class property remains high. Property buyers like the term 'primary', which can be used for a location or the quality of the building, although the two often go together because you tend to put up the best buildings on the most attractive sites.

✔ Overseas investors like the solidity of UK property.

✔ Property values tend to at least keep up with inflation.

Find out more about Investing at www.dummies.com/extras/investinguk.

In this part . . .

- ✔ Discover how to turn property into a paying proposition.

- ✔ Visit an investor's version of a casino — a place where you can lose your shirt or emerge with a huge pile of chips.

Chapter 19

Investing in Bricks and Mortar

· ·

In This Chapter

▶ Looking at the benefits and drawbacks of buying a property to rent

▶ Examining how to finance the property

▶ Choosing where to invest and matching the right tenant to the property's location

▶ Exploring property opportunities overseas

▶ Working through the tax return

▶ Starting out in commercial property

· ·

*B*uy-to-let was the fastest growing investment class in the UK during most of the first decade of this century. From being virtually non-existent in the mid-1990s it grew, along with prices for houses and flats, to more than rival many collective investment schemes. And if you believe some of the media, buy-to-let was the most talked about subject at dinner parties, other than the price of people's own property. After all, who wanted to discuss their sagging shares when they could boast of their burgeoning buy-to-let portfolios?

But buy-to-let enthusiasts forgot – or probably had never heard of – the number one investment rule: nothing is a one-way bet. They convinced themselves that buy-to-let couldn't fail; that both property values and rents would always rise. They also forgot not to place too much of their future in an investment that could be difficult, time consuming and costly to sell. Property isn't liquid like shares or bonds or cash at the bank. And that also applies to huge projects – shopping malls, office blocks, factory estates – where investors know they're in for the long haul.

The days of instant fortunes and dinner-party boasting are over (and even if they're not, you're still best not to go down that route!). But if you're careful, property investing can still provide a useful extra income over the years. In all property investing, the postcode is the vital component: location, location, location. In the most desirable, a property can be a wreck but still be worth millions. But don't overlook less-well-regarded areas. Very cheap property can be worthwhile, provided you can purchase it for little and rent it out for lots. You have to balance 20 homes bought for £1 million that bring in £2,000 a week against one £1 million house that may – or may not – rent for £2,000 a week.

This chapter gives you the need-to-know basics about investing in a buy-to-let property – the pros and cons as well as the mortgage, location, tenant and tax issues. In addition, this chapter introduces you to the idea of investing in commercial property, which could be the basis of your long-term pension-fund investing.

Buying Property to Rent: The Pros and Cons

Buy-to-let involves buying a second property (or third or fourth or sometimes even more) in addition to the one you live in yourself. You rent this extra home to a tenant, and if all goes well, you earn rent once a month and see your initial capital investment rise as well. You gain an income and increase your wealth at the same time. That's the theory, and it can work in practice, providing your expectations are modest, your time horizon is long and you do your homework.

Buy-to-let has grown into an established investment because

- Investors are often fed up with shares that they feel won't deliver.

- Investors want an investment with a solid feel rather than a piece of paper or a line on an Internet statement.

- Investors are looking for an investment they could get involved in – they want to manage something tangible rather than leave it to expensive managers.

- Investors don't want to be tied to expensive fund managers who all too often fail to perform.

- The whole idea appeals to many people who wanted to operate their own spare-time business.

- Mobile people always need somewhere to live but don't want to or can't afford to buy a property that they may have to quit at short notice.

- Property prices in many areas remain out of reach of first-time buyers. Because they must live somewhere, they have to rent.

✔ Interest rates for borrowers have become very low. And although mortgage firms are choosy about what they'll lend upon, they now see this activity as mainstream and no longer charge a huge interest-rate premium for buy-to-let loans.

✔ Estate agents have set up units to deal with rented property.

✔ Borrowing in order to purchase a property to rent is far easier than it once was, even if you still owe money on your original residence.

✔ Residential property is *uncorrelated* with other assets, which means it doesn't go up and down in line with shares or bonds or currencies. So investors can take a back seat when it comes to analysing day-to-day news, which doesn't concern them.

✔ Property has shown a remarkable consistency in making gradual gains. And unless the UK starts to build hundreds of thousands of extra homes (and in the right places) then demand will continue to lord it over supply.

Despite all the points in the list, a buy-to-let strategy isn't guaranteed. You may find yourself without a tenant, and you may lose money on the property because prices can fall as well as rise. Or you could find that your tenant refuses to pay and trashes the place upon leaving (and, by the way, unless you have insurance to cover bad tenants, you could spend thousands in legal fees evicting people you don't like). And you have to consider costs such as building insurance, maintenance (both regular and big one-offs such as a new roof), furniture and kitchen machines.

Some other potential drawbacks exist as well:

✔ **You can't get your money out in a hurry.** Selling a property may take a year or longer, especially if house price rises stall or go into reverse. If you need to sell in a hurry, you'll probably have to accept less. A number of firms offer instant cash for properties, but you won't get anything like the market value. They know you're desperate so you'll accept almost anything.

✔ **You need to be hands on, even if you employ an agent to deal with tenants.** Letting agents often limit themselves to certain tasks for their 10 to 15 per cent cut of the rent, so you must know what those parameters are and be prepared to do some DIY. You need to know what to do if a tenant reports a dripping tap – do you go round and do it yourself or pay a plumber?

✔ **Getting a portfolio of properties can be very expensive.** Most buy-to-letters just have one property, so they don't diversify. Putting all your spare cash into this one property is worse. But the more properties you have, the more time and effort it takes to maintain your investment.

A move into buy-to-let is far bigger than any move into equities, bonds or cash. You can't change your mind in a few minutes or even a few months' time. You may also have to do all the work yourself, including checking and cleaning the property between tenants – or if that sounds awful then you'll have to pay around 15 per cent of the rent to have someone else manage the property. And unless you've come up with a really good deal, that someone else will probably send you the bills for the cleaners on top.

Before considering affordability or whether buy-to-let is the right type of investment for your needs, use the negative points of buy-to-let as a checklist to see whether the idea even appeals to you.

Beds in sheds: Tempting but a no-no

Most buy-to-let landlords rent out their house or flat to one tenant such as a family or to a group such as a number of friends who are willing to share the property (although usually one of the group is deemed to be responsible for the rent and maintaining the property in a good condition). But others rent to a number of single individuals – each with their own room but sharing facilities such as the kitchen and bathroom.

For whichever course, landlords must be aware of the rules for *houses in multiple occupation* – or HMOs for short. In general terms, an HMO exists when three to six unrelated individuals share a property and its facilities – the rules don't apply to families. Special rules apply when five or more unrelated people share a house that's at least three storeys high. These are called large houses in multiple occupation and require a special local-authority licence.

With all HMOs landlords have additional responsibilities that include:

✔ Checking that there are safety measures to protect in case of fire. This includes smoke detectors in every bedroom and in every shared area. Additionally, the kitchen or anywhere used to cook must have a heat detector. Landlords must pay for a gas safety certificate every twelve months and ensure electrics are tested at least every five years.

✔ The property must be kept in good repair and not be overcrowded – there must be sufficient washing and cooking facilities for the number of tenants allowed in the property.

✔ Property owners must ensure there are enough waste bins for tenants.

Some landlords flout these rules. They decide to take on as many individuals as they can cram into the property – and then some more. At the extreme, they have more than one person sleeping in the same bed on a shift-pattern basis or they put beds in garden sheds or unused garages (usually bunk beds to maximise returns from the space). This is illegal and a number of landlords have been prosecuted and heavily fined. Some local authorities hire helicopters with heat-seeking devices to track down this practice.

Considering the Affordability Issue

Very few buy-to-let investors can afford to pay cash for their property purchase even though in some (admittedly not too desirable) locations, flats and houses can still cost under £50,000, especially if you buy *distressed* properties at auction (those that need some, or lots of, repair work before you can legally rent them out).

But even if you could afford to pay cash, you should never tie up so much of your capital in a property that it leaves you without an emergency fund or the ability to buy into other investment assets if you think the time is right. So most buy-to-let investors borrow money either out of necessity or to balance their portfolios better.

The price you see or even agree to isn't the property's real price. You also have to pay *Stamp Duty Land Tax* or SDLT (known as stamp duty). It is levied as a percentage of the purchase price. The more expensive the property, the higher the percentage. These rates can change from year to year, but at the time of writing they're as follows:

- ✔ Up to £125,000: 0%
- ✔ £125,001 to £250,000: 2%
- ✔ £250,001 to £925,000: 5%
- ✔ £925,001 to £1.5million: 10%
- ✔ More than £1.5m: 12%

You pay no tax on the first £125,000 of the purchase price. You pay 2 per cent on the next £125,000 – the amount that brings the price up to £250,000. When buying a property for £175,000 you pay nothing on the first £125,000 and then 2 per cent on the next £50,000, which adds up to £1,000.

On a home costing £450,000, the tax is nothing on the first £125,000, £2,500 on the next £125,000 and £10,000 (£200,000 at 5 per cent) on the final slice.

The stamp duty land tax on a home costing £850,000 would be £32,500 – the £450,000 example above plus a further £20,000 for the additional £400,000 purchase price.

And if you are affluent enough, the tax on buying a £2million property is £153,750.

This tax does not apply in Scotland. Instead, Scotland has a similar levy on property purchase known as the Land and Buildings Transaction Tax.

Besides stamp duty, you have legal costs, possibly a mortgage arrangement fee, a survey and, if you're letting a furnished property, an allowance for everything from curtains and chairs to cookers and cutlery. These extra expenses can typically soak up £10,000 to £15,000, and represent money you can't recoup. You may also find that borrowing to fund these extra start-up costs is difficult.

Before you can think about borrowing, you need to start with how much you can put down as a deposit and how much will be soaked up by other costs. And until you know what price range you can afford, you can't go out to look at potential investment properties.

Looking at the Buy-to-Let Mortgage

Lenders want to look at the colour of your deposit. No 100 per cent buy-to-let loans exist (and if they did, the interest rates would be prohibitive). And some lenders refuse to give mortgages on properties such as one-bedroom flats or flats above shops. Why? They won't lend because they see these properties as difficult to sell if they're repossessed. If banks think these properties are tough to get rid of, take that as a hint that they are. But if you're prepared to live with the risk, you could do very well by investing where others dread to go.

How much can you borrow?

Banks and building societies calculate a figure called *loan to value* (or LTV), which is the largest proportion of the property price that they'll lend you – the rest comes from you as a deposit. The LTV generally varies from 60 per cent to 85 per cent. Because you fund the balance, you need cash of between 15 per cent and 40 per cent of the property value.

If you have £20,000 to put up as a deposit, the least generous lender with a 60 per cent LTV would add £30,000, so you could buy a property costing £50,000. The lender with a high LTV (85 per cent) would convert your £20,000 into a loan of £113,333, so you could look at properties costing £133,333, or more than twice as much as the meanest lender's offering.

A higher LTV gets you a bigger property bang for your deposit bucks. But larger deposits often mean lower interest rates.

How much do you actually get?

Your deposit and the LTV set a maximum. But you may not get that amount.

When you apply for a loan to buy a roof over your own head, the lender looks at the property itself to check its condition, the proportion of its value that you want to borrow and, most importantly, your ability to repay the debt from your salary or self-employment earnings. But because many buy-to-letters already have a mortgage banging hard against the limits of their earnings, buy-to-let lenders use a totally different way of judging how much they offer you because they see this as a business-proposition property.

Instead of looking at how much you earn, buy-to-let lenders judge how much the property will earn for you. Most banks and building societies are now involved in this market, although some specialise in buy-to-let loans.

TIP

Moneyfacts (`http://moneyfacts.co.uk`), an online comparison site, is a good first source of information on who's lending and their basic terms.

The simplest formula is where you tell the lender how much rent you expect each month. Suppose that amount is £500 per month, or £6,000 per year. The lender then calculates how big a loan that monthly or annual amount would back.

Suppose that interest rates stood at 6 per cent. Then your £6,000 per year would, on pure mathematics, pay back enough each month to back a £100,000 loan – irrespective of your personal income. But few lenders are stupid enough to go for that amount, especially after the 2007–2008 credit crunch, which was caused – in part – by over-generous lending to buy-to-letters. And even though interest rates may be on the low side when the loan starts, there's no guarantee that will remain true over the 20- to 25-year life span of a typical buy-to-let mortgage.

Besides building in a safety zone against rising interest rates, you need to consider nasty things called *voids* – months where you have no tenant and hence no income, or where your tenant has disappeared while owing more than the tenancy deposit. (Buy-to-let veterans suggest you allow for two void months each year. If you beat that, count your blessings. But if your experience is worse, look for explanations. Maybe you're asking too much for the rent or the building is in a poor state of repair and hence discouraging to new renters.) And to cap it all, you have other, often unexpected, costs of ownership, such as repairs and maintenance.

Lenders insist that the rent more than covers the mortgage, so you don't run on empty if something goes wrong. Typically, the rent has to be anything from 1.3 times to 1.6 times the monthly outlay, a number called the *cover*. Some lenders drop the cover to a lower figure – especially when credit is easy – but others demand a high level of cover and then only assume that you're collecting rent in ten months of the year. A few lenders also demand that you've largely paid off the loan on your own home beforehand.

Although high mortgage cover sounds mean, it's really not. High mortgage cover protects you (as well as the lender) and gives you a cushion against the unexpected. Do you want to end up in *negative equity* where you owe the lender more than your property is worth? In that situation, the lender could come after you, even demanding that you sell your own home to finance your debt.

REMEMBER

Buy-to-let is a business proposition. So you face risks along the way.

Items to consider about the mortgage

Before you contact a mortgage company or mortgage broker for a buy-to-let loan, take a look at the following points. They'll save you time and stop dodgy mortgage firms pulling the wool over your eyes.

- ✓ **Fixed versus variable:** A fixed rate is where every payment for a set period is identical. Variable rates go up and down with interest costs in the economy at large. The fixed rate gives you security of payment for a period but sometimes at the cost of inflexibility and slightly higher interest rates. You can often set a fixed rate to match a tenancy agreement. Doing so is a good idea because raising a rent for a sitting tenant can be difficult.

- ✓ **Fees:** Some mortgages are fee-free, so you have nothing to pay initially. But this setup may be offset by higher costs later on. Otherwise, expect to pay from £500 to £1,500 as a fixed fee or between 0.5 per cent and 1 per cent of the loan. Fees are often set according to the rate you pay. A higher percentage means a lower fee, and vice versa.

- ✓ **Minimum amount:** Few lenders lend on properties worth less than £30,000 (if you can still find one!). If you want a portfolio of ultra-low-price dwellings, you must find a specialist lender, likely to be more expensive, or fund your purchases either from cash or by re-mortgaging your home.

- ✓ **Maximum loans:** Many lenders are happy to lend on more than one property provided you can come up with a deposit and finance the loan through the rent. Generally, lenders put a ceiling on the number of properties so that you can't have more than five or ten, and some lenders also limit the total lending on your portfolio at anything from £250,000 to £2.5 million.

- ✓ **Interest only or repayment:** You may have the choice of just paying the interest on the loan each month or paying this plus an extra amount, which reduces the loan to zero over the projected life of the mortgage. The first option costs less initially, so you can afford to borrow more with the same rental income backing. The second course is more expensive initially but you're repaying the capital, so the loan shrinks. This way, you get more back if you sell and have a useful cushion against higher costs if interest rates rise. The choice is more complex when you factor in tax – you get tax relief on mortgage interest and have to pay capital gains tax on any profit you make when you sell.

Buy-to-let is a commercial activity. Buy-to-let loans aren't covered by Financial Conduct Authority rules, which offer safeguards against misleading sales techniques aimed at mortgage customers who are buying their own home. The Financial Conduct Authority has shut down a number of dodgy mortgage brokers but that doesn't help to compensate victims of bad advice.

The Property Yield: A Comparison Tool

Buy-to-let isn't a magic way to make money. You need to compare its attractions against other asset classes, such as cash, bonds or shares. The easiest way is to look at the *gross yield*: what you get in rent before you spend on financing a loan. For example, take a £100,000 property rented at £500 per month. That's a £6,000 total for the year, so the yield should be 6 per cent.

But hold on. You may be spending on property-management firms such as estate agents and cleaners and you'll certainly be spending on insurance. Furthermore, you always run the risk of voids (months when you have no tenant). You're far better estimating the rent on ten months per year. Now, in this example, the annual rent falls to £5,000 and so the yield drops to 5 per cent – even less when you factor in the time you'll have to spend on the property, all those extra costs and the possibility selling could take a long time if you need the money out.

Now compare that final figure with what you may get from other assets such as shares or bonds. (This comparison ignores changes – up or down – in the value of the asset.)

The future worth of your investment depends on the state of the property market and the condition and location of your flat or house when you want to sell. Never forget that property values can fall as well as go up.

Property isn't like a bond where the yield and capital value are closely linked in a push – pull relationship. Instead, when property prices rise, you should be able to push up the rent so you get a double benefit. But when they fall, rents tend to go down so you get a double hit.

Think twice about the 'free' property seminar

'Free' property seminars claim they can make you a property millionaire overnight (or at least in just two to three years). Now, my idea of a millionaire is someone who can spend £1 million if he wants to. The seminar organisers' idea of a millionaire is someone who owes the bank £1 million in property loans.

The initial two- to three-hour seminar is free, but expect a heavy sell and not much in the way of learning about property. Most seminars feature a method where you apparently buy at a discount and then take another mortgage when the price rises and spend the excess. You can repeat the process over and over again.

The seminar organisers claim to be property experts. But what they're really good at is selling 'courses' and memberships for up to £10,000. You will learn something. But you'll learn even more with a book such as *Property Investing All-in-One For Dummies* (published by Wiley), which will also leave you with an awful lot of change from £10,000. These property seminars are get-rich-quick schemes that make the organisers rich.

Many of the seminar firms have gone spectacularly bust, taking their investors' money with them, often to the tune of many hundreds of thousands per person. They aren't regulated by the Financial Conduct Authority, so you can't get recompense. And the law doesn't seem interested – these property crooks know how to arrange the documentation.

Understanding Location, Location, Location

Location, location, location is the essential property mantra. It answers this question: Why is a two-bedroom flat in Belgravia some 40 times more expensive than a similarly sized flat in Barnsley, Bolton or Blackburn? With location, location, location, people pay not just for *what* they get but for *where* they get it.

But that doesn't mean that you can't invest wisely at the lower end of the market. Much may depend on what type of tenants you feel happiest with. You can provide fairly basic accommodation to students, extremely upmarket premises to top managers from abroad on short-term UK contracts or something in between. Remember that most rented property is let out for 6- or 12-month periods at a time – called an *assured shorthold tenancy*.

There's no substitute for walking around an area, sizing up the amenities, looking at estate agents and viewing properties. You can sometimes get a discount by buying *off plan*: buying from a developer who's selling units in a new or refurbished property before the building is completed (and sometimes before it's even started). In many cases, though, this discount is an illusion. Developers increase their price just so they can reduce it to convince buyers they're getting a bargain below market value. Lenders now recognise this trick, along with the fact that when a tenant moves in and the walls get scuffed, the value falls. Mortgage firms now usually base loans for new-build properties on 85 per cent of the official purchase price.

Buying off plan can be buying blind. Don't do so just because you see an advertised incentive. In some cases the properties are never built, so you could lose your deposit. This is even truer with overseas properties, which can be a veritable horror story.

Matching tenants to the property's location

Here's how to match your preferred group with the right property type:

- ✔ **Students:** They want low-cost premises near their college or university. You may be competing with subsidised halls of residence. Expect a fair amount of cosmetic damage, supply low-cost furniture (preferably from second-hand shops) and factor in long summer vacations when you may have no tenants. You may also have costs involved in installing fire and other safety regulations, to satisfy both the educational body and the local council. Also be aware of the houses in multiple occupation rules, which impose extra safety standards (see the earlier sidebar 'Beds in sheds: Tempting but a no-no'). Educational establishments only publicise your properties providing you prove that you maintain the house to these levels.

- ✔ **Employed young people:** An ideal target for many landlords. Look at areas with good transport and good employment opportunities. This group prefers to be near city centres and not stuck on a distant estate.

- ✔ **Families with young children:** Go for properties with gardens near schools. Public transport and access to shops can be important.

- ✔ **Professional high earners:** They want upscale properties and will pay for them. Many come to you through company deals, such as a firm renting your property for a long period and then installing staff members who need a roof over their heads.

Buying a house rather than a flat may involve gardening costs, especially in void periods. In some cases, local authorities can oblige you to keep the place in good order.

Considering properties in poor condition

Investment properties are cheap, but the term is generally a euphemism for houses and flats in poor condition. They can be profitable, however, provided that you pay for a full survey and then factor in the costs of bringing the property to a habitable condition. The period of repairs brings in no rent but involves outlays that you may not be able to fund through borrowing.

Here are a couple of additional, important points to keep in mind:

- ✔ You may have difficulty getting a mortgage until you carry out the repairs.
- ✔ Some investment properties are in rundown areas where you find it hard to attract tenants, although some landlords specialise in housing benefit cases. You could also miss out on future property price rises because the area is unattractive and, in the worst case, face losing a lot if the neighbourhood becomes unliveable.

Some unscrupulous firms have been advertising a scam with *managed investment properties*. Here's how it works: you buy a number of low-cost dwellings for £100,000 or £150,000 in total. The properties may be worth £15,000 each on the open market, but you end up paying £30,000 a time. According to these firms, the extra goes towards bringing the properties up to a minimum standard, including central heating and new wiring, so they can be let to housing associations. Sounds good, doesn't it? The scam is that no housing associations are prepared to buy and the firms themselves carry out no repairs, leaving you with rubbish properties. Meanwhile, the firms disappear with much of your cash. Some people have gone to prison for this racket but that doesn't help you get your money back.

Beware of so-called *rent guarantees*, which promise a fixed sum in rental income every year for five or ten years even when the property has no tenants. These guarantees cost. A five-year guarantee promising £5,000 a year could add £25,000 to the purchase price. Even worse, dishonest developers take this extra money plus whatever they can from you and then disappear. This has happened a lot in Bulgaria, Turkey and, to a lesser extent, in France and Spain. Remember that a guarantee is only as strong as the company making it. Unless backed by a highly rated international insurer, guarantees are rarely worth the paper they're printed on.

Getting Savvy with Attracting Tenants

Your buy-to-let is worthless without tenants. You also must be sure that the tenants are the type of people you want. The easiest way to find them is to hand the whole job over to a firm of estate agents who'll manage your property, find tenants, interview them and take security deposits. Some agents only work with tenants and call themselves letting agents, but you can use either term. The firm does these tasks in return for, typically, 15 per cent of the gross rent each month. Some agents specialise in finding companies that will engage in a long-term contract.

The estate agent's cut can be the difference between profit and loss. Successful buy-to-let investors need more than financial skills. You're managing a business, so if you hand management duties over to a third party, you need an agent you can trust on a long-term basis.

If you don't want to hire an estate agent to find tenants for you, consider using the suggestions in this section.

Advertising for tenants

Take a close look at the for-rent pages in your local newspaper. Doing so gives you some idea of how similar properties are priced. You can always go out and look at those properties or send a suitable friend if the flat or house is likely to appeal to a specific age group. You can then come up with a competitive and attractive advert.

Some people are put off if you only give a mobile phone number. Tenants are as entitled to know who they're dealing with as landlords.

Contacting local employers

Big local firms and educational establishments often look for suitable, safe and well-maintained properties for staff to rent. Some of the companies may want to enter a long-term contract in which the company does all the work, including repairs, in return for a fixed-rent agreement.

Using word of mouth

Often people ask proprietors of local corner shops and newsagents whether they know of places to rent. This is a cost-free advertising opportunity. Libraries and some supermarkets also have free notice-boards.

Going online

A number of sites list property for rent. But you should probably use this avenue as a backup, not a first method of attracting people. Some sites attract fraudsters who take money upfront for 'security' and then disappear. You don't want to be associated with them.

If you list your property for rent on the Internet, draw up an application form for potential tenants to provide their name, current address and work details. This form could be part of the online offering. Alternatively, get prospective tenants to email you and then you can send them a form. Always probe to see whether the potential tenants have any financial problems. They should have a bank account (or pay a large upfront deposit in cash). In addition, always ask for references and check them out thoroughly. Don't take anything at face value because forging references on a computer is easy.

Buying Overseas

Ever thought about buying an investment property in Albania, Bulgaria, Croatia or even the Cape Verde islands or Mongolia? Enterprising property developers cite these, and other locations, as the 'next big place'. But just because they say that, don't throw caution to the wind. After all, their job is to promote what they intend to build. When they have your money, their job is over.

You can even take 'free' inspection trips where you end up seeing a field and a set of drawings, and then the promoters of the development try to persuade you to put down a deposit.

The difficulty is that while your developer is building, so too are many others. The result is over-supply and under-demand. If you want to know what happens when building gets out of control, take a look at what's happened to property prices, and especially those sold to foreign investors, since 2008 in one-time hot spots such as Spain and Florida. There, far from luxury homes, the visitor sees rotting, half-built estates, doomed to be consumed by weeds.

This brings us back to location and demand. London, Paris, Hong Kong or Manhattan property is always expensive because these cities have limited space and very strict zoning rules. And big cities like these are attractive to people. So whatever is built is often snapped up at top prices.

In places that have empty fields and not much planning control, property can be substantially cheaper than in a crowded city, but you have to take a reality test – look at the location and demand, and the future supply, before buying property there as an investment. You could end up buying a luxury flat in a ghost city!

Of course, if you want a second home abroad for your own use then you're not buying an investment. You're purchasing a holiday or retirement property.

Being Aware of the Tax Issue

As far as HM Revenue & Customs is concerned, buy-to-let is a business and not an investment. You have to pay income tax on your profits from rentals, but you can deduct interest and the cost of adverts, repairs, insurance and council tax. You add what's left to your other income.

You're allowed to make a loss on your rental activity. And in some circumstances, you can carry forward losses against future profits. You must keep records, and many people employ an accountant (you can offset the fee against tax).

If, or when, you sell, you'll be liable for capital gains tax on any profit, although you can deduct your annual capital gains tax allowance if you haven't used it elsewhere. In some circumstances, you can deduct capital losses.

Because you can set the mortgage interest (but not repayment of the loan itself) against tax, many buy-to-letters go for interest-only mortgages to maximise the tax relief. Interest-only mortgages cost less each month, which makes a bigger loan more affordable.

Avoiding the land scam

Wouldn't you like to invest £10,000 and turn it into £100,000 in a few years' time with no risk? Well, who wouldn't! But when it sounds too good to be true, it is. Welcome to *landbanking*, a scam that has deceived thousands.

Here's how it works. Landbankers buy a field from a farmer at £10,000 an acre. The field has no planning permission. But they call investors saying that the field is a dead cert to get the go-ahead for housing. And when that happens, the value of the land will go up 10 or even 20 times.

The landbankers divide each acre up into ten blocks and sell each block for £10,000 to £15,000. So they sell the land bought at £10,000 for up to £150,000.

So far, no landbank site has ever received local authority permission to build. And given that most are just fields suitable for nothing more commercial than crops or horse grazing, none are likely to be.

Many landbanking firms have disappeared, leaving investors with a worthless piece of land that they can't even use to park a caravan or pitch a tent.

You have to voluntarily tell HMRC that you're engaged in buy-to-let within three months of starting. The tax people won't accept excuses such as 'I was waiting for a tax form' or 'I didn't know I had to declare this'.

Investing in Commercial Property

Commercial property, such as offices, factories, warehouses and retail premises, is a lower-risk investment with a good return if the price is right and it's the right property in the right place.

Commercial-property ownership is generally structured so that you need a minimum £50 million to £100 million to be considered a player – and even more to get a really diversified portfolio. However, some commercial-property investment opportunities exist for those whose fortunes lack most of those zeroes, usually via a specialist collective vehicle.

What's good about commercial property?

In a nutshell, here are the long-term benefits of commercial property:

- ✔ Rental yields are up with higher-risk corporate bonds but with less likelihood of financial problems.

- ✔ Rents tend to increase; some properties have automatic increases every five years.

- ✔ Demand for top-class property remains high. Property buyers like the term 'primary', which can be used for a location or the quality of the building, although the two often go together because you tend to put up the best buildings on the most attractive sites.

- ✔ Overseas investors like the solidity of UK property.

- ✔ Property values tend to at least keep up with inflation.

What's bad about commercial property?

Here are the drawbacks of investing in commercial property:

- ✔ It's illiquid, so buying and selling can take ages – many property funds can lock you in for 6 or 12 months if you want to sell your holding.

- ✔ Returns are very susceptible to interest rates. A substantial increase can wreck the best forecasts.

✔ So-called secondary properties, the rubbish that top-class tenants avoid, can be difficult to let. If you want to imagine secondary property, think of rundown shopping parades, decrepit factories or office blocks that no sensible organisation would want to be based in.

✔ Types of property can go out of fashion. Buildings can become obsolescent or subject to new, and expensive, environmental regulations.

How to invest in commercial property

You may already have some exposure to commercial property through a pension or other funds. Many packaged UK investments are also likely to have a percentage of property-company shares in the portfolio. But if you want more, this section covers some other, less bank-busting ways than going out and buying an office block or retail development.

Property-company shares

A number of property-owning companies are listed on the London Stock Exchange. Buying and selling their shares works the same as with any other quoted equity.

Some property-owning companies have enormous portfolios, but others focus on one type of property, such as office blocks or out-of-town retail parks. Bigger firms tend to concentrate on prime property, which they rent to top household-name firms. But a number of firms go for secondary properties, hoping to make more money out of cheap buildings that they rent to less-attractive tenants. Secondary property is generally more volatile.

Investors look at two factors beyond the portfolio constituents:

✔ **Dividend yield:** This is usually higher than the market average, with the highest returns coming from property firms that go for secondary properties. The normal investment rules apply. If the dividend yield is high then the capital gains are likely to be lower for the same level of risk.

✔ **Discount:** This is the gap between the value of the property firm's underlying portfolio less borrowings and its stock-market capitalisation. The stock-market value should generally be lower than the worth of the buildings owned.

Most property companies are now officially real-estate investment trusts (REITs). This structure gives certain tax benefits.

Property unit trusts

These are standard unit trusts offered by a small number of investment groups to those wanting a specialist fund. They're a mix of direct investments in property, property shares and cash. The minimum investment is usually £500 or £1,000.

Property bonds have nothing to do with *holiday property bonds*, a form of time-share where you can use holiday accommodation in proportion to your holding. Holiday property bonds aren't intended as a serious investment – they're for vacations.

Enterprise Property Zones

Enterprise Property Zones (or EPZs) are areas where the government is anxious to attract new commercial buildings, so it offers forms of tax relief to do the attracting. Investors with a minimum £5,000 to £10,000 can buy into these projects and gain tax relief on their investment. Investors who borrow to raise the cash can also offset interest payments against tax. The EPZ investor receives the rental income without any tax deduction, but must declare it.

The tax relief that comes with EPZ investment sounds like a good idea. But no guarantee promises that the property will be profitable, and investors usually sign up for 25 years – a very long time, especially because no clear or easy exit exists. You could be left with a property lemon. This option is for serious investors with serious money and is best approached by taking serious advice from a professional property person!

Chapter 20

Delving into Derivative Investments

*I*f you have a nervous disposition, you may want to skip this chapter. It's all about how you can lose not just your shirt but everything else you own. It covers the one investment opportunity in this book from which you can end up with more than *minus everything*, because not only can your investment money go down to zero, but you also can end up owing cash over and above those losses. Very financially painful!

That sounds unbelievably awful, and it can be. So why should you grit your teeth and read this chapter? Because these types of investments, called *derivatives*, are advertised everywhere. They include contracts for difference, spread bets, traded options and covered warrants, and because of their prominent publicity, you need to know about them, if only to say no to their apparent charms.

They are known as derivatives because they are investments based on stock, commodity and currency markets but where you go nowhere near buying the shares, metals or foreign-exchange contracts on which they're based.

Don't confuse these types of investment with putting your money into art, vintage cars, farmland or wine which, confusingly, are often called 'alternatives'. The alternatives I am discussing here are based on stock, commodity and currency markets. They are also called derivatives because they are 'derived' from underlying investments in shares, bonds, currencies or commodities. The following section describes derivatives in full.

All the financial schemes in this chapter are for experienced investors who can afford to make some losses. I reckon you should always stick to what you know. You're better being safe than sorry, whatever the adverts for these products make out!

Describing the Derivative

Think of a football match or other sporting event. The players are on the pitch, trying to score goals, notch up points, make runs or take wickets. They are actively involved. But there is a whole world which depends on their activity. Betting, for instance, is derived from these sports that take place on the field, track or tennis court. Financial derivatives are similar. The action in these specialised investments is derived from what happens on the 'pitch' where traders deal in real stocks, shares and other assets. They are one step removed from the real thing, just as someone betting on a horse race is not part of the actual event.

When someone bets on a football match, deriving the punt from the actual event, the gambling does not affect the game (unless there is bribery and corruption!). But financial derivatives are part of a two-way process. Changing values in the underlying 'real' assets affect those contracts derived from them. But – and this is the bit many miss – it's a two-way process. Investors buying and selling derivatives can change the value of the real assets.

What fans and critics say about derivatives

Fans of derivative investments say that they're cheaper and more flexible than dealing in conventional assets. These enthusiasts claim that these investments are the future, often pointing to overseas countries where their use is often more widespread.

Detractors say that derivatives are a visit to a posh betting shop; that they offer rapid, high-risk routes to financial wipe-out; that you should treat them no differently than a punt on an outsider in the 3:30 at Epsom; and that although they give the veneer of investment sophistication, the only winners are the bookies, specialist dealers and others who sell these schemes. It's

a fact that around four of five spread bets on financial markets (I discuss these in the later section 'Taking a Gamble with Spread Betting') end up with the investor losing.

This high ratio of losing bets to winning plays also applies to the other investment methods in this chapter. In practical terms, the only difference between spread bets, contracts for difference and many of the other super-risk strategies lies in the small-print legalities. They have, of course, the unifying factor that you can lose money really quickly – and in most cases lose more than you started with.

Getting into Gear for a Faster Ride

The big difference between the investments in this chapter and most of those elsewhere in this book is *gearing*, an arrangement in which a set sum of investment money potentially works harder for you but involves greater risk. Americans, and increasingly people in the UK, refer to gearing as *leverage*. The two terms are interchangeable.

To understand gearing, look at the difference between someone on foot and a cyclist. A pedestrian may cover 5 kilometres in an hour. But pedalling a bike, the same person may easily cover 15, 20 or more kilometres in an hour. The difference is due to the fact that the cyclist has gears that transform the leg movement into greater distance when her physical effort goes through the mechanism to the back wheel. And the higher the gear used, the farther the person goes. The energy expended may be the same as when walking or even less if the cyclist freewheels.

Logically, it would be better if everyone cycled. (And I love my bike!) However, bikes have disadvantages such as higher injury risks. Falling off a bike is easier than falling down as a walker. The gears are great when the going is good on the flat or downhill, but life can get tough on steep, uphill climbs. You get hit more severely by bad weather. And cycling has higher equipment costs than walking. The gearing advantage with a bike over walking has potential downsides.

With financial gearing, you buy a derivative of a share, a share index or bond for a fraction of its price. If the value of the underlying security goes the way you want, your investment moves up very rapidly in percentage terms. Get it wrong, and you can face total wipe-out (or worse).

To help you understand the concept, consider a simple example of a winning derivative investment scenario. For simplicity, I've chosen a ten-to-one gearing ratio so you get the equivalent of ten shares for the price of one. I could have selected lots of other numbers – the higher your gearing goes, the greater the win potential and the more frightening the chances of loss.

- **Conventional investment:** You have £1,000, and you buy 1,000 shares in a company called ABC plc at 100p each. The shares go to 110p. You sell and earn 10 per cent on your money, giving a £100 profit. Ignoring stamp duty, dealing costs and the spread between bid and offer prices, you now have £1,100, a 10 per cent gain.

- **Derivative investment:** Instead of buying the shares, you go for a derivative where you put down 10 per cent of the purchase price. You now have the equivalent of £10,000 worth of shares in ABC plc for the same £1,000. The shares go from 100p to 110p. But instead of having 1,000 shares, which have gained 10p, you now have 10,000, so your profit is £1,000. Ignoring costs, your £1,000 has turned into £2,000, a 100 per cent gain.

Now look at how you can lose:

- ✔ **Conventional investment:** Your £1,000 buys 1,000 shares in ABC plc at 100p each. The shares fall to 90p. You sell. You've lost £100 but still have £900 left. Not good news but not a total disaster, either. You could have instead held on, hoping for an eventual uplift and taken the dividends as well.

- ✔ **Derivative investment:** Your £1,000 buys the equivalent 10,000 shares in ABC plc at 100p each. The shares fall to 90p. You've now lost 10,000 times 10p, or £1,000, so your investment is worthless. Most alternatives don't pay dividends, and they have time limits, so you can't hold on for the longer term looking for a rebound.

Now suppose that the shares fall to 80p:

- ✔ **Conventional investment:** You've lost £200 or 20 per cent. Many investors would live with that, reasoning that downs (and ups) of this magnitude are normal, and that the shares will bounce back.

- ✔ **Derivative investment:** Bad news! If you play the markets this way, you've already lost all your money. But with some derivative strategies, including spread betting, it gets worse. You not only give up your £1,000 (equal to the first 10p of the loss on each share), but you also owe the spread-bet company £1,000 for the second 10p loss per share. If ABC plc suddenly goes bust and the shares are worthless, you have to pay the whole £10,000! Ouch!

Optioning Your Bets

If gearing is one side of a coin, where you increase your risk and, hopefully, your reward, then the options market can be the other side of the coin. Here investors try to work out what the value of a share or other asset will be over a fixed period – often three months. But first realise that at its most simple, an option is the right but not the obligation to purchase or sell something during this time, and you can't lose more than your original stake.

Imagine you want to buy a piece of art but don't know whether your partner will like it and you won't be able to check this for a week. You also know that many other art fans are hoping to buy this painting. You come to an arrangement with the art dealer where you put down a £1,000 option to guarantee you'll get the first chance to buy the artwork, which is worth £20,000. If you and your partner decide against it during the week, or never get back to the dealer, you lose the £1,000. Tough, but that's better than wasting £20,000. But suppose you decide you want the artwork. You now pay the £20,000 plus the £1,000 option money. That's more, but you have the comfort of time to make up your mind and the reassurance you'll get the painting at the price quoted. The dealer gets £1,000, and sees that as recompense for having taken the risk of being obliged to refuse someone who may have offered substantially more.

What's a stock-market option?

An *option* is a promise, backed by the stock market, that you can buy or sell a set number of shares (nearly always in parcels of 1,000 shares) in a company at a fixed price between the start day and the expiry date. You can generally choose between a number of expiry dates and a number of strike prices. A *strike price* is the value the shares have to hit before your option has any value. Remember that although this promise comes from the market, it does, of course, need another investor (or investors) to be on the other side of the deal. The company whose shares are involved knows nothing of all this.

Options are available on all sorts of investments, including bonds, shares and currencies. Equity options are the best known and the most likely to be chosen by private investors. Most are called *traded options* because investors can trade them on, buying or selling during the option period. In the art market example, you may sell your £1,000 option along with its right to buy the work at £20,000 for £2,000 to another painting purchaser who reckons this is really a masterpiece and worth £30,000. The second art fan acquires the painting for £22,000 – £2,000 to buy the option and £20,000 to the dealer. You've doubled your money – great if you've by now decided the painting wasn't your style.

Worldwide, you can choose from thousands of options. In the UK, traded options are available on nearly all the shares in the FTSE 100 index, as well as on the index itself.

Looking at the two sides of the options contract

Just as you need two to tango, you need two to create a market. In the non-financial example I use in the introduction to this section, the two sides are the art buyer and the art dealer.

In financial options, you can divide the world between those who gear up their investments with options and those who use them to reduce risk. And you can further divide it into those who think the price of the asset will go up and those who believe it will go down.

Start with a simple *call option*, where you purchase the right (but not the obligation) to buy a set number of shares in a particular company at a fixed price on or before a stated date.

This is how a call option works. You reckon the shares in ABC plc will be worth substantially more sometime over the next three months. You can buy an option to buy the shares in three months' time at 100p. The shares are now quoted at 95p – because you expect the shares to rise, you go for a strike price higher than the present quote.

You buy an option for three months at 10p on 10,000 shares for an outlay of £1,000. After the shares go past 110p (the 100p strike price for the option plus the option premium itself) you're 'in the money'. After one month, the shares stand at 120p. You then decide that's as high as they'll go, but you sell your option for 30p in the stock market to someone who believes they'll keep going up. Your profit is 10,000 times 20p, which is £2,000.

The new owner has to hope the shares will rise again. She's paid 30p for the right to buy shares in ABC plc at 100p, but only over the remaining two months. The shares have to top 130p before this buyer is 'in the money'. If the shares fall back, the option may still be worth something (but not 30p) to another investor who calculates it could be worth paying, say, 5p for the opportunity to purchase ABC plc shares at 100p.

As a rule, the longer an option has to run, the more it's worth. This is called *time value* – you may consider it as paying for more hope.

Protecting your investment with traded options

Suppose you own 10,000 shares in ABC plc. They're quoted at 95p, so your investment is worth £9,500. You also decide you need that money in three months' time rather than now, but you're not happy about the future progress of the company.

Instead of selling now and banking the £9,500, you *write an option* (where you offer shares that you own to an investor taking an option; you either deliver the shares at the agreed price and keep the option premium or, if the option taker walks away, you keep your shares plus the option premium) with a strike price at 100p. You now have the £1,000 option premium plus your shares.

If the shares soar, you lose out. You have to sell your shares for 100p to the option purchaser. But if the shares fall, you earn the cushion of 10p a share over the three months – and you still have your stake in ABC plc.

In the later section 'What are call prices and put prices?', I show some more detailed examples. In the meantime, rest assured that with these options, you can never lose more than your stake. So the person on the other side of this deal where you option your shares in ABC plc faces a maximum £1,000 loss. This person can't be forced to buy the underlying shares, so if ABC goes bust it's you who ends up with worthless shares, not the other person, whose loss is limited to £1,000.

Trading good news

The good news about options is that, unlike with some of the fancy stock-market structures in this chapter, with options you can't lose more than you invest. And you can make a lot of money in a short time. The bad news? Many (probably most) option trades expire worthless. But then what do you expect from a geared investment?

The greater the potential gain, the greater the risk of losing.

You can trade options at any time before expiry. They're worthless on expiry, so the nearer you get to that date, the less valuable they become – a process called *time value*, where you pay for hope. The amount you pay for the option is called the *premium*, and it goes up with time value.

What are call prices and put prices?

Each option series for an underlying share has two sets of prices:

- ✔ **Call prices:** These prices are for investors who think the shares will go up. They give the right but not the obligation for an investor to buy the underlying shares.

- ✔ **Put prices:** These prices are for investors who think the shares will go down. They give the right but not the obligation for an investor to sell at a pre-agreed price.

A call-option example

Say that Supafones plc (which would be my favourite phone company if it really existed) has options that expire on a fixed date each month. You can buy up to one month ahead or for longer periods. A snapshot on one day with a stock-market price of 194p per share shows that you can choose a 180p or 200p strike price. The 180p strike price is 'in the money' for call-option purchasers because the underlying shares are more valuable. The 200p strike price is 'out of the money' and has no immediate value because it's higher than the current stock-market price.

If you want to buy the call option at 180p expiring in one month's time, it costs 17.25p per share. So if the share price between now and then tops 197.25p, you have a profit.

If you think the price will go up even further, you'll do better buying the 200p strike-price series. Here, a one-month call option costs 5.5p. If Supafones tops 205.5p over the next month, you win. If not, your loss can't be greater than 5.5p a share.

Investors who want to take a chance on Supafones over longer periods pay more for their options – around 2p for an extra month.

A put-option example

If you hold the shares and want to put a floor under the price then take out a put option. Doing so gives you the right but not the obligation to sell, so you receive a set price. With my Supafones example, guaranteeing a right to sell in around a month at 200p costs 11p a share.

Have a look at some possibilities:

- ✔ The Supafones price falls to 150p. You win! You collect 200p for each share less the 11p premium. So you get 189p.

- ✔ The Supafones price stays unchanged at 194p. You lose. You get 200p for each share less the 11p premium. So you end up with 189p.

- ✔ The Supafones price soars to 250p. Your right to sell is worthless. You lose 11p per share, but some investors think this worthwhile to buy insurance-style protection. The share price may have gone the other way.

Always study how traded-option premiums move for a wide number of underlying shares before dipping your toe in this particular water. Options that have expiry dates each month rather than every three months are more heavily traded and tend to have lower dealing charges. Many strategies exist, but all involve either gearing up your investment or hedging your risk.

Strategies involving selling shares you don't own can bring limitless losses.

What is option volatility?

Winning on traded options requires having a good feel for the direction of a particular share. Will it go up or down? But you also need to know about *volatility*, the amount the shares jump around. High-volatility shares have unstable prices. The more volatile a share is, the greater the chance of the option making money but the higher the cost of the option.

You can take a bet on the volatility of the market as a whole through VIX, the Chicago Board Options Exchange's Volatility Index. You can deal on this via a stockbroker. But even if you don't – and that would put you into the overwhelming majority – looking at this measure is worthwhile so you can see whether the market as a whole is trending to being jumpy or to a period of calmness. No index can tell you what's happening in an individual share, of course.

You never own the shares or other securities with traded options and other forms of derivative trading. So you have no shareholder rights. You don't get dividends either. Both those who buy and those who write options calculate the value of expected dividends.

Taking a Gamble with Spread Betting

Dyed-in-the-wool gamblers used to bet on which of two moths would hit the light bulb first and frazzle. I suppose they still do. But long gone are the days of just betting on winners in horse or dog races, or football matches, or moths on a light bulb. Nowadays, a whole new range of gambling opportunities exists (mostly opportunities to lose money, but then that's the nature of punting). You can bet on the total number of runs scored in a cricket match or the points total at rugby. Both of these bets are irrespective of which side scored them or which one wins. You can take a punt on when the first goal will be scored in a football match or the number of players sent off for foul play in a month. You can take bets on house-price moves. And you can bet on shares, bonds, currencies, stock-market indexes and other financial matters.

If there are numbers, there can be a spread bet. Whether the numbers are total points scored in a rugby match or a share price, all spread betting works in the same basic way:

1. **The bookmakers try to second-guess the most likely result.**

   Perhaps it's a total of 50 points in a rugby match or a probable price of 50p for a share in a week's time.

2. **The bookmakers create a spread either side.**

   In this case, it could be 47–53, which is called the *quote*.

3. **The punters must decide to be either long or short of the spread.**

   If they go long, they think that the match will be more high-scoring or the share price will be higher than the bookmakers' quotes. If they go *short*, they're thinking of a low-scoring game or a poor share price.

4. **The punters bet so much per point or penny of share price movement.**

   There may be a £10 minimum.

5. **When the match is over or the share bet reaches its expiry date, the punters look at the result.**

In this example, assume a £10-a-point bet:

- ✔ Say that 60 points are scored at the rugby game. Those investors who went long win. They multiply their stake by the points over 53 to calculate their gain. So they collect £70. Those who went short lose. The bookmaker starts counting at 47, so they have to pay £130 (subtracting 47 from 60 and multiplying the resulting 13 by the £10-a-point stake).

- ✔ Say that the result is 40. Those who shorted the bet receive £70 (£10 for each of the points between 40 and 47), and those who went long lose £130 (£10 for each of the points between 40 and 53).

- ✔ Say that the result is 50 – in the middle of the spread. All bets are lost, and all participants owe the bookmaker £30.

Keep in mind that you'll have to pay costs as well as deal with the spread if your bet lasts longer than one day. This is usually based on a mutually agreed interest rate. Most spread-betting websites have a section where you can take a dry run, so you can practise betting on financial assets without incurring any costs or losses.

Spread betters on financial instruments can lose limitless amounts. They may have to put up margin money each day to cover losses if they want the bet to continue to the expiry date. But punters can take profits or cut losses whenever they want. They can also reset limits one way or the other. Spread betting is leveraged, so big gains and big losses can occur without putting up money to buy the underlying investment.

Worried that the value of your home will drop or that your dream property will soar in price well out of reach? By taking out a spread bet on the Halifax House Price Index, you can protect yourself. If you worry that property values will soar, take a spread bet on the index rising. And if you think that prices are about to plummet, take a bet on the index falling. Of course, the Halifax index is an average across the country and won't exactly replicate what's happening to the prices that concern you. And know that getting it wrong could cost you more than your shirt!

You can also bet on gold, oil, other commodities, many individual shares and currencies; in fact, you can find a bookie with a quote on almost anything that moves. If you want to bet, however, on which of two moths will hit the light bulb first, you'll have to do that yourself with your family and friends. To find out more about spread betting, a good title to have a look at is *Financial Spread Betting For Dummies* (Wiley).

Limiting Your Betting Losses with Binary Betting

The warning words *potentially unlimited losses* accompany almost everything written about spread betting and are often enough to make even those who like a flutter on football or a punt on a racing classic run a country mile.

Binary bets are different. They let you take a gamble on financial markets knowing that you can lose no more than your stake. The other side of this coin is that you also know exactly how much you could win – and it will be the same whether you're just a little or a whole lot right.

With a binary bet, you're either right or wrong. You could, for instance, bet that the stock market will be higher (or lower) at midday – or any time and on any share as well as the Footsie index. You're quoted 33–36. If you think it's going up then you bet a stake (£1, for example) at 36, costing £36. If you're right, you gain £64, based on 100 less 36. If you're wrong, you lose £36. If you think it's going down, your stake is £67, based on 100 less 33. Those who are correct pick up £33, whereas losers give up £67. A quote of under 50 means that the bookmaker thinks the market will fall; over 50 implies that the market is likely to rise.

You don't pay capital gains tax on winnings from spread or binary bets. Neither can you offset your losses against capital gains tax, however.

Getting Contracts for Difference – for a Different Kind of Deal

Contracts for difference, or *CFDs* as they're known to stock-market insiders, are a low-cost route for frequent share buyers who want a deal with, well, a difference. Instead of buying a share and holding it, the CFD investor comes to a deal with a CFD provider (usually a specialist broker) that at the end of the contract, one side or the other will pay the difference between the opening price of the contract and the closing price. Some 20 per cent of all UK equity deals are now through CFDs – so activity in this market can make a lot of noise in the short term.

You can trade CFDs on most large UK companies, share-price indexes and many foreign companies. You can take a position in a price fall as well as hope for a rising price. And because all you're paying is the difference, you get the advantage of leverage.

At the start of the contract, you may only have to put up a small proportion of the contract value. This amount is often around 10 to 20 per cent, depending on how volatile the share is. So expect a lower percentage for a dull utility share and a higher amount for a technology stock. But because your losses could eventually exceed this margin money, brokers often insist that you deposit a minimum of £10,000 before trading.

How CFDs work

Suppose that you decide shares in XYZ plc look cheap at 100p and expect them to rise over the next week. You want £10,000 worth. Instead of paying dealing charges of around 1.5 per cent, plus stamp duty, plus the cost of the underlying stock, which would add up to £10,200, you go to a CFD broker. Here, you put up 10 per cent, and you 'borrow' the other £9,000 from the CFD provider in return for interest at a preset but variable level.

For a week, this arrangement may cost £10. You'll probably pay 0.25 per cent commission on the whole £10,000 in costs (£25). You don't have to pay stamp duty.

A week later, XYZ shares can be sold for 120p, putting the value of your holding up to £12,000. If you sell, you receive a £2,000 profit less £30 selling commission (that's 0.25 per cent of £12,000). Subtracting this amount plus your interest and buying costs gives a total profit of £1,935. (Note, though, that if XYZ shares had gone down to 80p, your bill would have been £2,000 plus all the £65 costs.)

You can also profit if you correctly guess that a share price or an index will fall in value. This scenario is called *short trading*. Suppose that you think XYZ plc is going to fall in value. If you're right, you gain. If you're wrong, you lose. It's simply the preceding example turned on its head!

The benefits and drawbacks of CFDs

Here are some plus points of CFDs:

- ✔ You can go long (expect the price to rise) or short (expect it to fall).
- ✔ You have a wide range of shares and indexes to choose from.
- ✔ Commissions are low.
- ✔ You leverage your stake to increase profits.
- ✔ You don't pay stamp duty.
- ✔ You can hold CFDs for very short periods.
- ✔ You receive dividend payments where applicable.

But there are also drawbacks:

✔ You're gambling so although you can forget capital gains tax, you can't offset losses against capital gains elsewhere.

✔ They're bad value for long-term investors.

✔ Investors who go short must pay the dividend to the broker.

✔ Unless you can place a *stop loss*, a device to close a losing position automatically, your cash can bleed away very quickly.

✔ If you buy CFDs, the Financial Conduct Authority will consider you to be a professional and experienced investor, even if you aren't. So you can say goodbye to a large slice of your consumer protection. Beware of CFD salespeople phoning you out of the blue, promising big gains for small outlays. If it was really that easy, they wouldn't be bothering to cold-call you. And if you think signing up to the Telephone Preference Service, which is supposed to prevent cold calls, will help then think again. These nuisance callers always claim to have found your details because you filled in some form or another requesting them. If you ask which form that was, they say they don't know. Convenient!

Don't ignore the commission and other costs, even if they sound small. CFDs are intended for short-term trading. But frequent traders face huge costs. If you have a £10,000 deposit and trade on ten times leverage (that's playing with £100,000), each buy and sell round trip will cost you 0.5 per cent of the amount you're playing with at most brokers. That's £500. If you trade just once a week for a year at this level, you end up paying your broker an amazing £26,000 plus interest (say £4,000). You've got to be really good to make money after all of this. Longer-term traders soon find the initial savings with CFDs outweighed by the running costs and the lack of dividends.

Understanding Warrants

Warrants have been around for years. They often came with investment-trust launches as a free gift for the original investors. The traditional *warrant* gives the right but not the obligation to buy a set number of shares in the underlying trust (sometimes in other sorts of quoted concerns) for a fixed sum during a set period each year for a number of years.

A typical launch deal is to offer one warrant for every five shares bought at the original 100p. A £1,000 investor would get 200 warrants. These warrants then give the option to buy the underlying shares for 100p no matter what the price stands at during each September for seven years. After seven years, the warrants expire, worthless.

But warrant investors in this particular trust aren't limited to trading in September. While the warrants have value, you can buy or sell them at any time on the stock market. They're a long-term gamble on the price rising.

How about an example? Say that the warrant you received as part of an investment-trust flotation allows you to buy the actual shares for 100p in any July for the next five years. The underlying shares are worth 200p at the moment, but you want out. So another investor buys the warrant for 110p. The 10p extra is compensation for the hope value. Four years later, the shares stand at 400p. The warrant holder converts into shares. The bill is 100p, plus the 110p for the warrant, plus the interest cost of holding the warrant (there are no dividends), but the final reward is 400p. Not bad! But note that if the trust shares had slumped to 50p and stayed there, you would have wasted the 100p-a-time warrant money. Disaster!

So what's the point?

- ✔ Low cost.
- ✔ No stamp duty.
- ✔ You can buy a warrant for a sector, such as banks or pharmaceuticals, so you don't have to consider which bank or which pharmaceutical company to back.
- ✔ No annual management fees.

Betting on divorces – the next big thing?

Earlier in this chapter I say people can bet on anything, including which of two moths would burn first on a light bulb. Now a US fund manager has come up with a new idea: betting on divorce settlements. You can do this one of two ways:

- ✔ The less risky method is to join a fund that puts money behind divorce lawyers who work for clients who wouldn't otherwise afford their fees. Fund buyers hope that putting £50,000 of lawyer behind a divorcing person will produce more than that in alimony, or reduce the bill for the side with the money by more than £50,000. The lawyer gets a fixed fee and the fund takes a percentage of the winnings.

- ✔ You gamble on publicly available divorce settlement information using spread-betting techniques. You may think Celebrity A will end up with £5 million but the bookmaker is only going for a spread of £3–4 million. If you're right, you win – probably at the rate of 1p or one-tenth of 1p for every pound you're right. However, if Celebrity A ends up with nothing, you lose big time – even when the bet is for a tiny fraction of each pound!

And if you don't want to bet on divorce, you can take punts on almost anything else from the result of the next election in the UK, the US or many other places, to football transfers or the winners of literary prizes. You may still lose your money, but at least you're exercising some judgement so you may feel superior to those folk who feed the hungry mouths of fruit machines with their hard-earned cash.

Part V
The Part of Tens

Enjoy an additional Part of Tens chapter online at www.dummies.com/extras/investinguk.

In this part . . .

- ✔ Learn more about how to find a good advisor – they can make or break your investment strategy.

- ✔ Develop your own investment strategy – the most important factor in deciding how to invest your money!

Chapter 21

Ten Tips for Fact-Finding

In This Chapter

▶ Using your eyes and ears

▶ Searching the Internet

▶ Analysing tipsheets

▶ Examining media coverage

*T*he Rothschilds' financial fortune and banking empire was founded, so it is said, on the family receiving news before all others of the defeat of Napoleon at Waterloo by the Duke of Wellington (yes, the British did get some help from the Prussian army). The Rothschilds had organised a series of messengers and carrier pigeons so that they'd know the outcome first.

The stock markets of the time believed the French would win and priced investments accordingly. But because the Rothschilds knew the real result first – that the opposite outcome had occurred – they were able to take big financial bets against the markets and make the early 19th century equivalent of billions.

Now, as then, investment markets revolve around information. If your information is quicker, more accurate and better understood than that of others, you'll prosper. So this chapter explains how to build your own personal information bank. The Internet, the media and ever-increasing disclosure rules for stock-market-quoted companies can give you more facts, figures and opinions than you'll ever want or be able to use. On top of that, companies produce annual reports and other documentation that grow weightier with each passing year.

Before you build your information bank, you must decide what you want from it. You can't file away everything available on financial markets, so limit yourself to looking at the shares and bonds you already hold, or at an area of the market that interests you, such as government stocks (the UK version of government stock is also known as a *gilt*, the US version a *treasury* and the German bond is called a *bund*), emerging markets or construction company shares. And after you build your information bank, you have to make up your mind what to do with the info. Know that if you're still confused, keeping your money in the bank is okay. Know too that no such thing exists as an unrepeatable offer. You don't have to 'buy now while stocks last' because another deal is *always* coming along.

Taking a Look Around You

To build an information bank, your first move requires neither a computer nor a filing cabinet. It requires merely your eyes and ears.

You're surrounded by products and services from stock-market-quoted companies. The high street is full of them. So too are your food cupboards, wardrobes and home leisure areas. The fortunes or otherwise of these firms are ultimately based on the purchasing decisions made by millions of consumers. And that includes you. Acting on gut feeling can be a valid start to a share buying or selling decision.

All the boasting and blustering of a firm's top management are meaningless if the employees nearest to the consumers fail to deliver good service or if the consumers themselves aren't interested or prefer a rival.

Here are some potential investing areas to look at:

- ✔ **Fashion retailing:** If you and your friends stop going to a store then others are probably also shunning the outlets. Alternatively, you may start buying at a store that you previously thought had poor design or bad value. For real examples, look at the ups and downs of high-street fashion staples such as Next and Marks & Spencer. They've both had periods in the doldrums and times when their goods were cutting edge. Companies often churn out good profit figures for some time after customers have deserted them and may fail to reflect an increase for a year or two after consumers vote with their feet in favour.

- ✔ **Food retailers:** The state of the car park and the length of the checkout queue at key times, such as Saturday mornings, can speak volumes about the success or otherwise of a superstore firm.

- ✔ **Holiday companies:** It's a bad sign if their nerve cracks and they start to offer deep discounts on school-holiday months such as August or if they're cutting prices many months ahead of departure dates.

- ✔ **Furniture, carpet and do-it-yourself superstores:** These depend to a large extent on the number of people moving home who tend to buy new furniture and carpets and redecorate.

✔ **January sales:** Whether they're selling cars or clothing, watch out for companies that have too many sales. Winter sales and summer sales should be more than enough. When the company gets to pre-Christmas, half-term, spring and autumn sales, start to worry. These firms aren't efficient.

Going Online

I used to have a chunky bookshelf lined with volumes on how to invest online. They were all very worthy and offered useful information, stressing how the Internet has revolutionised share buying and selling for the individual. Then I bundled the lot and sent them to the charity shop.

Why? Because most of the stuff these books told me was out of date before I'd even read it. Sites they told me to visit that were free had erected paywalls (and vice versa). Sites had changed out of all recognition or had ceased to exist. So although in this section I mention a few of the sites I find particularly useful, countless sites offering investment advice exist and finding your own is far better than relying on a list in a book.

In any case, I found most of the books failed to make these vital points:

✔ A huge amount of duplication is on the Internet, so concentrate your searches to a few sites that you know how to navigate and where you trust the content.

✔ Information on the Internet isn't guaranteed to be accurate or even have a passing resemblance to the truth. Before you accept anything, ask yourself what your reaction would be if you saw this in a hard copy. Would you trust it?

Chat rooms or so-called investment communities are a waste of time. Why? They consist of clueless people posting messages to those looking for clues or, more dangerously, they consist of chat from people with a position in the shares looking to give their investments a boost by persuading others to join them. Some of this information is downright misinformation – and often the very opposite of the truth. Ask yourself why a total stranger hiding behind a pseudonym should be so anxious to help you by sharing thoughts. Remember the old stock-market saying: 'Where there's a tip, there's a tap.' That means that people only give you information (the tip) if they see an advantage for them in your acting on their information (the tap).

✔ The Internet doesn't change the fundamentals of investment. It just speeds up the flow of information and increases the amount by a massive margin.

✔ Using the speed of the Internet to make buy or sell decisions can deprive you of those vital few seconds when you pinch yourself and double-check that you're doing the right thing.

✔ Thousands (literally) of financial scam sites exist, and they're devoted to parting you from your money.

Those are the warnings. But the Internet has great value in building up your personal investment information bank as well, especially if you use it counter-intuitively – in a way that most other investors don't think about doing because they're too busy confusing themselves in the noise and rubbish of investment communities. This section helps you use the power of the Internet to build your information bank.

Websites come and go. Their names change. Their services alter. Their policy on what's free and what you have to pay for also varies over time. And much of the info on the Internet that's useful to investors is repeated over and over again on various different sites. So use search engines on a regular basis – that way, you won't be stuck with a few sites and you can get a fresh view on the investment world.

Exploring a Company's Website

The dotcommers' vision of a world free of shops, where all products and services are traded online, has, as of yet, remained a pipe dream. But although most people still stick to traditional ways of buying, the Internet has a big influence on their decisions.

Exploring the websites of companies can give you a great deal of insight into the companies themselves. To build your information bank, you need to assess the actual site, read the company's online report and read between the proverbial lines.

Your eyes and ears should always play a big role in your information-bank building, so when you're exploring a company online, take a look at how well designed the website is. Start off with the product or consumer area. Act as though you want the product or service. If the site is easy to navigate then it's likely to attract extra business. A bad site sends potential customers to the competition.

Assuming that the assessment passes your personal quality-control barriers, head off to the corporate section of the firm's site. This is often completely separate to the consumer side of things. If you enter 'ABC plc' into a search engine, you usually end up with the consumer site. But if you enter 'ABC plc corporate' you should find yourself where you want to be. On the corporate site, you should find a large amount of information about your target company, including press releases, company statements, recent stock-exchange filings, and annual and interim reports.

Understanding the nuances of a company website is akin to understanding a bank reference or a school report. It's what's missing that counts!

Don't expect web material from a company to mention the negatives. Where a firm has to reveal bad points publicly, it may well try to place them in a report in such a way that only the most wide-eyed reader finds them. In any case, no quoted company is yet obliged to keep a website. You can sometimes find negative opinions or information about a company by entering 'I hate ABC plc' or 'ABC plc sucks!' into a search engine.

Checking Out Other Sites for More Info on a Company

After you fully explore the company site, go back to your favourite search engine. Now you're looking for general sites, such as Bloomberg, Citywire or Yahoo!, which offer a brief company history, up to five years of past results, charts of past share-price performance, names of company officers, directors' share dealings, comparisons with rival companies and present share-price information. You should be able to look at past performance over a number of timeframes with reference to the market as a whole. You can usually access information on these sites without paying, although you may have to pay for higher-level and more specialised information.

Most sites give share prices delayed by 15 minutes unless you pay for a premium service that gives real-time numbers. Paying for real-time prices is probably only worthwhile if you're a short-term trader rather than a longer-term investor. Many share prices don't change that much from day to day, and those that are frequent movers often go up and down within narrow limits.

Signing Up for Stories

A number of investment websites will email you information on firms you select. You may have to pay for this info.

Tried and tested media such as newspapers are often 'investment game changers'. Fund managers and other stock market participants are more likely to take notice of something they see in a large circulation newspaper than on a website attracting few readers, if only because they believe their competitors will act on that information.

Broadsheet newspaper articles are usually archived and should be easy to find. Access to these articles may be free, but many newspapers, including the *Financial Times* and *The Wall Street Journal*, now charge a fee, although this is waived if you subscribe to the newspaper itself. Even those that don't charge you may demand that you register.

Information sites and other areas you look at online have a strange way of disappearing. Never be afraid to print what interests you. Otherwise, you may never find it again!

Bookmarking the Best Sites

So many information-bank sites are available for you to choose from that you could spend hours selecting one. But a huge degree of duplication exists. Your best bet is to try out as many of the general sites as possible and then bookmark two or three as your favourites. I find that ease of access and use come before clever features buried deep in the site.

Here are some sites to check out:

- **Association of Investment Companies (www.theaic.co.uk/):** The official site of the trade association for the investment-trust world. It has news and views from the association and member companies (not all the investment trusts on the market because membership is optional), plus info on how to understand the trusts and performance figures.

- **Citywire (www.citywire.co.uk):** This site is great at breaking news. It should be because it's staffed by experienced financial journalists who look for originality instead of merely re-running the material sent in by news services. You can get alerts on shares you hold or are interested in and find the usual mix of prices, information on companies and funds, and price charts.

- **Digital Look (www.digitallook.com):** A helpful site for those looking for a good source of company news and financial data from both the UK and the US.

- **FE Trustnet (www.trustnet.com):** This site is best known for its unit trust database, where you can find charts, performance figures and links to sites run by fund managers.

- **Financial Conduct Authority (www.fca.org.uk):** The official site of the Financial Conduct Authority, the UK watchdog for all financial services including investments and banking. It has advice, warnings and the all-important check on whether an adviser, broker or fund manager is authorised in the UK. Shun those not on its list.

- ✔ **Investment Management Association (www.investmentfunds.org. uk):** This is the site of the Investment Management Association, the trade body for the OEIC (Open Ended Investment Company – the technical name for unit trust) industry. It has past-performance statistics as well as details of its member companies and information on how to invest.

- ✔ **Morningstar (www.morningstar.co.uk):** A unit-trust and mutual-fund database; the one that many newspapers quote. It sorts out the performance of up to 80,000 funds worldwide over a wide variety of timeframes as well as carrying information on exchange-traded funds (ETFs). Also available is information on fund-management groups. On top of that, it has general investment news.

- ✔ **Motley Fool UK (www.fool.co.uk):** The UK site of the US Motley Fool phenomenon. Although it has been cut back over the past few years, it still has lots of education features and sets out to show how you can invest without paying commission or fees to professionals. It's good on direct share investment and on why the professionals add little or no value. The site is sometimes too self-reverential and referential for many people's tastes.

Reading Specialist Magazines

Specialist share magazines, such as *Investors Chronicle* and *Shares*, can be part of your information bank. The weekly magazines won't burn too much of a hole in your pocket. You can expect to spend £250 or so a year on each one. *Investors Chronicle* also has a website aimed at subscribers.

These publications are good as archive material because they often cover results from companies that aren't big enough to make it to the pages of daily newspapers. They can be helpful in portfolio building, often running their own selections with the reasons for each choice.

They can sound authoritative, but be warned that many of the articles are written by junior staff who are unlikely to write anything other than the orthodox view at the time.

Examining Tipsheets

Tipsheets are small publications devoted to telling you exactly what to buy and sell. They tend to concentrate on small companies where a few purchases or sales can move the share price substantially.

Tipsheets are generally far more expensive than mainstream publications such as *Investors Chronicle* or *Shares* magazine. Some charge up to £1,000 a year for a few pages, or an email alert or two each month. Literally dozens of tipsheets are on offer. They're regulated by the Financial Conduct Authority (or should be! Never take any notice of tipsheets that are outside the City watchdog's control). Tipsheet writers are supposed to reveal any holdings they have in shares they recommend, although this usually goes no further than a vague statement.

Tipsheets should indicate when shares are difficult to buy and sell. They often recommend illiquid shares where the gap between what buyers pay and what sellers get (this is called the *spread*) can be enormous. Pushing shares like this can enable tipsters to mark up great successes! For instance, if they push a share at 4p and it goes up to 5p, they can claim a 25 per cent gain. That sounds brilliant. But now look at the reality. The share that appears at 4p costs 4.5p to buy. And when the share goes up to 5p, sellers only get 4.5p. On this example, the 25 per cent gain has disappeared altogether! And that's before counting the cost of stockbroker fees.

Here are a few additional titbits about tipsheets:

- Most tipsheets have low-cost introductory offers. You sign up for a direct debit for three to six months at a bargain rate, which, unless you cancel it, automatically moves to the far more expensive rate after that.

- Some go for a scatter-gun approach and tip a large number of shares in each issue, hoping that one or two are bound to be winners. Others are more careful.

- No evidence proves that any tipsheet is consistently good. But if you like the idea, try a few to find one that suits your risk/reward profile and the sort of share you like to invest in. One or two tipsheets specialise in sectors such as technology or investment trusts.

- Tipsheets advertise their successes and ignore their failures. They aren't obliged to reveal the date when they made the tip in any advert or when the sheet suggested selling, so know that the successes may be several years old when market conditions were quite different.

Following the Regulatory News Service

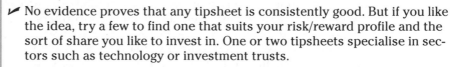

The keep on top of it all investor needs information straight from the horse's mouth. And nothing comes as fast or as authoritative as the news coming straight from the company, whose shares you own or might consider buying.

It's called RNS or *Regulatory News Service*. RNS consists of statements that companies are legally obliged to make in a form that is consistent with stock market regulation. All UK-quoted companies have to report at least twice yearly to shareholders as well as issue statements on a number of other occasions, such as during takeovers, the issuing of new shares and significant director-level changes. Firms reveal all this information to the stock market via the RNS, which gives equal prominence to an announcement from a company worth £10 billion or more and to one worth £10 million or less. The RNS feed from a company must contain all this information. Other news sources such as newspapers or websites look for what they consider to be interesting. As an investor or potential investor, your interest may not be the same as theirs. RNS puts every company and every fact that it must reveal on an even playing field. Companies generally put up RNS statements on their own websites.

Sifting through the City Pages

Most investors rely on newspapers as a primary source of information and also for comment on the stock market and other investment issues. So you need to know how City pages work, the decisions editors make and why some companies receive so much more coverage than others.

Keep these points in mind:

- ✔ **City pages aren't just aimed at investors**. They have to attract at least some other readers to justify their expense. Companies with a high-street presence, such as retailers and banks, get more coverage than manufacturing concerns or mining companies, no matter how important these companies may be. The first group is interesting to non-investor readers and the second is deemed boring.

- ✔ **Reporters can't be everywhere at once**. They concentrate on companies they consider sexy. They may even take that word literally. For example, reporters write about some companies because they're in the fashion world – cue a picture of a scantily clad model. Reporters also concentrate on controversial companies, including those whose directors are deemed to be greedy fat cats or where big losses are occurring.

- ✔ **Public relations agencies play a major and growing role**. Most quoted companies hire PR firms whose job it is to ensure that good news gets into newspapers and bad news is hidden away or, preferably, ignored – or, even better, gets turned into good news.

- ✔ **Few journalists dig deep enough to expose powerful people and companies doing things they shouldn't be**. Investigations cost time and money – most media organisations now have little time and practically no money. And they worry about legal ramifications.

Keeping a healthy degree of scepticism

Be wary when looking at information that's offered to you on a plate. Remember that you're being told something by a perfect stranger that could make you poorer or richer. Always ask why you're being told this, and what's in it for the person telling you.

But more generally, always remember that very little is black and white in investment. A large amount of what you're told is opinion, and whether you can trust it may depend on the track record of the person giving you this material. Is the person right? As with anything else in investment, you rarely find an easy answer. What's important is to see where the cheers and the jeers are coming from.

Chapter 22

Ten Helpful Hints for You

*W*hen it comes to investing, you won't be 100 per cent right in what you do even if you read and inwardly digest every word of this book, or even dozens more volumes as well. But if you figure out nothing else about investment, the key lesson to remember (and here you can score maximum marks) is that it's your money, your needs (and the needs of those who depend on you) and your life that count. Losing your hard-earned savings is, sadly, much easier to do than growing them. So stop everything you're doing and don't invest a penny until you've read this chapter.

Define Where You Want to Be

Really basic questions here: what do you want from your money? Who do you want to benefit? And can you afford to lose anything? Investing isn't a game like rugby or bridge where you hope to score more than your opponents.

Always know what you want and where you're going. Don't be afraid to say that your aspirations are modest. And don't be nervous to admit that you enjoy taking a risk if you do and when you can afford to. But don't forget to put a limit on your more speculative investments.

Protect What You Have

You'll feel worse if you lose what you have than if you miss out on an investment opportunity. That safety-first option can also apply to your life and salary. Insuring the first is generally inexpensive. Buying protection against losing your earning capacity through illness – critical illness policies and income protection plans – is more expensive, but consider protection if you're the breadwinner in the family.

Always check on the cover you already have from other plans and from employment before taking on more.

Pay Off the Home Loan

Most people have mortgages. Getting rid of the home loan as fast as possible is the best risk-free use you can make of spare cash because you'll save a fortune on interest payments. So do it. Ensure that paying down the home loan is at the top of your list of tasks.

Equally important, never remortgage to a larger loan to pay for an investment venture; or to buy a car; or to pay for a holiday. An investment must be consistently very clever to produce more than the interest rate on a personal loan or even a mortgage. Such investments are very unlikely.

Accept Losses

Not all your investments will work. Full stop. Some of them will fail to gain as much as the best or even the average. Others will lose money absolutely. As an investor, you have to be tough. You have to accept that there will be days, weeks, months or even years when the signs are negative and the price screens are red with losses. Don't forget that a loss is only a loss (and a profit only a profit) when you close out the position by selling.

Don't get too worried about newspaper headlines showing one-day percentage losses. The market typically goes down in big lumps and rises in bite-sized amounts. Quality is what counts. If your investment has real potential, stick with it. Otherwise, cut it out. Ask yourself if you can still justify the investment purchase you made.

What's really tough is the first time you accept that you've backed a real turkey and the only exit is a fast one. But it's like cutting out dead wood. You'll come out of the situation knowing more, feeling stronger and looking happier. Promise.

Take Your Time

Time and patience have been the great healers of investment difficulties. Or at least they have been for the past century or so, and there's no reason for a change. So time is on your side. Panic is pointless, but you can profit when others rush to sell indiscriminately. If you can keep your head when all those around you are losing theirs, you should end up well ahead.

This works the other way around too. Don't get sucked into a buying vortex unless you're very disciplined, with a clear and firm exit route.

Do the Groundwork

Are you willing to do the hard work involved with investments? This groundwork includes selecting and monitoring, and making tax returns, even if you opt for an easy portfolio-building method such as picking with a pin and then holding on. You can't make gains without some pain.

If you don't want to make any effort, you can hand all your money over to a professional investment company (some will provide your tax return details as well), but there can be no guarantees that you'll get good value for your cash.

Get a Handle on the Odds

Nothing's wrong with taking bigger-than-average risks that others may consider little better than playing roulette or backing horses, provided that you're clear about what you're doing and you can afford the losses.

Don't forget that big risks really do mean slim chances of winning. Try to get a handle on the odds. The big mistake previous investors in precipice or high-income bonds (two just-about-legal scams from the start of this century) made, other than taking notice of commission-chasing advisers, was that they didn't get a handle on the odds. They didn't compare the most they could gain with the most they could lose. Their top gain was a few percentage points a year more than a risk-free bank account. Their loss – and a lot lost big time – could be as much as all their investment. (Okay, the advisers didn't exactly publicise the downsides, so only those who really understood could do the calculations, and they wouldn't have been stupid enough to buy.) You wouldn't toss a coin at the start of a game if you had to call heads and there were nine tails! If a chance exists that you could lose all your money, to invest you need a really substantial chance of multiplying it many times.

Know When to Sell

Knowing when to sell is really tough. So set yourself some rules. What about selling when an investment makes a certain percentage gain or loss? Or giving it a fixed period of time? Or determining a need, such as a home improvement, family occasion or retirement, where you'll require cash and then selling when that need's time comes, no matter what?

Read the Small Print

Cigarette packets must now have a large percentage of their surface covered in health warnings. Yet no rules exist for the prominent display of wealth warnings on investments. Even if they're buried away, phrases such as 'investments can go down as well as up' mean something. Sellers and product providers cite them as a defence if things go wrong. If you don't believe how much those who push rubbish packaged products depend on almost invisible get-out clauses, look at the scandals of the past two decades with endowment mortgages, precipice bonds and split-level investment trusts. No guarantee exists that some new, 'sure-fire' route to success won't turn very sour.

Take time to read *all* the material. Then ask for the worst possible scenario in writing. If the reality is even worse, you may have a case for compensation. Don't get complacent just because no big scandals have hit personal money for a year or two. They never go away, and turn up in unexpected places.

Wake Up without Worries

The last 30 years have seen some of the most amazing financial-market manias ever. There was the collapse in the Japanese Nikkei index, which has fallen by around three-quarters since its late-1989 peak; there was the bursting of the high-tech bubble in 2000, which led to some stocks losing 99 per cent or more of their value; and, biggest of them all, the 2008–2009 bank crash, which wiped trillions (and still counting) off the world's worth. Trillions? That's 12 zeroes, which is an awful lot of money, whether it's pounds, dollars or euros.

Your investment strategy and portfolio should allow you to go to sleep happily and to wake up without worries. Sensible investing is about not losing out to insanity. If it looks too good to be true, it probably is. No magic solutions exist. And don't even think about defying gravity.

Index

About the Author

Tony Levene has been a financial journalist for nearly 40 years, after spending a year or so teaching French beforehand. He writes on issues ranging from investment to consumer rights – sometimes both at the same time. Over his career, he has worked for newspapers including *The Guardian*, *The Sunday Times*, *Sunday Express*, *Daily Express*, *The Sun*, *Daily Star*, and *Sunday Mirror*. He has also published eight previous books on investment and financial issues. He lives in London with his wife Claudia. He has two 'grown up' children, Zoë and Oliver, and a cat, Pandora.

Dedication

This book is dedicated to Claudia, for her patience during the book's gestation; to my son Oliver for persuading me to write the very first edition; and to Zoë for her suggestions and approval of my initial chapters way back when I started *Investing For Dummies*. I would also like to thank my brother Stuart for giving me sanctuary away from phones and other distractions whilst I wrote much it and the subsequent editions.

Author's Acknowledgements

I would like to thank the publishing team at Wiley for their patience and help during the various stages of this book. And a special thank you to Iona Everson for all her work in turning my manuscript and amendments into *Investing For Dummies*

But most of all, I would like to acknowledge Peter Shearlock. Peter, whom I first met at school when we were both aged 11, was responsible for starting my career as an investment writer and has helped me invaluably along the way. He gave me my first lessons in the irrationality that often characterises financial markets and introduced me to 'City characters' ranging from spivs and chancers to the epitome of blue-blooded respectability. It is this variety that makes investing so fascinating. Thanks Peter.

Publisher's Acknowledgements

We're proud of this book; please send us your comments at http://dummies.custhelp.com. For other comments, please contact our Customer Care Department within the U.S. at 877-762-2974, outside the U.S. at (001) 317-572-3993, or fax 317-572-4002.

Some of the people who helped bring this book to market include the following:

Project Editor: Iona Everson

Commissioning Editor: Annie Knight

Proofreader: Kerry Laundon

Publisher: Miles Kendall

Project Coordinator: Sheree Montgomery

Cover Image: ©iStock.com/olm26250.

Take Dummies with you everywhere you go!

Whether you're excited about e-books, want more from the web, must have your mobile apps, or swept up in social media, Dummies makes everything easier.

Visit Us

Like Us

Follow Us

Watch Us

Join Us

Pin Us

Circle Us

Shop Us

FOR DUMMIES®

A Wiley Brand

BUSINESS

978-1-118-73077-5

978-1-118-44349-1

978-1-119-97527-4

MUSIC

978-1-119-94276-4

978-0-470-97799-6

978-0-470-49644-2

DIGITAL PHOTOGRAPHY

978-1-118-09203-3

978-0-470-76878-5

978-1-118-00472-2

Algebra I For Dummies
978-0-470-55964-2

Anatomy & Physiology For Dummies, 2nd Edition
978-0-470-92326-9

Asperger's Syndrome For Dummies
978-0-470-66087-4

Basic Maths For Dummies
978-1-119-97452-9

Body Language For Dummies, 2nd Edition
978-1-119-95351-7

Bookkeeping For Dummies, 3rd Edition
978-1-118-34689-1

British Sign Language For Dummies
978-0-470-69477-0

Cricket for Dummies, 2nd Edition
978-1-118-48032-8

Currency Trading For Dummies, 2nd Edition
978-1-118-01851-4

Cycling For Dummies
978-1-118-36435-2

Diabetes For Dummies, 3rd Edition
978-0-470-97711-8

eBay For Dummies, 3rd Edition
978-1-119-94122-4

Electronics For Dummies All-in-One For Dummies
978-1-118-58973-1

English Grammar For Dummies
978-0-470-05752-0

French For Dummies, 2nd Edition
978-1-118-00464-7

Guitar For Dummies, 3rd Edition
978-1-118-11554-1

IBS For Dummies
978-0-470-51737-6

Keeping Chickens For Dummies
978-1-119-99417-6

Knitting For Dummies, 3rd Edition
978-1-118-66151-2

FOR DUMMIES®

A Wiley Brand

SELF-HELP

Cognitive Behavioural Therapy For Dummies
978-0-470-66541-1

Creative Visualization For Dummies
978-1-119-99264-6

Mindfulness For Dummies
978-0-470-66086-7

LANGUAGES

Spanish For Dummies
978-0-470-68815-1

Polish For Dummies
978-1-119-97959-3

British Sign Language For Dummies
978-0-470-69477-0

HISTORY

The Tudors For Dummies
978-0-470-68792-5

Medieval History For Dummies
978-0-470-74783-4

British History For Dummies
978-0-470-97819-1

Laptops For Dummies 5th Edition
978-1-118-11533-6

Management For Dummies, 2nd Edition
978-0-470-97769-9

Nutrition For Dummies, 2nd Edition
978-0-470-97276-2

Office 2013 For Dummies
978-1-118-49715-9

Organic Gardening For Dummies
978-1-119-97706-3

Origami Kit For Dummies
978-0-470-75857-1

Overcoming Depression For Dummies
978-0-470-69430-5

Physics I For Dummies
978-0-470-90324-7

Project Management For Dummies
978-0-470-71119-4

Psychology Statistics For Dummies
978-1-119-95287-9

Renting Out Your Property For Dummies, 3rd Edition
978-1-119-97640-0

Rugby Union For Dummies, 3rd Edition
978-1-119-99092-5

Stargazing For Dummies
978-1-118-41156-8

Teaching English as a Foreign Language For Dummies
978-0-470-74576-2

Time Management For Dummies
978-0-470-77765-7

Training Your Brain For Dummies
978-0-470-97449-0

Voice and Speaking Skills For Dummies
978-1-119-94512-3

Wedding Planning For Dummies
978-1-118-69951-5

WordPress For Dummies, 5th Edition
978-1-118-38318-6

Think you can't learn it in a day? Think again!

The *In a Day* e-book series from *For Dummies* gives you quick and easy access to learn a new skill, brush up on a hobby, or enhance your personal or professional life — all in a day. Easy!